D0841978

THE ETERNAL FOOD

SUNY Series in Hinduism
Wendy Doniger, Editor

◆

Prepared under the auspices of the International Commission on the Anthropology of Food

THE ETERNAL FOOD

GASTRONOMIC IDEAS AND EXPERIENCES OF HINDUS AND BUDDHISTS

Edited by
R. S. Khare

STATE UNIVERSITY OF NEW YORK PRESS

Published by
State University of New York Press, Albany

Printed in the United States of America

For information, address State University of New York
Press, State University Plaza, Albany, N.Y., 12246

Production by Diane Ganeles
Marketing by Dana E. Yanulavich

Library of Congress Cataloging-in-Publication Data

The Eternal food : gastronomic ideas and experiences of Hindus and
Buddhists / edited by R. S. Khare.
p. cm.—(SUNY series in Hinduism)
Includes bibliographical references (p.) and index.
ISBN 0-7914-1057-9 (CH : acid-free).—ISBN 0-7914-1058-7 (PB :
acid-free)
1. Food—Religious aspects—Hinduism. 2. Food—Religious aspects—
Buddhism. I. Khare, R. S. (Ravindra S.) II. Series.
BL1215.F66E84 1992
294.5′446—dc20 92-3270
CIP

10 9 8 7 6 5 4 3 2 1

Contents

Note on Transliteration

The text uses Sanskrit, popular Hindi, Marathi, Kannada, Tamil, and Sinhalese words, phrases, citations, and proper names, essentially by reflecting two disciplinary styles of transliteration—anthropological and Indological. *Both* styles are followed to reflect the current practices and their emphases. This is exemplified in cases like Viṣṇu and Vishnu, Upanishad and Upaniṣad, and *prasāda* and *prasād* (even prasad). Frequently employed words like "karma" and "dharma" are not italicized, unless there is a special reason. All other technical terms, phrases, or sentences are italicized and explained by a contextual gloss. The glossary provides further identification of some crucial words, phrases, and concepts.

Regional cultural usages and expressions follow their styles, adding richness, precision, and clarity to ways food "speaks" in India. As for the transliteration of Sanskritic (and Sanskritized Hindi rather than Hindustani) words, the standard scheme is followed, where long vowels (e.g, ā, ī, ū) and aspirated and nonaspirated consonants are distinguished (e.g., *bh, ph, kh, gh, ch, jh, th, dh*). Similarly, the cerebral consonants (*ṭ, ṭh, ḍ, ḍh, ṇ,* and *ṣ*) are distinguished from those dental (*t, th, d, dh, n,* and *s*). Also, we have *c* as in church, *s* as in sugar, and *g* as in goat.

Note on Translation

Illustrations

Preface

This is a book about the ways in which the Indic (primarily Hindu and Buddhist) cultures approach *food* as an "essence" and experience within personal and social life. With emphasis on expressive aspects, contributors to this volume discuss food for its cultural—learned and popular—characteristics across the subcontinent's varieties of "texts," regions, and languages. The accounts try to illustrate aspects of the rich "food culture" Indian civilization provides. However, the book does not propose to describe systematically the empirical diversity of food and culinary habits; nor does it attempt to deal with changing gastronomic practices of castes, sects, and ethnic groups of contemporary South Asia, and its emerging public culture around culinary traditions.

Instead, the book focuses on the long-term sharing Hindu and Sinhalese "food cultures" provide, encoding and enhancing some distinct notions of Indic essence, experience, and aesthetics. Our accounts rest on an interdependence between textual, aesthetic, ritual, customary, and popular descriptions and discourses. These try not only to read the "internal language" of food-markers and meanings, but also help uncover those creative intimations, interpretations, and reasoning patterns which may constitute a distinct aspect of Indian civilization and its contribution to world culture.

An example of such a distinct reasoning pattern is the way India (as distinct from Western thinking) *conjoins* food's cosmological, moral, social, and material qualities within a comprehensive order of essence and experience. As the papers of this volume variously emphasize, food in South Asia intimately concerns bodily conditions, social experiences, emotional states, literary expressions, religious practices, and philosophical ideals. For the Hindu, food is a part of the *revealed* knowledge (*śruti*); it is an extension of the noncontingent and the self-evident. If food this way truly acquires a pervasive cosmic presence within the Hindu life, it does so *not* by dichotomizing and excluding the practical aspects. Instead, the "practical" becomes an experiential ground as much for testing the Hindu's ability "to live the textual ideals" as for "testing" the inner worth of moral ideals against actual life experiences. Food thus becomes synonymous with one's life's refining essence and subtler experiences until the ultimate goal of life is reached (whether it is liberation or something else). Conceptually, food for the Hindu is not simply a medium *of* expression (nor only a symbol *of* or *for* culture) but rather a direct essence and expression of the ultimate Reality itself. As such, it is, in a most fundamental way, always *prior* to such contingent qualifiers as status, sex, age, and social and religious duties.

The implications of such a cultural ideology of food are wide ranging and require systematic investigation *across* the domains of idea and practice. If the Hindu's food, for instance, stands as a moral value which is *prior* to various social, age, and gender distinctions, what implications does such a conception have for practical issues, and the Hindu's approach to them? Instead of being either "neutral" or simply age-gender "bound," does such a conception of food produce a distinct perspective (along with its own blind spots) on *how* food reaches all creatures—intimately, collectively, and as a "basic right" within a universal moral order? Popularly, only the creator or the divine ultimately ensures its availability to all creatures. This perspective is maintained despite the common knowledge that, in practice, social and economic factors strongly constrain food availability and adequate diet. For the Hindus, the moral order continues to receive attention as "the ultimate cause."

Though we have limited our attention in this book to only some shared "essences and experiences" of food mostly within the Hindu cultures and regions, the Hindu and Buddhist ideologies of food deserve a full comparative account on their own grounds. Within such a study must also be considered the question of *how* these traditions deal with issues of "food and women" and "food and female principle." Only such studies will better prepare us to consider the problems "food and gender" studies raise, as conceptualized in the West and imported into contemporary South Asia.

The accounts in this book recognize the woman's presence and role in an implicit way, essentially by context of discussion and by level of idealization. Our contributions mention the woman's role within ideal, ritual, expressive, and aesthetic contexts. However, this is *no* substitute for more systematic studies of the subject of women and food within South Asian societies and cultures. There is much to learn here, with comparative views from inside the culture and outside. But we must simultaneously recognize that the "gender focus" inevitably brings with it the Western-style politics of Western "individual's" rights and a politics of protest and counter-privilege that is far removed from the conjoining Indic ideologies of food essence and experience. In such a juxtaposition, it is crucial that we are able to treat the import, without privileging it, to let the people's own knowledge and sense freely appear.

The papers collected in this volume have gone through a rather long and complicated journey. We (the late Professor M. S. A. Rao and I), as organizers, conceived of "some sort of publication" soon after a group of Indian and American scholars had participated in a conference on Food Systems and Communication Structures, held during January 2–6, 1985, at the Central Institute of Indian Languages, Mysore, India. With our decision to publish selected papers, we asked the contributors to revise their presentations for publication, while we looked for two or three additional contributors to strengthen the volume's dominant focus. However, before these steps could be completed, Professor Rao unfortunately fell ill and died. Just about the same time, my own engagements, one year-long fieldwork trip and other research and teaching priorities, intervened, forcing me to postpone the project for a rather long period. Meanwhile, understandably, three contributors decided to publish their papers elsewhere (though three new ones joined—Aklujkar, Moreno, and White). I could return to the book only in late 1989. The present collection is a result of this second, rather "revised" effort, which owes most to the continued patience and faith of the "original" and new contributors included in this book.

Though the authors of this book reflect a diversity of disciplines and perspectives (some planned and some fortuitous), all attest to the cultural depth and sweep food evokes on the subcontinent. How does the subject enjoy as distinct and comprehensive a conceptual-practical discourse structure in India (vis-à-vis the West) as our papers here suggest, requires still further exploration. Similarly, we need to know more about how food in India continues to show its two Janus-like faces—one with a core of ideological essentialism and perpectivism (as with the Hindu and the Buddhist, in two different ways), and the other with problems, contradictions, and conflicts encountered in practice. The third—modern—face of food is still under construction, but it is not likely to simplify picture.

The Mysore Food Conference, held during the Sixth International Institute for Semiotic and Structural Studies (1985), was made, in part, feasible by a travel grant from the Smithsonian

Institution, Washington D.C., for the North American scholars. From the other side, the Central Institute of Indian Languages and the Central Food Technology Research Institute, both of Mysore, provided the conference and its participants with a venue, an intellectual ambiance, and generous hospitality. As is most often the case, this book also reflects only a fraction of the rich intellectual (and culinary) fare we had shared during the conference. This is indeed the occasion to thank the aforementioned institutions for their help, alongside a number of local hosts and individual scholars. Among those who must be mentioned are Ms. Francine Berkovitz of the Smithsonian Institution, the (then) directors of the two Mysore institutes, Dr. E. Annamalai, Dr. B. L. Amla; Professor D. P. Pattnayak, Dr. Ashok Kelkar, and, most of all, the late Professor M. S. A. Rao and his entire family in Mysore, for feasting us at his home on the occasion of the 1985 New Year.

Besides those included in this volume, the main participants of the 1985 Mysore Conference on food studies were Professors Mahadev Apte of Duke University, Judith Goode of Temple University, Ashok Kelkar of the University of Pune, David Knipe of the University of Wisconsin-Madison, Jayant Lele of Queen's University, McKim Marriott of the University of Chicago, M. S. A. Rao of the University of Delhi, and Rajendra Singh of the University of Montreal. Professors Walter Hauser and Murrey Milner of the University of Virginia, and Dr. P. K. Misra of the Anthropological Survey of India made useful comments. I acknowledge with thanks contributions from these (and several other Indian) colleagues who joined us in exploring humanistic and social-science based "food studies" on the subcontinent.

I am also grateful to Rafael Alvarado and Bruce Koplin for helping me revise different drafts of the typescript, especially by their expertise in word processing ("the only way to go," in their words).

This book is dedicated to the memory of Professor M. S. A. Rao, who as the Convener of the South Asian branch of the International Commission on the Anthropology of Food and Food Problems, had proposed the Mysore Conference.

R. S. Khare

Acknowledgments

The editor, authors, and SUNY Press gratefully acknowledge the following permissions granted for material used herein:

The University of California Press for "The *kathā* of Sakat: two tellings" (Susan Wadley, translator) in Stuart Blackburn and A. K. Ramanujan, eds., 1986, *Another Harmony: New Essays on the Folklore of India;* also for "The Karma Eater" in *Karma and Rebirth in Classical Indian Traditions,* 1981, by Wendy O'Flaherty.

Academic Press for material from *The International Journal of the Sociology of Law,* 1980, vol. 8:297–317. T. Selwyn, "The order of man and the order of things."

Columbia University Press for material from "Children" from *Poems of Love and War,* 1985, by A. K. Ramanujan.

Penguin Books Ltd. for the translation of the poem "Milk is left over . . . " by Basavanna, from *Speaking of Siva* by A. K. Ramanujan, 1973.

K. M. George, copyright holder for his translation of "When Death is on a Holiday" by Kunjan Nambiyar, in K. M. George's *A Survey of Malayalam Literature,* Asian Publishing House.

Introduction

The papers assembled in this volume investigate food in India and Sri Lanka for its wide-ranging cultural meanings and uses. The special focus is on the cultural essence and experience foods evoke among Indians.[1] Several papers discuss the issue of food essence and aesthetics, with special attention to Hindu saints and the divine, where foods, firmly grounded in moral ideals and practice, represent a cosmic, divine principle at one level and a most immediate and intimate semiotic reality at another.[2] Food in India involves cultural characteristics not commonly associated with food in the contemporary West,[3] for the subject routinely concerns matters of this world as well as the otherworld. Food is integral to India's cultural philosophy, since it comprehensively reflects the essence and experience of Indians at personal and collective levels. Food in India is never merely a material substance of ingestion, nor only a transactional commodity. It is synonymous with life and all its goals, including the subtlest and the highest. Sometimes highly abstract (approximating the linguistic, aesthetic, and even nontransactional or supratransactional "grammars") and sometimes palpably tangible (as a physical substance and "bodies"), this food asserts such a life-guiding presence that it concerns, one way or another, the thought and practice of the entire Indic civilization.

No wonder that such a conception of food is conducive to producing a comprehensive semiotics and semantics of food. There is widespread common understanding that foods in India routinely grade people's caste rank, help cure ailments, and reflect innate personal dispositions and spiritual pursuits and attainments. In its sweep and depth, food in India affords the Indianist a cultural lens to see beyond such basic dichotomies of his analysis as the ideal and the practical; self, body and the other; and abstract and concrete.

However, since our subject—a systematic study of food as a comprehensive cultural language—is still in initial stages, a suitable background discussion is needed for approaching the subject.

Once we have that, we will first identify those major cultural ways in which food plays a pivotal role for the expression and communication of the Hindu world and its distinctness, and second comment on how the papers of this volume illustrate a few aspects of the Hindu's comprehensive approach to food.

Food as a Subject of Study

Recent studies of food and culture in India repeatedly demonstrate that the varied properties of "eating and feeding" proceed according to one's social rank, customary rituals, sectarian values, and even implicit philosophical positions (e.g., Dumont 1980; Marriott 1968, 1976; Khare 1976b; and Khare and Rao 1986). In this way, the Indian food routinely produces a "semantic density" (to use Edwin Ardener's [1982, 1–12] phrase) of its own, often to comment on Hindu cultural expression and communication of the worldly or the otherworldly. We thus encounter a comprehensive cultural language that food develops with the help of "event richness" and "simultaneities" in meanings. All papers in this volume contribute toward such a discussion of food in India.

Our present discussion derives from the studies of food done earlier *in situ*—within caste, ritual, kinship, and traditional economics. What such traditional accounts and ethnographies offer us provides the necessary background for launching the next phase of food studies. If the earlier research repeatedly tells us that food is socially crucial within the Indian's world, we now systematically explore the issue of how Indians communicate about themselves, and their aesthetics and worldview with foods in a distinct—and uniquely comprehensive—way. If foods, in such a view, become clusters of moral expressions and meanings, they also reflect the constraints of the practical world and the imperatives of personal survival, on the one hand, and spiritual liberation, on the other.

A sociological initiative in such a direction was reflected in the studies of McKim Marriott, who employed "food transactions" as a primary explanatory device for discussing the internal organization of village caste ranking (Marriott 1968). In several studies, Marriott expanded on the Hindu logic of food transactions to grasp the more general cultural "construction" of the Hindu world and cosmology (Marriott 1959, 1976, 1989; Marriott and Inden 1977). Though his later attempts virtually abandon explicit reliance on food transactions, he started on this road with help of the example of intercaste food handling. The example perhaps allowed Marriott to conceive of the Hindu world as a "flow of substances" (e.g., Marriott 1987; 1989).

Though a distinct advancement over the earlier *in situ* food studies, Marriott's approach still does not accord food that comprehensive attention which the Indian and his world demand. In this volume, we argue that the Indian food system has much to reveal if we approach it as a subject of study by itself and test its explanatory powers across wide-ranging contexts. This, in turn, necessitates a brief review of some recent food-focused studies. The prewar, or early, phase of food studies in India mostly appeared within heterogeneous administrative reports and monographs produced on different "castes," "tribes," and administrative "districts" of India. Among the early exceptions would be Charlotte Viall Wiser's *The Foods of a Hindu Village of North India,* completed in 1936 and published in 1937, as a part of the studies of the Bureau of Statistics and Economic Research of the United Provinces. Similarly, for good knowledge of indigenous scholarship on the Hindu tradition and everyday life, one may mention C. Auddy's *The Diet of the Ancient Hindus,* published in Calcutta in 1916; A. K. Sarcar's *The Food and Dietary Customs of the Ancient Indians,* published in 1929; and J. C. Roy's *Food and Drink in Ancient Bengal,* published in 1948. A more systematized account of food in classical texts appeared with Prakash (1961).

Of these, Wiser's study comes nearest to what we now call the "anthropology of food and nutrition," for it anticipated some developments of the seventies. Such early studies require a systematic review as much for our better understanding of Hindu gastronomy as for recognizing a crucial place of the interdependence between Hindu diet and health (e.g., the Ayurvedic-Unani-Homeopathic complex of popular medicine in India consider dietary control to be integral to any effective treatment).

The recent phase, starting with the sixties, increasingly produced *field-based* inquiries on such subjects as vegetarianism (e.g., Sharma 1961; Khare 1966) and "food offerings" to the deities (e.g., Yalman 1969). Such attempts explicated a sociocultural institution, principle, value, or worldview in terms of food handling. The approach still continues in various ways within anthropology, only with increasing diversity of analytic concerns (e.g., on food and political relations, Appadurai 1981; on food and historical changes in a regional political economy, Breckenridge 1986; on food's place in regional socioreligious organization, Cantlie 1984; on food in temples, rituals, myths, literature, and popular culture, Ferro-Luzzi 1977, 1985; and on food practices under migration, Rao 1986). Several studies of the food system in India began in the seventies. They treated food as a cultural construction and made it a dominant subject of analysis in all of its complexity. Some called it the "anthropology or comparative sociology of food and food problems" (Douglas and Khare 1979). Concerned with comprehensive food, food policy, nutrition and hunger studies, investigators of this persuasion are consolidating their work, especially within American anthropology. Such studies either feed back into sociocultural analyses and perspectives, or develop into distinct nutrition and hunger-study specialties (for a sense of the range of studies already going on in this field, see Messer 1983).

A comment on these new developments and their value to our interpretive approach is in order. Under extreme domination, trauma and torture, food control becomes the prime weapon for determining others' survival. To the survivor, food becomes the dramatic minimum, with powerful psychological and social consequences. Appropriate accounts of the impact of extreme hunger on the human body, conducted from several directions, illustrate the controlling force of food on culture (e.g., Ruth 1987; Ngor 1987; Szymusiak 1986; and Scarry 1985). Though we lack such studies on India, we know that moral criteria every day crowd the issues of the food, physical body, and self-identity of the Indian (e.g., besides the Hindus, see Mahias 1985, on the Jains; Murphy 1986, for the Muslim feasting and fasting).

As I shall propose later on, cultural studies of food need not ignore the wide-ranging issues of policy and praxis, from food as commodity within regional histories to the current issues of international political rights to food and the problems of distributive justice. Anthropological research can contribute to such "critical" food studies, once we give the needed attention to the "entitlement" and "the right to food" debates (e.g., see Sen 1981, 1984; Tilley 1983; and Alston and Tomasevski 1984). And thus we also address the issue of food's shaping of culture. The purpose of mentioning such a direction of research is more than incidental for our volume: it relates to a deep-seated value conflict within the Indian system—the fact of unequal entitlements to food, on the one hand, and the ideal of morally just access to food by all creatures, on the other (Khare 1976b). In order to handle such internal conflicts, the Indian, especially the Hindu, draws upon the internal dynamics of his cultural ideology. If we consider the three major models of the Hindu "essence and experience" of food (chapter 7 in this book), we find that such models and meaning systems produce three correspondingly distinct but overlapping discourses—ontological and experiential, transactional and therapeutic, and world-critical (see section IV). To concern ourselves with the "semiotics" of Hindu foods is often to deal with a combination of these discourses for one significant reason or another.[4] But before we can discuss these, we must briefly consider certain essential and distinct semantic properties of food within the Hindu world.

Self-Evident Truth

Food among the Hindus is "self-evident" because it is a dimension of none other than the Creator himself and is integral to the formation of cosmos. A cosmic (rather than anthropocentric) "logic" thus controls the production and circulation of food within creation, and it is a manifestation of Brahman, the ultimate Reality, as the Upanishadic sayings assert (see chapters 7 and 8 in this volume). It is ideal and material at once. It therefore does not admit such Western dichotomies as code and substance, symbol and reality, and ideal and practical. To the Hindu, food also does not "represent" Brahman, but it is actually a part of this ultimate reality, Brahman. In this world and beyond, the cosmic moral order (*dharma*) regulates the availability of food to all creatures. Hindus regard such a truth as self-evident, requiring no further proof and admitting no doubts. When body and self are concerned, food is considered as one of the five "sheaths" (*annamayakośa*) which "clothes" the soul (*jīva*; the other four sheaths being those of life-breath, mind, understanding, and bliss). Thus, food directly matters to the formation of a Hindu's inner being and its becoming from one birth to the next.

Defined by such a distinct cultural ideology, food is "meaningful" to the Hindu throughout his life. As we know, multiple schemes of food classification establish the rules about *appropriate* eating and feeding practices (for some classical rules, see Manu IV, 205–225; V, 5–56; for an ethnographic description of some food practices among the Hindus, see Khare 1976a; for intercaste food transactions within a village, Marriott 1968). The general message of such an approach to food and food transactions seems unmistakable: one must specify as many contexts, conditions, and qualities of foods to be eaten (or not to be eaten) as possible, because the internal states of one's being, within this world and beyond, remain intimately connected to the moral quality and condition of what one eats. Whatever one eats has manifest and hidden, and immediate and remote, consequences on one's body and being (Manu IV and V; Kane 1974, chaps. 21–22). Food in India is therefore never simply a material substance; it is never only what the eyes see. The unseen karma and dharma of the giver and receiver energize it, circulate it, and color it.

Food thus exemplifies in India its multilayered semantic density. It is a moral (i.e., dharma-ordained) substance, a semiotic field, and a comprehensive "discourse" (i.e., a "text of meaningful actions" in Paul Ricoeur's sense; Ricoeur 1981). Thus if food expresses the cosmic truth, showing its ultimate control by the dharma-based principles of cosmic creation and maintenance, it also expresses itself with intricate social-ritual (and karma-dharma) distinctions, classifications, and customary actions, releasing discourses on meaningful action concerning how food, body, and self need to be handled in each other's terms to achieve the Hindu goal of liberation. However, this picture remains incomplete unless we also note that, despite such elaborate schemes, food still retains for the Hindu unpredictable (even mysterious) consequences, and thus requires ever more vigilance in its handling. This character of food is in some important ways a "limitless field" where language, speech, and action continuously work in each other's terms.[5] Once we become used to approaching food within such an expanding paradigm of significance and interpretation, we will see how often major rituals centrally locate "food acts" and "events" because they extend, and even magnify what speech and action want to convey. Foods quickly absorb good as well as bad words and intentions, producing what mythologies and the popular culture abundantly illustrate as a concern with "cursed" and "blessed" foods (for example, see O'Flaherty 1976).

Such "speaking food" culminates in producing a non-dichotomous linkage between the Creator, body, and self (Nikhilananda 1963, 272, 275–276, for the *Taittirīya Upanishad*'s formulations of this link). Here food is at once an exhaustive moral product and a cosmic process, an ideal construct (i.e., popularly the *annadevatā*) as well as a "generative commodity" (*anna* or *annaja*). If hunger reminds us of the material food, Hindu food still demands that we treat it as a comprehensive moral language that is "partly interior, subjective and rooted in regularities of the human mind, and partly exterior, objective and rooted in materiality" (Ardener 1982, 10, for characterizing the nature of language).

Food is self-evident to the Hindu in another way. It is for the coveted pursuit of one's own liberation. Food here is the necessary "helper" until all exchanges *cease* between self (*prāṇa*), body, and the world; even the renouncer feeds himself until the absolute Brahman is realized. Within the worldly life (*saṁsāra*), however, food plays a double role—enlightening when approached with austerity and self-control and degrading when sought for sensual indulgence. Within the second frame, sensual food becomes a part of the hall of Māyā's mirrors, deluding and destroying the indulgent. Unscrupulous pursuit of food and eating in daily life is known to invite diseases and shorten life. Under extreme austerities (*tapas*), on the other hand, any eating is considered a hindrance.

Such a close and intense relationship of food to self (and its spiritual welfare) makes food a subject of "heightened intersubjectivity" among the Hindus, where they routinely take into account the moral backgrounds and powers of those who handle food. Food readily absorbs the qualities of its "carriers" or "feeders" (in Hindi *khilānéwālé*). If a saint renders food auspicious and blessed, an ordinary person's covetousness, accumulated karmas, ignorance, and moral lapses as surely taint it. Even a saint's lapse pursues him from one birth to the next, until rectified (for the case of Ravidas, see Khare 1984, 40–46; O'Flaherty 1976, 73–77).

Three Major Discourses

Based on the "thread-soul" ideology where food becomes simultaneously a moral and material essence, Hindu India pursues its comprehensive gastrosemantics in terms of three major cultural models and their corresponding discourses. The first discourse on food—ontological and experiential—is concerned with the cultural "givens" within the "worldly" sphere (including food's classifications, taboos, intrinsic qualities, normal meal patterns, dietary restrictions, and notions of sufficiency and insufficiency). It includes one's passage along the designated social-ritual phases (*varṇāśramadharma*), on the one hand, and on a "path" of spiritual welfare (*atmakalyāṇa*), on the other. The second discourse—transactional and therapeutic—concerns itself with the maintenance and promotion of comprehensive body-soul "wellness" (including the prevention and cure of various diseases by diet and medicine) by recognizing interdependence among different intrinsic properties of foods, the eater and his actions of giving and receiving. The third discourse—world-critical—shows the limits of the first two as it concerns itself with such ultimate issues as the reality or illusion of the world, and the roles ("inner," or spiritual and "outer," or physical) of foods in enhancing one's spiritual knowledge (*jñāna*) and "inner sight" (*antaradṛṣṭi*) for attaining liberation (*mokṣa*).

The three food discourses, in other terms, are concerned with (a) worldly life and becoming, (b) healing and happiness, and (c) self-control and salvation. Each discourse deals with issues of cognition and experience, self and cosmos, and ideology and action. Each discourse is characterized by its own distinct praxis—the first does so by keeping the soul-Brahman principle at the center of all spiritual paths and pursuits (yogas); the second by following dietary and ritual regulations organized along one's physical state and social stages in life (e.g., *varṇāśramadharma*), for fulfilling dharma and achieving personal health and "wellness" (*svāstha* and *kalyāṇa*); and the third by pursuing fasting, austerities and renunciation for attaining liberation. Finally, and most importantly, the three discourses overlap and work interdependently within a Hindu's life; they exhibit contextually varying distinctions—but no immutable dichotomies—along thought, feeling, and action.

In Indian sociology, the three discourses have been unevenly studied so far. At present we know most about the second discourse, and less about the first and the third. For these two discourses, often classical or other learned texts still best inform us how India develops its distinct gastrosemantic conceptions by linking the healing of body to the healing of soul, with a critical view of the worldly, the ephemeral, and the unjust (*adharma*). Issues of justice and fair play, for instance, engage the classical lawgiver Manu as he enunciates the basic principles of food classification and hierarchical food use. He deals with issues of social priority in food distribution, justifying his hierarchical view of moral justice and fair play (for the basic internal structure of the discourse, see Manu IV, 205–225; V, 5–56).[6] Manu of course does not see hierarchy and justice as mutually incompatible. His ultimate authority for rendering the conception and distribution of food unequal-but-just resides with the Creator:

> The Lord of Created beings (*Prajāpati*) came and spake to them, "Do not make that equal, which is unequal. The food of that liberal (usurer) is purified by faith; [that of the] other [man] is defiled by a want of faith" (Manu IV, 225).

The contemporary Hindu's food discourse is often an ambiguous critique of this foundational structure of the Hindu cosmic order. It remains ambiguous because, on the one hand, it renders hierarchy as unjust under the influence of modern values, and, on the other, keeps subscribing to the primacy of the traditional hierarchical order (e.g., in terms of the ideology of *varṇāśrama* model). Similarly, the contemporary Hindu's popular food values involve him in another anomaly as he constructs his personal and group identity on the superiority of vegetarianism. They conflict with the classical, Vedic values of meat eating. Vegetarianism, as the anthropologist well knows, defies a simple, consistent caste rank correlation (otherwise all Brahmans will only be vegetarians). Vegetarianism perhaps involves several rival historical forces and value paradoxes in Hindu ideology, pointing to us other properties of such food discourses.[7]

But such paradoxes only increase the force and subtlety of gastrosemantic discourses for the Indian. In foods reside all the major constituents and "essences" that cause physical ailments and influence personal temperament, emotional fluctuations, longevity, and salvation. With foods the Indian regulates his mental states and aesthetic feelings, and secures spiritual gains. To the spiritually adept, foods reveal as well as filter the thoughts, feelings, and experiences of others (and their own). The discerning know, as Mahatma Gandhi used to say, that food can either aggravate or subdue the primary sources of worldly bondage—anger, lust, greed, and infatuation.

Though the Hindu, Buddhist, and Jain on the subcontinent may largely continue to share the preceding profile of food praxis (and we have employed the word "Indian" in such a comprehensive sense), we must emphasize that each stakes a claim to a distinct philosophic ideology and "food culture." And this means that, once considered in detail, their gastrosemantic discourses will also be distinctly different. Thus, if food and eating constitute a "multiform" but single Ultimate Reality to the Hindu, they are subjects of severe austerity and denial for the Jains, and largely a practical matter of maintaining life (without extremes) for the Buddhist. If the Hindu approaches eating with self-control, the Jain finds eating ideologically risky (if necessary) and the Buddhist approaches it as a part of his "middle path".[8] Still, for all the three, food may variously enter the issues of being and becoming, healing and social sharing, and self-discipline.

A Comprehensive Food Culture

The chapters assembled in this book may be better understood with the help of preceding three cultural discourses on Hindu food. The chapters concern themselves chiefly with two aspects—ritual and literary, especially as they are interrelated in India. Chapters predominantly concerned with religious matters, often deal with mythological figures, saints, householders, and the divine. Those concerned with literary and aesthetic aspects serve to underscore the breadth and depth of comprehensive expressions foods enjoy in India. They specifically show how the Hindu and the Buddhist convey their generally overlapping experiential, aesthetic and communicational richness within ceremonial as well as everyday life. All papers, together, approach food for its properties of wide-ranging presence, semiosis, circulation, and communication across the physical, human, and divine domains. Hindu saints, ritualists, and the divine particularly treat food as a bridge between this-worldly and otherworldly spheres, making it a ground for divine-pervading sensual and suprasensual experiences. Thus the Hindu's food (alongside his body) becomes one of the most exhaustive mediums within which the discerning realize the ultimate unity of the material and spiritual existence.

As an aesthetic experience, food also acquires distinct literary, culinary, worldly, and popular expressions. Open to the worldly, everyday experience, different foods and "food contexts" readily evoke wide-ranging sayings, common wisdom, and special feelings and moods. Not confined to the sacred and the profound, Indian food also expresses the ordinary and the witty. The sacred and the secular readily conflate, denying room for a rigid dichotomy or division between them. Further, as this volume attempts to deal with the learned and popular cultural meanings of food, and food contexts, it deals with a variety of "essences" and exchanges shared by the saintly and the divine, the sensual and the suprasensual, and the commonsensical, the poetic, and the ironical.

The chapters of this book are arranged to reflect a complementary relationship between ritual, mythological and literary properties India variously assigns to food. Though dominated by the sacred, the ritual easily slips into the domains of "common knowledge," the secular and the practical (and vice versa; see chapters 6 and 8 in this volume). However, to familiarize the reader with major shared rules, meanings and actions of the Indian world, we start with the rich and varied roles saints, sadhus, sages, and devotees have played in increasing the signifying power of food in India. More than representation, such food evokes an universal essence and triggers vast experiences—poetic, intuitive and mystical.

Khare, White and Aklujkar substantiate this issue in different ways as contemporary saints, mythological sages, and medieval saint devotees employ food to pattern their crucial communications with devotees (Khare), share intimacies with the divine (Aklujkar), and play out status conflict among themselves as antagonists (White). If the ritual, semiotic and experiential aspects concern Khare's paper, White's mythological material draws attention to status via edible and abominable foods, especially as the spiritual and temporal powers collide for domination. Aklujkar's Maharashtrian saints complement this conflict model by juxtaposing to it the power of divine love and the divine-devotee intimacy. They celebrate the food which communicates oneness as well as multiplicity, intimacy and (or denial of) hierarchy, and knowledge and experience. They express with food their exalted, unifying devotional attitudes and worldviews, on the one hand, and messages of social reform (or protest), on the other.

Such a range of concerns introduces what Khare calls the "semantic density" of the holy person's food. At the center is the cultural logic of "conjoining" several "gastrosemantic triangles" (e.g., food, body and self or *ātman*), establishing multiple appropriate interrelationships between the inner and the outer, spiritual and material, and general and particular. Pursuing two cardinal cultural formulations—you are what you eat, and you eat what you are—Khare finds that the Hindu sages, sadhus, and yogis have evolved a comprehensive gastrosemantic discourse according to their spiritual "paths" (*mārga*) and associated philosophies. The chapter, then, demonstrates the "conjoining logic" of Hindu foods, where semanticity and the semiotic productivity of food are corroborated for a range of cultural situations—from the Ayurvedic to the Tantric, to even the contemporary Gandhian.

Concerned with textual (often mythological) materials, White's exercise specifically focuses on a Kṣatriya sage's (Viśvāmitra's) dog-eating abomination and its prolonged consequences for his controversial quest for a Brahman sage's status. White amplifies on the long-recognized "inner conflicts" between asceticism and caste status within the Hindu world and food's crucial role in them. Framed by the polar opposition between the abominable "dog-cookers" (*śvapacas*) and the cow-worshipping Brahman sages (*brahmarṣis*), and engaged in prolonged status battles between the

Brahmanic authority of Vasiṣṭha and the ascetic power of the dog-eating Viśvāmitra, the story allows White to investigate the underlying ambiguous "rhetoric" which food produces within the Hindu world. Do sages really become what they eat?

While the orthodox traditions answer the question in the affirmative, the heterodox movements dispute such a resolution. They have produced mediating concepts (e.g., a Kṣatriya renouncer—*rājarṣi* like Viśvāmitra), on the one hand, and, as White shows with mythological evidence, anomalous conditions (Triśaṅku's bodily transfer to heaven), on the other. Corroborating a quality of Hindu gastrosemantics, White notes how "food" (milk, cow, dog, cooking and eating, and forcing others to eat and drink abominations) yields within his study "so many rhetorical expressions for the tensions inherent to the processes of pollution, purification and redemption in a hierarchized society." As Viśvāmitra, in distress, justifies saving his life by eating the hind quarters of a dog, he exemplifies for the ordinary Hindu defensible limits of permissible behavior during dharma-in-crisis (*āpaddharma* or *dharma saṁkata*), on the one hand, and a relentless pursuit of asceticism for acquiring superior spiritual (and *varṇa?*) status, on the other.

If food thus becomes a crucial rhetoric for expressing status and power conflicts with two famous mythological sages, Maharashtrian saints approach food for substantializing the power of divine love, carving out a distinct form of "feasting" (emotional, literary, and spiritual) to let food aesthetics and poetics create each other. Aklujkar shows how such "feasting" occasions a wide variety of aesthetic and literary expressions, characterizing intimacies of deity and devotee. Such a food flouts normal social rules by valuing love over hierarchy, informality over formality, and feeling over reason and rules. This chapter provides the climaxing Bhakti paradigm later saints (including Khare's contemporary sadhus) have followed. Not only that, it links up with the paradigmatic *annakūṭa* feast of Krishna which Toomey analyzes as a "feast of love." On such occasions, food yields waves of polyvocal discourses where status and love, transaction and nontransaction, and reason and emotion test each other's limits. Riding waves of divine love, the Hindu experiences the extraordinary by handling food.

The next two chapters (Toomey and Moreno) extend the discussion of how love empowers food, body and life, especially in the presence of the temple-enshrined divine. Both chapters deal with gross (*sthūla*) and subtle (*sūkṣma*) properties of the divine body and divine leftovers (whether acceptable or unacceptable). However, while

Toomey places feasting food (*annakūṭa*) within some of the emotive moods of Vaiṣṇava devotion and its spiritual aestheticism (*bhāvas* and *rasas*) in the north, Moreno deals with Lord Murukan̲'s "food washings" (*pañcāmirtam*) as a material-Ayurvedic-aesthetic-divine substance (*rasa* or *rasam*). Once in contact with Lord Murukan̲ of the south, these washings "become" him. Both contributors remain careful not to oversimplify the messages (gross and subtle) the food thus creates for the devotee and his world.

Toomey's discussion of the *annakūṭa* feast as a "mountain of food" and a mountain of love illustrates the ideal of reciprocal love. In his words, the feast is a "gastrohyperbolism," a reversal of the ascetic model of food, yielding "meta-communicative effects," where, as a Krishna's devotee had remarked, "we share everything with everybody." The semiotics of the "mountain of food" (*annakūṭa*) builds on a homologous, metonymic prism—Krishna, Govardhan hill, and the *annakūṭa,* where each refracts on the other two, producing a three-way "mirroring" among Krishna, hill, and food. Krishna is the hill, as well as being beside it, in a "split or double image" (as Toomey's lithograph, figure 4.1, shows). Though sensuality within Krishna's devotion has a specialized conceptual character and development, it does not exclude popular-cultural characterizations, where a Krishna's devotee is a *masta* (i.e., essentially an informal, carefree, and uninhibited) person, and therefore often a glutton as well.

The *annakūṭa* feast has a formal and an informal face, varying with the sectarian differences of the devotees (i.e., along the Vallabhite and Caitanyaite sects) and reflected by Krishna's iconic and aniconic forms and the sect-prescribed modes of food offering. In the Vallabhite setting, which is formal and hierarchical, the regal child Krishna takes 95 minutes to eat the enormous meal in seclusion, while his informal ("natural" or aniconic) counterpart, the "lotus mouth" (or a crack) in the Gobardhana hill, is the instant enjoyer (*rasika*) of his devotee's food, before everybody. But either way, Krishna enjoys such abundant faith and love from his devotees via abundant food that the feast directly "becomes" (in quality and quantity) his body and his divine grace.

The divine body in Moreno's chapter acquires a distinct material (and pragmatic) emphasis. Besides feeding, he is concerned with divine washings and leftovers because they renew and revitalize the devotee's body. As Moreno observes, to consume the deity's leftovers (including washings) is not only to experience the divine within, but it is also "to regenerate certain lost qualities in [devotees'] bodies, so that slowly they become more like the body of the god." Not unlike Krishna's mediation of the natural hill (gross) and the spiritual love (subtle) at the Mount Govardhana, Murukaṉ, "the essence (*rasam*) of the hills," concerns himself with the body and well-being of the devotee.

Taking a distinct "substance-altering," healing view of the deity's body (after McKim Marriott's ethnosociology), Moreno finds Murukaṉ made up of nine metalloids and various herbs, along with the poisons that carry healing and restorative powers. The god becomes the " 'doctor of the dark age,' " where the god's body, with appropriate food offerings and washings, is kept in "thermic" balance (i.e., a balance of heat and cold along the seasonal variations). Caste groups reflect this scheme of "substance"-based distinctions, Moreno tells us, by assigning among themselves distinct thermic characteristics. God, food, *therme,* caste, and life enter into mutually reinforcing relationships here to corroborate the "substance flow." And such a discussion of God-food (*pañcāmirtam*), for the purposes of this book, also remains cognitive, intersubjective, and expressive (like Toomey's), though the chosen markers are different. Moreno's account relegates the faith, emotion, and otherworldly pursuits (*sraddhā, bhāva,* and *adhyātama*) of the devotee in the background in order to focus on a particular "science" of "substance flow."

Such a language not only interrelates the divine body with the human but renders the former in terms of the latter. Our concern increases with the constitution and healthy functioning of the human body, bringing a focus on the primary constituents and Ayurvedic humors—*guṇas* and *doṣas*. Seneviratne's paper allows such a discussion within a changed context (Sinhalese Buddhists of Sri Lanka) and a changed (practical, everyday) ethics and aesthetics. (Yet there is *no* break with the rest of the book because Seneviratne skillfully builds on a basic *sharing* between Buddhist and Hindu notions of food, body, Ayurveda, and the related aesthetics.) Sinhalese meals involve "moments of perfect aesthetic appreciation," showing how the Ayurvedic and culinary qualities (*guṇas* alongside *rasas, dhātus* and *doṣas*—flavors, essences and humors) constitute a language of essential coherence. The Sinhalese Buddhist demonstrates this property best as he relates food cooking within one's house (external) to that within one's body (internal). Cooking and digestion unify diverse foods; spicy cooking, as Seneviratne puts it, "unifies the separateness inherent in the raw items." The Buddhist food aestheticism, though philosophically so different from the devout Hindu saint's, still converges on a shared sense of intersubjectivity and reflexivity as it locates flavor in foods and meditative bliss in flavors.

The preceding chapters variously depict a range of cultural essence, experience, and meaning the Indian foods convey. Though by no means representative of the entire Hindu "food culture," they show how two main frames of analysis (drawn from social science and humanities) intertwine within India's gastronomy: If one deals with diversity in terms of a few primary cultural principles and models, the other directly celebrates the diversity of gastronomic rites, aesthetics, and literary expressions (learned and popular). The last two chapters of the book illustrate two general interpretive exercises.

Khare focuses on certain dominant cultural models and meanings that constitute the "essence" and experience of Hindu foods.[9] Thus, the Hindu's food, like his world, is found to be grounded within five elements, three strands, five senses, three humors, six savors, and nine feelings, to let the Hindu achieve his four goals of life (for a schematic discussion of such a multiple chain of distinctions, especially within a distinct philosophical—nondualist—frame, see Satprakashananda 1965, 315–334). To view food this way as a product of strings of "constituents" is also to see it as a karma-dharma evolute (*kendraja*), requiring ethical control and regulation every day in adult life. At another (subtle) level, the same constituents allow the Hindu to treat food as an entirely conceptual (*mānasika*) essence and supratransactional presence (or even a devotional attitude or *bhāva*; see Aklujkar's chapter). As a presence, food thus routinely—and "eternally"—passes from gross to subtle, and vice versa, within the Hindu universe.

Within the lived world, the Hindu awards multiple values to food by status (*varṇāśrama*) and "path" (*mārga*) values (elaborated further according to the criteria of personal faith and spiritual maturity). Such characterizations apply until the cosmic-moral essence of food is not personally "realized" as a part of one's spiritual progress. Ideally, there is no notion of food without such a cosmic scheme.

Defined by the preceding properties, Khare approaches Hindu food in terms of three cultural models—ontological and experiential (i.e., based on the "thread-soul" or *éktā*), transactional and therapeutic (karma-dharma or *anéktā*), and world-critical and world reforming (Bhakti-Shakti or *sraddhā*). These models help him to show how food, in essence, must *conjoin* this-worldly with otherworldly, and sensual with suprasensual concerns. In evidence, as several chapters of this book show, innumerable Hindu sages, sadhus, poets, and wisemen (*jñāni-vijñāni*) have been prominent "synthesizers" of such models of food and their discourses.

On the other hand, Ramanujan arranges a "bouquet" of diverse contexts, markers, and figures of expression, identifying the Hindu's "gastroaesthetics," but again within a unified system of signification. He repeatedly illustrates how the Hindu forges interdependence and unity between this-worldly and otherworldly aesthetics and poetics. He treats food for its density of meanings—for its unlimited semiosis, and he adduces examples of moral metaphors and practical parables for their powers of semiosis—by denotation, connotation, and contextual suggestion. Showing how food metaphors expand into a shared discourse on gustatory and aesthetic "tastes" (*rasa, ruci,* and *asvāda*), he arrives at aesthetic discourses—learned and popular—in India that variously underscore a distinct, deep yogic principle—"experience is in the experiencer."

With the help of preceding comments, we hope that the reader will discover numerous other shared affinities between any two (or any cluster of) chapters in this book. We may find India's food conversing with us in several languages, acquiring a variety of faces and voices in a variety of conditions and criticisms of human condition. I allude to one development below.

Toward A New Turn: Critical Food Studies

India's distinct models and experiences of food provide us with certain distinct properties of India's cultural accounting of itself as a civilization. Food illuminates India's ideality, morality, reflexivity, materiality, and cosmology in various ways, showing us the depth as well as sweep of such a scheme. Conjoining materiality, practice, and experience, food in Hindu India stamps one's being and becoming; it runs through the personal, social, pragmatic, spiritual, and ideal domains, assuring the depth of meaning and purpose that the chapters of this book variously attest to. Food does not merely symbolize; it just *is* one of the self-evident truths on which the Hindu world rests.

Such a comprehensive formulation should benefit interdisciplinary food studies because it helps to enlarge and enrich our aspectual food descriptions, classifications, prohibitions, and transactions. As we found, food in India at once concerns "material and health sciences," layered meanings, intersubjective dialogues, emotional experiences, and multiple (and open-ended) cultural "texts" and their interpretations (learned and popular). Such food provides repeated clues to distinct characteristics of India's "cultural reasoning." Confined to the Hindu and the Sinhalese Buddhist food schemes, this book, however, by no means exhausts the range of "food discourses" in which India engages. There still are many other crucial directions and dimensions to account for. And one of the ways to conclude this introduction is perhaps to comment on another possible direction India's food studies could take in the future.

Food is as much a subject for moral regulation and contemplation as a substance for ingestion to maintain life. If its handling necessitates transactions at one level, its essence resides at another level, in morally just (*dharma saṁgata*) availability to all creatures, and within the entire creation. Evaluated for dharma-ordained notions of justice in everyday life, food seldom is a decision-neutral cluster of symbolic-reflexive discourses (see the preceding discussion of the "third discourse"). It becomes a comprehensive moral-jural "text," where different meanings of dharma, rights and obligations, unresolved personal dilemmas, and scales of practical priorities compete with one another. Such food engages us in issues of competing notions of just dharma and associated ethical-jural problems encountered within personal and collective life. White's chapter on Viśvāmitra's moral dilemmas as "dog-eater" comes nearest to considering such an issue.

A new aspect of critical food studies in India could thus be inaugurated if food were viewed as *more* than a customary (ritual or material) transactional commodity, to let the changing notions of the "just" and the "unjust" food (for hunger and survival) receive greater attention, with associated notions of (and debates on) distributive justice. We need to know about this aspect as much in classical and customary India as in contemporary times. The subsidized ration shops in modern India (for "fair" food distribution to the weak and the poor), on the other hand, demand that we critically examine assumptions of the internationalized Western ideology of economic individualism and egalitarianism (usually translated as "rights" and "entitlements" to food; e.g., Eide 1987; Sen 1981, 1984). Such a Western value scheme clearly assumes a different value basis for distributive justice than that produced by the dharma-karma forces of the Indic world. And yet as negotiations between the two distant positions go on in contemporary India, strategies of conflict as well as accommodation emerge every day, rendering food as that moral-material "commodity" that continues to speak in the language of karma-dharma even as the political language of Western-style rights is learned for asserting personal security and survival. Such a step *expands and deepens* the Indian's social, economic, and political communication via foods (for a general discussion of "linkages" between commodities and society, see Douglas and Isherwood 1979).

For India, we could start by examining notions of distributive justice (as a dimension of dharma and *nyāya*) in a wide variety of religious texts, history, and folklore. Anthropology could join the discussion by "writing" appropriate ethnographies on just and unjust notions of food (and hunger), and on the conditions (and justifications) of differential rights and entitlements to food. Some recent anthropological and philosophical critiques, once read with such a subject in mind, may encourage us to open food studies to recent critical cultural, political, and jural thought (e.g., see Marcus and Fischer 1986; Walzer 1983; Singh and Lele 1988).

Notes

1. The term "Indian" is used throughout to include the Sinhalese cuisine in a cultural, *not* political, sense. Its general conceptual affinity with Hindu food and the Ayurvedic system is equally striking, and H. L. Seneviratne, our contributor on the Sri Lankan Sinhalese food system, confirms such an overall sharing. For these reasons (but without erasing specific distinctions prevalent between the Hindu and the Sinhala), our usage of such words as "Indian," "Hindu," and "Sinhalese" in this book will emphasize a generally shared civilizational content and perspective on foods. Similarly, following other contributors, I continue to employ "Indian" to refer to the dominant Hindu or Hindu Indian cultural characteristics, though there is no intention to reduce India to Hindu society and culture.

Since food in India is a notoriously wide-ranging practical and philosophic subject, I must remark on another stipulation. When referred to as an abstract or cultural moral/collective construct, I use "the food" or "food" (in singular). Everyday diversity is usually indicated by "foods." Other contributors vary, though all of them refer to both senses of food. One contributor (Moreno, chapter 5) even capitalizes the word to refer to India's distinct philosophical notions of food. I purposely have not edited out this diversity of usage because I think it conveys a shared awareness in our analysis of food systems.

2. Explicated later on, "speaking food" encapsulates the cultural sense of a Hindi phrase (*anna péta sé boltā hai*), which my informants—householders and saints—variously employed to refer to the fact that food yields

speech. Food is a "live" presence for him, with many faces, "tongues," and meanings.

3. The issue is important enough in some ways to receive attention at this point. I particularly want to draw the reader's attention to the conceptual rather than practical or functional aspects of this distinction. India's frequent identification with food shortages, famines, and droughts may lead one to think that all this attention on food must be, after all, a consequence of India's longstanding food problems. The West, in contrast, has simply moved beyond such a phase and therefore shows a different attitude toward food—scientific when its production is concerned and casual when its distribution and everyday eating are concerned. Though there may be some historical truth in such a difference, when the recent past is concerned, the cultural approach to food in India, I suggest, has been distinct in some fundamental—ideological—ways. Food is not just a symbol *of* or *for* the cultural but it *is* integral to the Hindu's ultimate reality in the same way as "self" or "soul" is.

4. Charles Peirce's semiotics has recently attracted the attention of some anthropologists working on India (e.g., Singer 1984; Daniel 1984). Its analytic approach is generally found "suitable" to Indian culture. However, more work is needed to examine the "fit" between Peirce's schemes and India's own longstanding theories of logic, meaning, and epistemology. Exercises on food may help explicate more fully how Indian culture goes about interrelating syntactics, semantics, and pragmatics to each other, to produce context-dependent and context-free identities of self.

I prefer to use the term "semiotic" in a more general, dictionary sense to refer to "a general philosophy of signs and symbols" which deals with their functions and meanings in different "languages" (*Webster's Ninth New Collegiate Dictionary* 1985, 1070).

5. Once interpreted in as general terms as intended by the Indian, "speech" (*vāṇī* or *bhāṣā*) stands for both *langue* and *parole*. Such speech, as the classical authorities always emphasized, closely guides and affects every act and every thing, including foods. For example, Manu (IV, 256) proclaimed, "All things (have their nature) determined by speech; speech is the root, and from speech they proceed; but he who is dishonest with respect to speech, is dishonest in everything."

"Speech" in such a usage includes norms, good practice, intention, feeling, intuition, and insight. All of these together also shape the moral content and texture of food.

The chapters of this book variously argue that the Hindu food is a highly inclusive and sensitive cultural language, where the material and the symbolic, concrete and abstract, and the sensual and the suprasensual cannot be dichotomized. When such properties are distinguished by context, it is not at the expense of the underlying tendency toward the ultimate unity.

6. For an anthropological discussion of the point that discourses tend to engage in exerting and justifying a distinct form of control, see Parkin 1982, xlvi–xlviii.

7. Vegetarianism is a good example of how later Hindu culture reinterpreted the meat eating prevalent within the Vedic times and fashioned it as an ideological weapon for grading and justifying the practice among those socially near (as with the Brahmans and Kṣhatriyas of different regions), and downgrading and excluding those the "distant other." For a recent analysis of meat eating and its "ecological placement" and medical use in Ayurveda, see Zimmermann 1987. As I have remarked elsewhere, from the point of view of those at the periphery (i.e., Sudras and Untouchables), vegetarianism proved to be a dual weapon—of social dominance as much as of spiritual self-discipline (Khare 1984).

Paradoxically, on the other hand, when a vegetarian Hindu knows that his ancestors practiced and promoted meat eating, he does *not* see sufficient reason for changing his vegetarian value preference. Classical India's food values thus contradict those prevailing. Though, according to the traditional logic, the original practice should be the most authoritative guide, popular Hindu culture chooses to ignore such logic in favor of the prevailing preference. It is a clear case not only of reinterpretation but also of reaching and maintaining an opposite cultural judgment within a traditional order.

8. On the Buddhist position on food in different stages of life, I profited from a discussion with my colleague Professor H. L. Seneviratne, and he provided me with a general commentary on food within Buddhism.

9. My two chapters in this book, along with the "Introduction," are presented as interrelated readings. They grew out of the paper originally prepared for the Mysore conference in 1985. Thus the gastrosemantic "triangles" discussed in the first chapter have unavoidable conceptual kinship with the three models of food essence and experience (*anna* and *annadevatā*), on the one hand, and with the three—ontological and experiential, transactional and therapeutic, and world-critical—discourses, on the other (chapter 8).

References

Alston, P., and K. Tômasevski (eds.)
1984 *The Right to Food.* Utrecht: Martinus Nijhoff Publishers.

Appadurai, Arjun
1981 "Gastro-politics in Hindu South Asia." *American Ethnologist* 8:494–511.

Ardener, Edwin
1982 "Social Anthropology, Language and Reality." In *Semantic Anthropology*. A.S.A. Monograph 22. David Parkin (ed.). London: Academic Press.

Auddy, C.
1916 *The Diet of the Ancient Hindus*. Calcutta: Thomas.

Breckenridge, Carol A.
1986 "Food, Politics and Pilgrimage in South India, 1350–1650 A.D." In *Food, Society and Culture*. R. S. Khare and M. S. A. Rao (eds.). Durham: Carolina Academic Press.

Bühler, Georg (trans.)
1886 *The Laws of Manu, The Sacred Books of the East*. Vol. 25. Delhi: Motilal Banarsidass 1964 [quoted as "Manu" in the text].

Cantlie, Audrey
1984 *The Assamese: Religion, Caste and Sect in an Indian Village*. London: Curzon Press.

Daniel, E. Valentine
1984 *Fluid Signs: Being a Person the Tamil Way*. Berkeley: University of California Press.

Douglas, Mary
1966 *Purity and Danger*. London: Routledge & Kegan Paul.

1975 *Implicit Meanings: Essays in Anthropology*. London: Routledge & Kegan Paul.

Douglas, Mary, and Baron Isherwood
1979 *The World of Goods*. New York: Basic Books.

Douglas, Mary, and R. S. Khare
1979 "Commission on Anthropology of Food: Statement of Its History and Current Objectives." *Social Science Information*. Vol. 18, no. 6:903–913.

Dumont, Louis
1980 *Homo Hierarchicus* (Revised Complete Edition). Chicago: University of Chicago Press.

Eide, Asbjørn
1987 "Report on the Right to Adequate Food as a Human Right." Economic and Social Council, United Nations Commission on Human Rights. Mimeographed.

Ferro-Luzzi, Eichinger G.
1977 "The Logic of South Indian Food Offerings." *Anthropos* 72:529–556.

1985 "The Cultural Uses of Food in Modern Tamil Literature." *Annali dell' Instituto Universitario Orientale* 45:483–502.

Kane, P. V.

1974 *History of Dharmaśāstras.* Vol. 2 (pts I and II). Poona: Bhandarkar Oriental Research Institute.

Khare, R. S.

1966 "A Case of Anomalous Values in Indian Civilization: Meat-eating among the Kanya-Kubja Brahmans of Kātyāyan Gotra." *Journal of Indian Studies.* Vol. 25, no. 2:229–240.

1976 *The Hindu Hearth and Home.* Delhi: Vikas Publishing House.

1976b *Culture and Reality: Essays on the Hindu System of Managing Foods.* Simla: Indian Institute of Advanced Studies.

1984 *The Untouchable as Himself: Ideology, Identity and Pragmatism among the Lucknow Chamars.* New York: Cambridge University Press.

Khare, R. S., and M. S. A. Rao (eds.)

1986 *Food, Society and Culture: Aspects in Food Systems of South Asia.* Durham: Carolina Academic Press.

Lele, Jayant K., and Rajendra Singh

1985 "The Politics of Nutrition and Food Symbolism: A Plea for the Discourse of the Unprivileged," typescript.

Mahais, Marie-Claude

1985 *Déliverance et Convivalité.* Paris: Fondation de la Maison des Sciences de l'Homme.

Marcus, George, and Michael M. J. Fischer

1986 *Anthropology as Cultural Critique.* Chicago: University of Chicago Press.

Marriott, McKim

1959 "Interactional and Attributional Theories of Caste Ranking." *Man in India.* Vol. 39, no. 92–107.

1968 "Caste Ranking and Food Transactions, a Matrix Analysis." In *Structure and Change in Indian Society.* Milton B. Singer and Bernard S. Cohn (eds.). Chicago: Aldine Publishing Company.

1976 "Hindu Transactions: Diversity Without Dualism." In *Transactions and Meaning.* Bruce Kapferer (ed.). Philadelphia: Institute for the Study of Human Issues.

1987 A Description of SAṂSĀRA: A Realization of Rural Hindu Life. Chicago: Civilization Course Materials (University of Chicago).

1989 "Constructing an Indian Sociology." *Contributions to Indian Sociology*. Vol. 23, no. 1:1–39.

Marriott, McKim, and Ronald Inden
1977 "Toward an Ethnosociology of Indian Caste Systems." In *The New Wind: Changing Identities in South Asia*. Kenneth A. David (ed.). Chicago: Aldine.

Messer, Ellen
1983 "The Household Focus in Nutritional Anthropology: An Overview." *Food and Nutrition Bulletin*. Vol. 5, no. 4:1–12.

Murphy, Christopher P. H.
1986 "Piety and Honor: The Meaning of Muslim Feasts in Old Delhi." In *Food, Society and Culture*. R. S. Khare and M. S. A. Rao (eds.). Durham: Carolina Academic Press.

Ngor, Haing
1987 *Haing Ngor: A Cambodian Odyssey* (with Roger Warner). New York: Macmillan.

Nichter, Mark
1986 "Modes of Food Classification and the Diet-Health Contingency: A South Indian Case Study." In *Food, Society and Culture*. R. S. Khare and M. S. A. Rao (eds.). Durham: Carolina Academic Press.

Nikhilananda, Swami
1963 *The Upanishads*. New York: Harper Torchbooks.

O'Flaherty, Wendy
1976 *The Origins of Evil in Hindu Mythology*. Berkeley: University of California Press.

Parkin, David (ed.)
1982 *Semantic Anthropology*. A.S.A. Monograph 22. London: Academic Press.

Prakash, Om
1961 *Food and Drinks in Ancient India*. Delhi: Munshi Ram Manohar Lal.

Ricoeur, Paul
1981 *Hermeneutics and Human Sciences* (Ed. J. Thompson). Cambridge: Cambridge University Press.

Rao, M. S. A.
1986 "Conservatism and Change in Food Habits among the Migrants in India: A Study in Gastro-dynamics." In *Food, Society and Culture*. R. S. Khare and M. S. A. Rao (eds.). Durham: Carolina Academic Press.

Roy, J. C.
1948 *Food and Drink in Ancient Bengal.* Delhi: Munshi Ram Manohar Lal.

Ruth, Richard
1987 "The Psychology of Food and Starvation: Some Implications for Anthropology." *ICAF Occasional Report* V. Charlottesville: International Commission on the Anthropology of Food and Food Problems, University of Virginia.

Sahlins, Marshall
1976 *Culture and Practical Reason.* Chicago: University of Chicago Press.

Sarcar, A. K.
1929 *The Food and Dietary Customs of the Ancient Indians.* Calcutta.

Satprakshananda, Swami
1965 *Methods of Knowledge: Perceptual, Non-Perceptual, and Transcendental According to Advaita Vedanta.* London: George Allen & Unwin.

Scarry, Elaine
1985 *The Body in Pain: The Making and Unmaking of the World.* New York: Oxford University Press.

Sen, Amartya
1981 *Poverty and Famines: An Essay on Entitlement and Deprivation.* Oxford: Oxford University Press.

1984 "The Right Not to be Hungry." In *The Right to Food.* P. Alston and K. Tômasevski (eds.). Utrecht: Martinus Nijhoff Publishers.

Sharma, K. N.
1961 "Hindu Sects and Food Pattern in North India," in *Aspects of Religion in Indian Society.* L. P. Vidyarthi (ed.). Ranchi: Bihar Council of Social and Cultural Research.

Singer, Milton
1984 *Man's Glassy Essence: Explorations in Semiotic Anthropology.* Bloomington: Indiana University Press.

Szymusiak, M.
1986 *The Stones Cry Out: Memories of a Cambodian Childhood, 1975–1980.* L. Coverdale (trans.). New York: Hill and Wang.

Tilley, Louise A.
1983 "Food Entitlement, Famine and Conflict." In *Hunger and History.* Robert I. Rotberg, and T. K. Rabb (eds.). New York: Cambridge University Press.

Toomey, Paul M.
1986 "Food from the Mouth of Krishna: Socio-religious Aspects of Sacred Food in Two Krishnaite Sects." In *Food, Society and Culture*. R. S. Khare and M. S. A. Rao (eds.). Durham: Carolina Academic Press.

Walzer, Michael
1983 *Spheres of Justice: A Defence of Pluralism and Equality*. New York: Basic Books.

Webster's Ninth New Collegiate Dictionary
1985 Springfield: Merriam-Webster Inc. Publishers.

Wiser, Charlotte Viall
1937 *The Foods of a Hindu Village of North India*. Lucknow: Bureau of Statistics and Economic Research of the United Provinces.

Yalman, Nur
1969 "On the Meaning of Food Offering in (Buddhist) Ceylon." In *Forms of Symbolic Action*. Robert F. Spencer (ed.). Seattle: University of Washington Press.

Zimmermann, Francis
1987 *The Jungle and the Aroma of Meats: An Ecological Theme in Indian Medicine*. Berkeley: University of California Press.

1

Food with Saints: An Aspect of Hindu Gastrosemantics[1]

*

R. S. Khare

The Cultural Language of Food

Recent cultural research on food systems has increasingly shown that human foods convey wide-ranging sociocultural meanings and viewpoints. They explain and interpret interrelationships between nature and culture (Lévi-Strauss 1966b; 1969), and among social rules, conditions, taboos, and boundaries (Leach 1964; Douglas 1966, 1970, 1972). Foods also help explicate diverse relationships across the semantic, nutritional, and economic domains. They simultaneously implicate the symbolic and material conditions of a society (e.g., Sahlins 1978, 170–179; Douglas 1984). Though we now know that social rules and cultural values pattern food, we need to know more about its "language-like" properties of signification and communication for such issues as self and the cosmic order. A whole range of symbolic processes pervade such a food, making it highly communicative (for a general semiotics of food, see Barthes 1961; 1972, 62–64, 78–80). Such food becomes a part of the medium addressing issues of ontology, emotion, faith, and personal experience.

India provides us with virtually an inexhaustible repository of instances where food loads itself with mundane and profound meanings. The subject is so central to the culture that we have called it *gastrosemantics*, to refer to its unusual powers of multiple symbolization and communication via food.[2] Embedded within his quest for self-identity and ultimate reality, the Hindu's food "loads" and "unloads" meanings and messages as it passes through diverse domains of existence—physical, human, and divine. We will consider in this paper how food conveys a range of meanings and experiences that *conjoin* the worldly to the otherworldly, and the microcosmic (i.e., affairs of *jīva*) to the macrocosmic (i.e., matters of *sṛṣṭi* and the ultimate reality, *Ātman* or Brahman). The Hindu world rather demands that its food "speak" a language that conjoins the gross and the subtle, body and spirit, the seen and the unseen, outside and inside, and the particular and the general.[3]

The Hindu food meets this goal by representing extensive interrelationships between the three corners of the gastrosemantic triangle—"self," food, and body (including the societal; for the Hindu's "self," see Bharati 1985), and by becoming a principle of the eternal moral order (dharma) and cycles of creation (*sṛṣṭi*). Food becomes a reflexive medium for conceiving and experiencing interpenetrations of food, mind, and breath, most often by the yogic control of one's body and what one eats. In anthropological terms, food becomes a powerful, polyvocal interlocutor between matter and spirit, and body and self.[4] Such a "language" transforms according to one's life-stage (*āśrama*) and the path of spiritual pursuit (*mārga*). But whether it is a householder, a saint or a renouncer, food, body, self, and personhood remain guided by some universal principles (discussed below), and these hold key to a proper understanding of food to the issues of ontology and ultimate reality.[5] In the following discussion, I shall emphasize the food of the Hindu holy person, always a yogi (i.e., a conjoiner) of some sort.[6] He most often influences the gastrosemantics of the rest of the society in a distinct way. Householders routinely look up to him for guidance. In sickness they go to him for cures and healing; in everyday life, they approach him as a guru.

Within the Hindu system, therefore, self, food and guru are found to be the "companions" (with appropriate signs, relations, and presences) in that comprehensive and surpassing yogic sense which includes issues of physical body, society, and culture. Several recent sociological accounts of Hindu food and culture variously underscore the issue (e.g., Dumont 1980; Marriott 1968, 1976; Khare 1976a; Appadurai 1981; for a bibliography, see Khare and Rao 1986). Some attempts particularly focus on special signifying properties of Hindu foods (e.g., Daniel 1984, 125, 184ff, 278–287, on analysis of the body or "food sheath" in terms of coconut, rice, and ghee; Cantlie 1981, 182–217, for sensitive food-self dialogue among the devout Assamese; Khare 1976b, for cultural conceptions and classifications).

We focus on Hindu interrelationships between food, self, and the ultimate reality by two crucial cultural formulations: First,

"You eat what you are," and second, "You are what you eat." These are integral to the Hindu's authoritative tradition. The first is well grounded in the *Gītā* (XVII, 7–10), where foods are classified according to the three "strands" or dispositions (*guṇas*) that humans betray.[7] The second formulation bases itself on the Upanishadic instruction—pure nourishment leads to pure mind or nature (*ahāraśuddhau sattvaśuddhi*; see Hume 1985, 262). As a corollary, therefore, a healthy body is considered to be a byproduct of discriminating and controlled nourishment. Diseases follow from flaws—moral, mental, and physical. Holy persons rigorously control these and produce examples for the householders to follow.

If the first formulation says to the Hindu that one eats according to one's karma-inherited moral dispositions, then the second asserts that food can affect what one is, or can be.[8] The Hindu and his social order work to unite the two axioms, even if they are contradictory in logical terms. The Hindu does not tire of emphasizing in one breath that one's food preferences reflect his or her given moral dispositions (*guṇas*), and yet (with the yogi model in mind) that he or she should always select, regulate, control, and improve one's food to pursue health and spiritual goals.

The Hindu gastrosemantics thus deals with both of these tendencies in everyday Hindu life in a conjoining (hence meaningful) manner. Though people universally mean with food, Hindu gastrosemantics focuses on interrelating (back and forth) diverse moral and material conditions within comprehensive, conjoining schemes. The Hindu renders the moral, economic, and political spheres of food interdependent, even as each may contextually vary in its domination and control of life (for a semiotic discussion of food politics in India, see Lele and Singh 1985). The Hindu holy person exemplifies the same distinct tendency in a time-honored way when he integrates food with life's ideals and everyday experience.

Classical texts treat food extensively in aphorisms, dialogues, and discourses in relation to different phases of life (*āśrama*) and paths of yoga (see Kane 1974). Crucial to such discussions invariably is the situation of the moral agent (*jīva*) and its karma and dharma. Food relates directly to this moral agent. Our studies of this concept are still preliminary, though we gain from a series of recent comparative studies on the subject, whether called a being, a soul, a person, or a self (e.g., see Mauss 1985; Hollis 1985; Lukes 1985; Carrithers 1985; Sanderson 1985; Bharati 1985; and Khare 1984). Hindu's self (microcosm) is only a projection of the Ātman (the universal Self). Cosmos, including food, is visualized within this Self (macrocosm). One's self is a reflection of Self. Such a preoccupation engages the holy persons, who as yogis are "conjoiners" of one sort or another. This ideology is their foundation for approaching varied forms of eating, feeding, and sharing of food among humans, and within cosmos.

We will pursue within this chapter the position that food is integral not only to the Hindu's learned and popular versions of world, but it is uniquely owned up by saints, ascetics, and yogis for a civilization-wide commentary on life, over the centuries. And as we concern ourselves with the latter, we will also be able to observe on certain distinct styles of Hindu knowledge, experience, and its communication.

"Speaking Food" of the Holy: Three Contexts and Expressions

The Hindu holy person handles food to serve clearly designated moral and spiritual purposes, including efforts to alleviate human sorrow and suffering and to bring one nearer to liberation (*mokṣa*). Renouncers and sadhus do not view food as a commodity. They do not trade in foods to earn profit (denying them the classical goal of *artha*), and they neither hoard nor covet. They similarly should not cultivate their palate. Put another way, a holy person must regulate and control food only to cultivate his or her spiritual power. He masters his desires and senses by fasting and minimal eating. With increasing self-control and austerities, his sight and touch make food express special powers and messages. Detached from food, as we will see below, he makes food "speak" and "act" on his behalf. His food conveys his blessings and curses. As blessing, his food heals, uplifts, and brings good fortune to the faithful. As leftovers, his food guides disciples toward spiritual experiences and divine imminence (Babb 1987).

(a) Food for Sustaining Life . . . āhāra, bhikṣā, and vrata-upavāsa

Within the Hindu world, food is necessary to remain healthy and stay alive. Food is viewed as the source of all strength in the *Upanishads:*

> [Sanatkumāra said:] Food is, verily, greater than strength. Therefore if a man abstains from food for ten days,

> even though he might live, yet he would not be able to see, hear, reflect, become convinced, act, and enjoy the result. But when he obtains food, he is able to see, hear, reflect, become convinced, act, and enjoy the result (*Chāndogya Upanishad* VII, ix, 1; see Nikhilananda 1963, 341).

One is enjoined to stay alive, in extremity, by eating forbidden or abominable foods. Today's Hindu knows that the sages have done so under *āpaddharma* (dharma under distress; see chapter 2 in this book). Applicable to householders and holy persons alike, such life-saving pragmatic strategies render food procurement necessary for all—even the staunchest yogi or recluse.[9] There is no provision for death by starvation (in contrast to the Jains). Under normal conditions, all dharma-upholding persons, householders, and renouncers must regulate their eating (i.e., discipline one's *āhāra* or *bhojana* and *vihāra*; *Gītā* VI, 17). They must fast, control their senses, and view food as a cosmic sacrificial process and product (e.g., *Gītā,* III, 14).

Though all holy persons must eat, not all "handle food" (as does a householder by storing and cooking), nor must all beg. Yet all Hindus, whether saints or householders, extract special messages and portents from food. But saints especially encode foods with special messages as they go about eating, producing leftovers, and creating "blessed foods" (with sight, touch, giving by hand, or by verbal command; see Babb 1987). They convey equally well by fasting, maintaining silence, or favoring specific fruits and flowers (*phala-phūla*) for granting boons (*vardāna*) to devotees. Still, not all holy persons may engage in such transactions (*vyapāra*). Some may "rise above" such a necessity and bless simply by "willing" (*sphuraṇā*; literally "flashing on the mind").

Within the Hindu world, one should eat only enough to live. Fasting therefore is a necessary moral underside of eating, and it intensifies one's food-self dialogue. Fasting also emphasizes the dominance of soul over body. Non-eating, like eating, thoroughly affects one's physical, social, psychological, and spiritual states. By context, one may fast for dharma as well as accumulating *tapas.* With the help of Mahatma Gandhi's case, I shall illustrate the significance of fasting, especially when located within the food-body-self triangle. As a saintly householder, he neither begged to feed himself nor did he heal others as a "miracle worker."[10]

The issue of spiritual fasting was central to Gandhi's life and writings (e.g., see Gandhi 1957, 1959, 1965; for others' general evaluation, see Woodcock 1971; Bondurant 1971). Fasts opened the "inner eyes" of Gandhi. He fasted to resolve moral dilemmas and to decide on a course of personal or political action. He wrote, "My religion teaches me that whenever there is distress which one cannot remove, one must fast and pray" (Gandhi 1965, 8).

Prayers, another form of communication between self and the divine, complemented Gandhi's spiritual fasts. If fasting meant to him "abstinence from evil or injurious thought, activity or food," prayers concerned "the heart which knows God by faith" (Gandhi 1965, 10). Prayers not only enhanced the power of his fasts but the two became inseparable for him, demanding that he completely identify himself with them. Both were powerful "languages" for him. "Pure fast" for him was devoid of all selfishness, anger, lack of faith, and impatience. It was a form of *tapas* (austerity) that started with a strictly regulated small meal (*svalpāhāra*). In support, he interpreted the *Gītā* (Gandhi 1965, 52–53):

> The *Gita* enjoins not temperance in food but "meagreness"; meagreness is perpetual fast. Meagreness means just enough to sustain the body for the service for which it is made. The test is again supplied by saying that food should be taken as one takes medicine in measured doses, at measured times and as required. . . . A "full" meal is therefore a crime against God and man. . . . Hence the necessity for complete fasts at intervals and partial fasts forever. Partial fast is the meagre of measured food of the *Gita*.
>
> What is enough [food] is a matter of conjecture, therefore, of our own mental picture. . . . So what we often think is spare or meagre [diet] is likely to be more than enough. More people are weak through over-feeding or wrong feeding than through underfeeding.

Genuine fast for Gandhi underscored "a great deal of truth in the saying that man becomes what he eats. The grosser the food, the grosser the body. Plain living is said to go hand in hand with high thinking. . . . Plain living may itself be said to be a mode of fasting" (Gandhi 1965, 50).

A genuine spiritual fast thus speaks in the language of one's soul; such a fast enhances the sincerity of prayers, and the two together "work wonders." But the "right spirit"—an unflinching determination, a morally unimpeachable motive, a genuine humility (i.e., avoidance of "I-ness"—*ahaṁkāra*), and control over all the organs of sense—made the fast and prayers what they were for Gandhi.[11]

With such an approach, Gandhi not only builds on the popular Hindu intuition concerning the absence of opposition between spirit and matter, but he also comes very close to the classical "sheath" (*koṣa*) theory of interdependence between body, food and mind, and perception and experience:

> Just as there is identity of spirit, so is there identity of matter and in essence the two are inseparable. Spirit is matter rarefied to the utmost limit. Hence, whatever happens to the body must touch the spirit and whatever happens to one body must affect the whole matter and the whole of spirit. . . . But all my argument is useless if it cannot be sustained by practice (Gandhi 1965, 50–51).

For him, for example, mental deliberation, determination, recollection, and control of egoism (or "I-ness") were vital for proper fasting (and for its proper—nonviolent—expression; for example, see Gandhi 1965, Bondurant 1971, for a discussion of the Rajkot fast undertaken for the uplift and reform of the Untouchables in 1939). He variously underscored the popularly known interdependencies between food, body, and mind (the "inner-organ"); the relationship were at once pragmatic and spiritual.[12] Simultaneously, he warned against the "dangers of [inappropriate forms of] fasting." Unless one was scrupulous and careful, he repeatedly emphasized, the noble dialogues fasting produced between food and self, and food, self, and polity could easily disintegrate, resulting into coercion, fear, and violence.

Gandhi frequently expressed his concern for the control of influence fasts, as acts of austerity, exerted over others. He entered fasts to tackle the problems either with his body and self or the Indian body politic. Either way he illustrated the "revolving door" approach of the Hindu to spiritual fasts and their inevitable social influence:

> The fact is that all spiritual fasts always influence those who come within the zone of their influence. That is why spiritual fasting is described as *tapas* [religious austerity; literally "consuming by heat"]. And all *tapas* invariably

exerts purifying influence *on those in whose behalf it is undertaken* (Gandhi 1965, 44; my interpolation and italics).

(b) Saint's Healing Foods: sant prasād sé davā aur duvā[13]

Hindu holy persons in everyday life freely recommend special diets, herbs (*jaṛībooṭī*), and fasts for treating diseases, undesirable psychological dispositions, and mental tardiness. The enormous banyan tree of the Ayurveda provides them with congenial therapeutic ground, while their learning of healing from gurus and saints equips them with actual skills. As comprehensive healers, they freely dispense healing foods and herbs. Over time, they acquire the dual therapeutic-spiritual authority which even *vaidyas* (or "doctors") cannot dispute.

In principle, the holy person can heal with or without intention. He himself may not fully know the powers he possesses. His spiritual presence and contact are automatically considered beneficial to the body as well as the soul. Such qualities make gurus, sadhus, and saints the "ultimate healers." They cure all the three "fevers" (i.e., of the body, ill-fortune, and evil circumstance—*dehika, daivika,* and *bhautika tāpa*). If they are known to cure incurable bodily diseases, they also treat the "disease" of transmigration—*saṁsāra* (also called *bhavaroga*).

These holy healers respond according to a person's physical condition, age, sex, life-phase (*āśrama*), spiritual path (*mārga*), and psychological dispositions (*prakṛti* and *pravṛtti*). Though some sadhus in Lucknow were adept even in the "science of pulse and humors" (*nāṛī aur doṣa vijñāna*), most depended on their "spiritual" powers. The general principles governing their healing were that (a) only disciplined daily eating and living (*āhāra-vihāra*) ensured health and longevity; (b) healing foods required firm resolve and faith; and (c) such foods should adjust with a patient's age, gender, and karmic condition (for food, disease, and karma, see Khare 1976b).

However, for the Hindu, a holy person's healing foods or prescriptions can seldom be equated to that of a doctor's. Only the first one infuses (intentionally or unintentionally) his spiritual powers into whatever he prescribes. Devoid of any motive of economic profit or fame, and impelled by service to the needy and suffering, the holy person is the ideal healer. He ideally practices desireless action (*niṣkāma karma*). But one only rarely comes across such a healer. He appears only by the divine will (Hari *icchā*). He heals both the body and the soul of a person. Whatever he gives, whether flowers, herbs, roots, fruits, or elaborately cooked foods, it heals as no other medicine can. Even the dying are brought back to life (i.e., when the physicians have given up—*jab sab doctaron né javaab dé diyā*).

No wonder therefore that major Ayurvedic doctors in India are also found practicing selfless austerities and devotion. Prabhu Datta Brahmachari (1977, 19–20) mentions cases of *vaidyas* who treated not only free of charge but also refused to eat or drink water at the patient's house during such visits (even if they were of the appropriate caste status). In popular thought, rigorous self-discipline in diet and austere life style considerably enhances the efficacy of an Ayurvedic doctor.

Thus a holy person acts like a "doctor," and a doctor like a holy person. To paraphrase Brahmachari (1977, 18), a sadhu writing as a "doctor," Ayurveda's responsibility does not end with curing the body. Its goal is actually liberation (*mokṣa*). Its attention is not on the body but on one's soul (*ātman*). Body is after all ephemeral; it is destructible. One desires "diseaselessness" or health (*ārogyatā*) because it enables one to progress toward liberation.

The issue is mentioned thus by a doctor in the same book: "Ayurveda came about because of this sage tradition [of compassion toward those suffering]. So many times ancient sages have promoted Ayurveda. . . . Whenever sages, seeing human misery, have overcome with compassion, then, they have organized a significant new phase for augmenting and completing the [science of] Ayurveda." (Brahamachari 1977, 8; my interpolations).

(c) Super-Foods with Sadhus, Yogis and Devotees: alaukika prasād and sukṛta phala[14]

Since a genuine sadhu or renouncer views food in the context of faith, austerity, and devotion, he sees what eludes the ordinary. To him food is what self is—in the "seen" (gross) as well as "unseen" (subtle) dimensions. His austerities (*tapas*) empower self, and his self, the food. He blesses his devotees by accepting devotees' offerings and by returning them as his leftovers. Though milk preparations, sweets, and flowers are most often so exchanged, special offerings attract specific meaning and messages. For instance, rice pudding (*kṣhirānna*) may represent auspiciousness, fertility, and spiritual grace for many. Fruits received from a saint are "read" for hidden messages because foods readily acquire the intrinsic properties (*guṇa, doṣa,* and *rasa*) of the transactors and their intentions.

Some fruits represent maleness (banana), and others femaleness (orange); some represent astrological planets by color and shape, while others speak about the saint's equalitarianism.[15] Blessed sweets (*misṭhānna; mīṭhā prasād* in Hindi) widely connote divine agreeableness, desirable ritual consequences, convergent social goals and concerns, and auspiciousness (Toomey 1986, for Krishna's Vrindaban). "Fruits, leaves, and flowers" constitute a devout's normal food offerings (*naivédya*) to the divine, within homes and in temples (on different properties of *prasād,* see Khare 1976b, 92–110).

Some saints become widely known by the food they eat most, or bless with (e.g., a saint was known as *Payahārī* because he drank only milk to subsist; see *Bhaktamāla* 1969, 302). A famous *maunī* sadhu (i.e., a saint with vow of silence) in Lucknow was known to bless with sweets and flowers. Known as the flower-bearing saint (*phūlwālé bābā*), he was never seen without these accompaniments. Devotees believed that these appeared miraculously before him during his night worship and contained supernatural powers. His devotees had developed a whole language of interpretation for the sweets and flowers received from him. For example, red flowers meant auspiciousness and progeny, white stood for true knowledge (*jñāna*), and yellow for prosperity, family happiness, and personal fame. Flowers and foods were the saint's ubiquitous language of communication, though he complemented it with suitable eye contacts and bodily gestures.

Deities, in turn, essentially authenticate such a gastrosemantic paradigm of communication shared between the divine, saints, and their devotees. Popular devotional literature in different parts of India underscores how deities routinely "speak" through foods (e.g., see such hagiographies as *Bhaktamāla* 1969, and *Bhaktavijaya* 1982). Major saints often establish the models of (and for) such a total communication. Invariably, within such stories, a deity sides with his devotees when challenged by orthodox Brahmans, priests or other ritualists. For example, the deity refused the food offerings of the Brahmans to receive the same from the Untouchable saint Ravidas. He "came in his lap" to eat from him. This model underscores the superiority of love over social status or wealth, and it derives from Krishna's acceptance of leftovers from his devotee (Vidura) over the elaborate feast from a vain king (e.g., Duryodhana).

The deity even sustains a true devotee when the devotee does not (or cannot) feed or protect himself (since he is usually lost in devotion). The deity even cleans and tends him when sick (and then cures the sickness). The divine grace is known to come to those who feed other devotees and who offer them hospitality even at a great personal cost. (Illustrating these properties is the story of Madhava Das Jagannath in *Bhaktamāla* 1969, 540–551). With Mīrā Bāī, the famous woman saint of north India, the deity neutralized poison to prove his commitment to devotees.

Faith, devotion, otherworldly aestheticism, and saintly compassion thus charge the saint's food with special powers and messages. The contemporary religious culture widely recognizes this devotion-induced transformations of food. For example:

> One time he [Raghunath Gosain, a Caitanyaite saint] became indisposed and worshipped his deity [Lord Jagan Nath] mentally (*mānasika pūjā*), feeding him with rice and milk. He ate the same afterwards as offering (*prasād*). Its essence (*rasa*) pervaded his mortal body [just as the actual preparation would.] When a Vaidya practitioner felt his pulse [to treat his disease], he declared that the saint had just eaten rice and milk. O! gentlemen [says the commentator], how much more could I emphasize that you understand it all yourself (from *Bhaktamāla* 1969, 553; my translation and interpolation).

The devotional literature abounds with such examples (whether Vaishnava, Saiva, or Sakta). For example, the deity once fed the saints Rupa and Sanatana rice pudding, since they desired it (see *Bhaktamāla* p. 594). Since the deity remains at the beck and call of a genuine devotee to this extent, the devotees rigorously control their desire for food.

Simultaneously, once he has become spiritually accomplished (a *siddha*), a saint's speech is instantaneously realized. Whatever such a saint says or desires, occurs, especially for others' welfare. For such saints, speech and action, and thought and food become coextensive. It is a good example of Hindu's idea of gastrosemanticity. Thus, "As a devotee was mentally (*mānasika*) offering buttermilk to the deity, a disciple touched the saint's feet and startled him, and in the lap of the devotee spilled the actual buttermilk [for everybody to see]." (This case was related to me by an informant-Bhakta in Lucknow during 1986.)

A climax of such deity and devotee intimacies occurs when the two share their saliva via food. For instance,

> [Once Vallabhācārya] had the milk-*prasād* given to [saint] Paramānandadāsa in order to find out whether or not Krishna [the deity] found the milk-offering well prepared and rich in flavor. Since [the deity] is passionately fond of milk, giving milk as *prasād* to a Vaiṣṇava [devotee], who had received [the deity's] favor, is just like giving him the ecstasy (*rasa*) of union with the [deity] in the [divine sport]. If the [devotee] praises the taste of the milk-*prasād,* then it may be taken as certain that [the deity] is indicating, through that [devotee], that he enjoyed the milk.

The interpretive account of the episode continues:

> "Since Paramānandadāsa drank some of the saliva from [the deity's] lips along with the milk, he plunged into experience of the *rasa* [love-permeated, selfless devotion] of all of the nocturnal [divine] sports." (From the *Vārtās,* on Paramānandadāsa; see Barz 1976, 156–157.)

For the devotional and popular Hindu culture, these are examples of gastrosemanticity par excellence. The divine-tasted milk-*prasād* in the above example transports the devotee into a direct and powerful spiritual experience (*ātamika anubhūti*). For Paramāndadāsa, such an experience is beyond all the conceivable materiality or symbology of foods; it represents the most exalted divine intimacy. At this level, food, deity and self become co-extensive, collapsing our two opening formulations—"you are what you eat" and "you eat what you are"—into one supreme divine essence and experience.

Experience and Expressions

Not only do such examples produce a commentary on the dichotomous "opposites" (i.e., the *dvanda* as represented by matter and spirit, food and mind, and self and the other), but they also illustrate some general properties of the Hindu cultural logic. The Hindu's food pursues a nondichotomous logic and language suitable to convey the unity of expression and experience. Food to him is one of the most versatile interlocutors, and his saints and the divine elaborate, enrich, magnify, and empower it to transcend normal channels of signification and communication. Relying on more than ordinary logic, such Hindu food, like other crucial principles (dharma, karma, *ātman,* etc.), expresses itself most where faith (*viśvāsa*), practice, suggestion (*vyañjanā*), experience (*anubhava*), and intuition (*pratibhā*) converge.

Let us now return to our opening allusion to the Hindu's gastrosemantic triangle (food-self-body). With "self" (referring to *jīva* and its "I-ness" but culminating in the realization of Ātman) at the apex, food and body must cater to self's purposes and priorities. Given this Hindu view, the basic source of all gastrosemantics must also come from self and its journey within the creation. But such a triangle, by definition, is *multiform* (i.e., it is capable of transformation, and it produces varying signification by cultural context and purpose). It is manipulable. Thus, once we juxtapose this triangle to our general analytic triangle (i.e., food-language-self or food-discourse-self), we may see how the two interrelate, especially since the Hindu system treats language and discourse as a function of self (and its *manas*), while this "mind" depends on food (*anna*) and breath (*prāṇa*). The food thus also becomes the basis for breath and mind, underscoring an interplay between gross (*sthūla*) and subtle (*sūkṣma*) constitutive elements. Similarly applicable to food is the triangle of the three basic "qualities" or constituents of nature (*sattva, rajas,* and *tamas*). In life, such triangular "qualities" (*triguṇas*) swirl within oneself and outside, attracting an interplay of food with innate strands (*guṇas*), flaws (*doṣas*), moods (*bhāvas*), aesthetics (*rasas*), and attachments (*rāgas*). Whether one is a renouncer, a householder, or a woman, these triangles remain the generating source for food's multiple meanings and "voices" within the Hindu universe.

We may decode the food-breath-mind triangle a little further to emphasize the point that the Hindu cosmological constituents stand squarely behind the food. For example, breath (*prāṇa*) via food yields the *buddhi* (intellect), which, in turn, works in terms of five sensory organs, five organs of action, five subtle elements, and five gross elements (for a summary discussion and schematic representation of such cosmological constituents, see Satprakashananda 1965, 314; for a recent anthropological interpretation in "cubes," see Marriott 1989). However, all of this conceptual and semantic complexity translates into a simple, direct, and forceful principle: One should practice self-control via austerities to control the swirl of preceding triangular constituents of the world (*triguṇātmaka saṁsāra*). And only a genuine relationship between the divine and devotee, guru and disciple, and learned texts and practice ensures such a goal, where food becomes a crucial link between finite (body) and the infinite (soul). Food and body become soul's sheaths (*koṣas*), and not the otherway round.[16] Yogis, sadhus, renouncers, and gurus (even sagely householders) in India continuously try to "realize" this truth. They remind themselves that only their bodies are perishable; they are not. Since the *ātman* alone is real, it is considered capable of creating bodies (and the foods it needs). As Ramakrishna Paramahaṁsa said even food cooking conveys them a message:

> As potato and brijnal when *siddha,* i.e., when boiled properly, become soft and pulpy; so a man when he becomes *siddha,* i.e., reaches perfection, is seen to be all humility and tenderness (see Abhedananda 1946, 74).

But the devotional movement, where the deity takes over the devotee's life and his senses, complicates the above austere picture. Both food and body are divinized, and they return center stage with a divine-inspired substantivity and aesthetics. As our devout saints illustrated, they employ creative expressions to convey how a devotee "tastes" the divine name (*bhagvānnāma kā rasāsvādana* in Hindi), and "eats" and "drinks" the divine praise by his ears (*karṇāmṛtapān*). All senses thus immerse themselves in the divine's presence, making the double entendre a standard fare of devotional expressions. We illustrated such usages—semiotic "switches"—in the previous section with the help of an ancient classical text (*Chāndogya Upanishad*), a medieval saint (Purandaradāsa), a recent sage (Ramakrishna), and a contemporary "great soul" (Mahatma Gandhi). The following, again the master stroke of a saint, employs a battery of such switches which lights up the relationship between self (*aṁśa* or a part) and the divine (*aṁśī* or the whole), morality and aesthetics, and expression and experience.

> For the milk-made delicacy of Rama's Name, the sugar is Krishna's Name, and the Name of the Lord Viṭṭhala, the ghee; mix, put it into your mouth and see the taste! Take the wheat of Ego, put it into the milk of dispassion and pound it into soft flower and prepare it into fine vermicelli, boil it, and put it into the vessel of your heart, fill it with water of feeling and cook it with your intellect; take it on a plate and eat; and when you get a belching, think of the Lord Puran-

dara Viṭṭhala, who is of the form of joy. (Purandaradāsa [1480–1564] quoted in V. Raghavan 1966, 128–129).

With such expressions, joyous and blissful relationships between food and self, food and deity, and self and deity redraw the nondualist ideal with a definite purpose. Here emotion, intimacy, experience, and insight become the lifeblood of the Hindu's being and becoming (compare "ethnosociological" accounts; see Marriott 1976, 1989). We also experience a corresponding metamorphosis in the "substance" of body and self, self and food, and self and cosmos.

When dealing with historical saints and leaders, we also should be able to investigate the role of historical forces in Hindu gastrosemantics. These constitute an equally important but a separate subject of inquiry. We at present have very little idea of how history and politics in India may have shaped the symbolic loading (or reloading) of Hindu foods, with appropriate modification and expansion of tropic devices.[17]

Foods with Saints

Now we can make some general comments on the gastrosemantics of the holy food. The pervasive unifying logic of the Hindu food derives from the nature of the Hindu's cosmology. The Creator of the Hindu universe is a yogi, a conjoiner. Like him, food's cosmic place and meanings are therefore held self-evident and indisputable; they are found one with the rest of the cosmic moral order (in Hindi *brahmāṇḍa kā sanātana dharma*; for basic pronouncements in the Upanishads, see Hume 1985, 153, 284, 290). In practice, the food-body-self and self-dharma-cosmos paradigms work together to reveal the vast meaningful range within which the holy person places foods. The ascetic, orthodox or not, constantly approaches foods and food exchanges to proclaim and maintain his self-identity and to conjoin by yoga one's various bodily and spiritual states. To holy persons more than householders, foods constitute a comprehensive yet delicate and subtle language, marked with a wide array of cosmic, social, emotional, karmic, and spiritual messages. Foods, always imprinted by the transactor's *guṇa*-clusters, produce indirect (as in meditation or dreams) as well as direct (as by health or sickness) consequences for the yogi.

Suprasensual messages can come to the holy with every meal, every day. He therefore remains specially attentive to those foods that produce sluggishness, spiritual disquiet, and immoral thoughts (e.g., onion, garlic, and heavy, spicy preparations; or the *tāmasika* foods). Prohibited, impure, and inauspicious foods predictably produce maximum impact. Meat and liquor, for example, cause prolonged spiritual upheaval, while dishonestly earned foods are known to cause internal disquiet (even diarrhea, as some of my informants insisted). For an advanced yogi or an ascetic, all foods have a psychic signature, and he must therefore strictly regulate and control his daily meals.

Food in India speaks in several subliminal languages—biopsychological, humoral, moral, and spiritual—for exemplifying the Hindu's conjoining reasoning across wide contexts (for diverse examples, see Nichter 1986; Breckenbridge 1986; Cantlie 1981; for the logic of "appropriateness" in medicine and food, see Zimmermann 1987). Though the Hindu food logic, in practice, elaborately recognizes regional distinctions and differences for establishing dietary regulations and transactional controls, it still remains grounded in the classical principles of the *mahābūtas* (elements), *guṇas* (intrinsic moral dispositions), *doṣas* (flaws), and life-goals (*puruṣārthas*). These schemes address the issues of the Hindu's "quality of life." The general distinctions of superior and inferior, and the controlling and the controlled, also emerge from these paradigmatic principles. If all social distinctions of the householder's food ultimately must anchor themselves in this ground, which is subtle, suprasensual, and largely unseen, the saint emphasizes how food conjoins the worldly to the otherworldly:

> Food continually changes its face: left uncooked, it rots; once in the stomach, it becomes blood, muscle, bone, marrow, and finally semen; the waste returns to the soil to feed the plants. Holy persons change this food into a blessing by their mere sight or touch, while the impious beings taint it in unseen ways. Foods must therefore be always handled with care. They should be given generously but eaten only with regimen [*saṁyama*]. Fasting and self-control bring one nearer to liberation, while indulgence brings disease and degradation. Our food handling tells a lot about our souls (a Vaishnava sadhu from Lucknow, recorded during the summer of 1984).

A yogi's food rests with the classical Upanishadic notion of food as one of soul's "five sheaths" (*koṣas*—food, breath, mind, intellect, and bliss). Though constituting the outermost sheath, food successively transforms itself into the innermost (and the subtlest) experience—spiritual bliss (*ātamānanda*). Each succeeding subtler sheath represents to the yogi a transformation and transcendence of the one before. He "experiences" how the moral food substance (*anna*) changes into the rarefied breath, the breath into mind, the mind into (still rarer—*sūkṣma*) intellect, and the last into bliss (*ānanda*). Put in analytic terms, such a transformation of the concrete into the abstract by the Hindu saint, to borrow Paul Ricoeur's (1978, 165) phraseology, "precedes, accompanies, closes, and *envelops* [the] explanation" of the Hindu universe.

A saint starts in life by recognizing the fact that one's food varies according to different life-phases (*āśramas*), religious paths (*mārgas*), and goals (*puruṣārthas*). But he usually focuses on one of the major paths (e.g., devotion, knowledge, ritual action, or Tantra), to inform his food ethic and aesthetics. For instance, according to my interviews with Lucknow saints, *bhakti* views foods to yield a language of increment (*vṛddhi*), completeness (*purṇatā*), auspiciousness (*mangala*), intimacy (*ghanisṭhatā*), emotional states (*bhāva*), and noncontingent self-surrender to the divine (*pūrṇa prapatti*). On the other hand, tantra employs tabooed foods (*maṁsa* and *madirā*) as instruments for mastering the sensual temptations, to achieve unique spiritual powers, and ultimately liberation. Yoga, in all its forms, employs them for systematic self-control, and self-denial until the body, mind, and spirit (*ātman*) "speak" in "unison" (the *Gītā*'s *"yuktiyukta"* lifestyle) for the desired spiritual goal.

The same food-sheath (body) that a yogi thus manipulates for spiritual control reappears before the Ayurvedic doctor to help him prevent or cure his patient's diseases. A good doctor in India keeps close watch on his patient's diet; it is integral to any effective diagnosis and treatment. As we saw, today's swamis and saints generally share the same cultural paradigm as they heal the faithful with blessed foods (see also Kakar 1982; Babb 1987). Such an approach to food sets the basic perimeters of the Hindu's gastrosemantics. Food speaks to one's body and soul at once (see Bhagat 1976, 216–218; Kane 1974). It is most of all about one's traversing the distance between this world and liberation.

Notes

1. This paper is a revised version of the presentation made during the Colloquium on Food Systems and Communication Structures held at the

Central Institute of Indian Languages in Mysore, India, during January 2–6, 1985.

In this paper, in many ways, I have drawn on my field notes collected on the subject during the summers of 1984 and 1986, in Lucknow, the capital of Uttar Pradesh. I am indebted to various sadhus and *munis* (Hindu and Jain) who discussed food with me in so many contexts and guided me to some saint-written Hindi literature on the subject of diet and health. During and after the Mysore conference, Professors A. K. Ramanujan, Jayant K. Lele, and Rajendra Singh offered me helpful comments on the paper. I am thankful to them. However, the responsibility for the final version rests only with me.

2. Gastrosemantics may be generally defined as a culture's distinct capacity to signify, experience, systematize, philosophize, and communicate with food and food practices by pressing appropriate linguistic and cultural devices to render food as a central subject of attention. To refer to the cultural depth and density of meanings foods invoke, I will employ "gastrosemanticity." However, since general semantic studies of food and food handling are still rare (e.g., Bascom 1951; Lévi-Strauss 1966; Lehrer 1969) and they require a separate general comparative discussion, I will concern myself here only with the Hindu case and its contribution to gastrosemantics and gastrosemanticity.

3. In the context of the recent anthropological efforts which have tried to correctly identify the predominant Hindu cultural "logic" of relations (e.g., Dumont's [1980] notion of "encompassment" and Marriott's [1976, 1989] recognition of the Hindu's emphasis on "movement" and "fluidarity"), we find "conjoining" to be a pervasive, fundamental process, encapsulated and expressed ubiquitously by the civilizational conception of *yoga* (and its practitioners—*yogis* or conjoiners). Etymologically related to root *yeug,* yoga, like "conjoining," leads us to devices appropriate to "put or bring together" to "make [things] continuous" or "unite" (*American Heritage Dictionary:* 1979, 282 and 1550). Yoga and yogi, the conjoiner, continue to have a prominent place within the Hindu's world ever since the Vedas.

4. Disassociating it from its specific religious and historical meanings in the West (especially the moral/material dichotomy), I use the term "spiritual" in general terms, to refer to those Hindu notions of *unity* which a *jīva* or *jīvātman* seeks at gross and subtle levels, within this world and beyond, while pursing the goal of liberation (*mukti*). Various notions of body and bodilessness are also included within such a formulation of the spiritual or the otherworldly (*ādhyātmika*). The Hindu holy personages exemplify the "conjoinings," seen and unseen, which show how the soul (*ātman*) triumphs over the ephemera—body and rebirth.

5. It is an important conceptual perspective for our analysis of the Hindu world. Here the differences across a twice-born householder, a renouncer, a woman, and a Śūdra are treated as rearrangements (or varia-

tions) of such general principles as karma, dharma, rebirth (*saṁsāra*), and liberation (*mokṣa*), and intersected by such "paths" as devotion, knowledge, and yogic austerities (*bhakti, jñāna,* and *tapas*). A correct understanding of the Hindu's conception of "differences" is necessary before we can satisfactorily address what the householders and renouncers represent to each other and mean to the Hindu world.

6. As may have been evident, I use the phrase "holy person" or saints to refer to a wide variety of yogis, sadhus and *sants,* including the renouncers, *paramahaṁsas,* and *avadhūtas.* This is because no single word adequately conveys the entire ground that food attracts. Simultaneously, I employ the word "yogi" to refer to that basic Hindu tendency to conjoin—to forge meaningful links between diverse experiences, contradictory ideas, opposed values, and conflicting activities. I employ the word "saint" in a general way, without any encumbrances from the Western Judeo-Christian theologies and their traditions.

7. All references to the *Gītā* in the chapter are to R. C. Zaehner's 1969 translation and annotation of this classical text. However, sometimes in my text, I have purposely retained some popularly conveyed senses and interpretations from my field discussions, conveying to the reader an idea how today's Hindus widely regard the *Gītā* a "living"—life-guiding—text.

8. The two formulations must account for a whole range of analytical categories—culture vs. nature; morality vs. ecology and physical evolution; customary habits vs. nutrition; and the spiritual vs. the corporeal. At another level, the first formulation ("you eat what you are") emphasizes ontology while the second ("you are what you eat"), the process of becoming. The Hindu food, as a self-evident essence of cosmic creation, tends to forge metonymic and contiguous links in all directions, and at all levels (gross and subtle, seen and unseen, and cosmic, spiritual, psychomoral and physical).

9. Jains, in comparison, extend the notion of austerity (*tapas*) and renunciation (*tyāga*) to giving up of eating, until, under certain circumstances, one can cast off one's bodily frame. Hence, if eating is a necessary, life-preserving action for the Hindu ascetic (*jivandhāraṇa ké hétu karma*), it is ultimately a dispensable act for the Jain.

10. The cultural significance of this case remains undisputed. Gandhi variously reformulated and redirected fasting to suit his personal and political goals. However, if he developed it as a distinct political instrument of *satyāgraha* (nonviolent noncooperation), he also assigned fasting more tasks for personal health and spiritual needs. Fasts were self-cleansing to him, enabling him to hear his "inner voice." Gandhi's unorthodox "experiments" in fasting influenced even the orthodox Hindus.

11. Gandhi's example also helps us illustrate some properties of Hindu gastrosemanticity. Fasts helped Gandhi cleanse his body and mind

(*antaḥkaraṇa,* literally the "inner organ"). This "inner organ" of the Hindu has cognitive, affective, and conative properties. It converts sense impressions into ideas and, according to the classical Indian epistemology (e.g., see Satprakashananda 1965, 53), it produces diverse mental states or functions (*vṛtti*), including faith and volition. Gandhi's use of "mind," however, takes after the popular meanings of *antaḥkaraṇa,* where it usually stands for one's "heart and mind." Either way, thc Hindu system conveys the same general message: Controlled eating and fasting help inculcate inner purity, a resolute mind, a clear memory, and a penetrating spiritual insight.

Gastrosemanticity rests on this range of interdependence, and on the fact that "self" (*jīvātman*) and food are two forms of the same self-evident verity—the Absolute Brahman.

12. The whole subject of how food affects mind within the Indian system requires systematic attention. Popularly, people recognize a close relationship between mind (i.e., mental states and functions) and foods. Some medicinal foods are known to enhance intelligence (e.g., *āmlā* or *Emblica officinalis,* cow's milk or cream of wheat—*niśāsta* in north India; also the appropriate Ayurvedic preparations of herb *brahmi*). Others retard intelligence or disturb sanity (*buddhināśaka*). Usually these are intoxicants or poison foods that are extremely "hot," "heavy," and disorienting (e.g., certain poisonous meats, fruits and chemicals, including *dhatūrā* or thorn apple and *saṁkhiyā* or arsenic).

Still others cause only the loss of one's equanimity (*buddhibhraṣṭaka*). Gandhi found, for example, that his sexual abstinence depended on food which "should be limited, simple, spiceless, and, if possible, uncooked" (Gandhi 1957, 209).

13. The phrase comes from one of my Lucknow informants, interviewed in the summer of 1986. Ample popular literature is readily available in India on the subject. For the Hindi region, for example, a famous (ordained) sadhu writer and political activist from Allahabad, Prabhu Datta Brahmachari (1977), wrote his book "to provide traditional ways to reduce fatness (*motāpan*)." A well-known Ayurvedic pharmaceutical firm—Sri Vaidyanatha Ayurveda Bhavan—commissioned and published the book and an Ayurvedic "doctor" wrote the foreword in praise of the saint, who was found "full of *tapas* and compassion and welfare for the common public."

Similarly, a homeopathic doctor (Chauhan 1987) concerned himself with remedies by diet—*Bhojan ké dwārā Cikitsā,* with English title, "Let Food Be Thy Medicine." A Jain saint, Muni Kalyan Sagar, provided this book his testimonial, and the author published the picture of the saint blessing him and his book. Such writings underscore the longstanding reciprocal linkage recognized between food, saints, and Ayurvedic medicine.

14. "Fruits" (as *phala* [food] and *"phala"* [a shorthand for the consequences of one's karma]) have double meaning in the present context. Gods and saints, as they bless with foods, read and *modify* one's past karma. This

is as widespread a notion among the contemporary Hindu as that of karmic fate (*bhāgya*). (For a commentary on this issue from the south, see Daniel 1984). The divine grace (*bhagvadkṛpā*), similarly, is considered to overpower one's bad karmas, whether accumulated in the past or the present (*prārabdha* or *duṣkrata* karmas). See also note 15.

15. The word *phala* or *phalama* (see Apte 1965, 689–90), as already noted, refers to fruit-as-food and fruit-as-consequence of past action (karma *phala*). Now we may also add to these the popular notion of *raśiphala* (astrological consequences). Thus, when a saint blesses the faithful with food, several different languages of "fruits" (*phala*) stand behind one another to convey multiple meanings to the faithful.

Equally importantly, food must reflect the overarching equalitarian ethic and attitude of the Hindu saint. Examples abound in hagiographies. A Brahman saint, described in *Bhaktamāla* (1969, 276–277), lived and ate with an Untouchable on his own. He did so with the support of the divine, Lord Jagdish, but much to the chagrin of Brahman priests. Another saint (*Bhaktamāla* 1969, 272–276), Lalacharya ji, performed the last rites for a person of unknown *jāti* in the face of protesting Brahmans. Unperturbed, he feasted god Vishnu's attendants (*prasāda*), when Brahmans turned down his invitation. The saint-blessed food thus often carries a message of social reform (see chapter 3 in this book).

16. The usual anthropological characterization of Hindu food emphasizes its indeterminate (i.e., social and ritual) qualities. We need to widen the scope of our studies to include how food (finite) is overtaken by certain notions of infinite. Food in such contexts becomes a rich subject for philosophical anthropology.

The Hindu system discovers in food a firm experiential ground on which to integrate the material with the moral, the sensorial with the intuitive, and to extend the subjective into the mystical (for the role of intuition [*pratibhā*] in Indian epistemology, see Kunjunni Raja 1963). In such a perspective, food is much more for the Hindu than what food ordinarily is within the "seen" world. In the Hindu's universe, to employ Ricoeur's (1978, 34) expression, food "wills the 'whole,' which thinks the 'whole,' and does not rest except in the 'whole.'"

17. Hindu gastrosemantics is *not* immune to historical forces, though some aspects of the food system may be more open to such forces than certain others. In a macrosociological perspective, the production and distribution of food in independent India are increasingly under the influence of technological developments, on the one hand, and "public cultural" redefinitions, on the other. Even the strongly regionalized Indian cooking, as Appadurai (1988) argues, is trying to evolve into a "national cuisine."

Food consumption, especially within households on everyday basis, on the other hand, still continues to show substantive cultural continuity (i.e., morally conjoining logic) over time. The unifying moral conceptions of food, self, and cosmology, as discussed in this chapter, continue to define the mammoth Hindu majority.

References

Abhedananda, Swami
1946 *The Sayings of Ramakrishna.* Calcutta: Ramakrishna Vedanta Math.

Abbott, Justin and N. R. Godbole
1933 *Stories of Indian Saints* (Translation of Mahipati's *Bhaktivijaya*). Delhi: Motilal Banarsidass, 1985.

American Heritage Dictionary of the English Language
1979 (ed. William Morris) Boston: Houghton Mifflin Company.

Appadurai, A.
1981 "Gastro-politics in Hindu South Asia." *American Ethnologist.* 8:494–511.

1986 "Theory in Anthropology: Center and Periphery." *Comparative Studies in Society and History,* 28:356–361.

1988 "How to Make a National Cuisine: Cookbooks in Contemporary India." *Comparative Studies in Society and History.* 30:3–24.

Apte, Vaman Shivram
1911 *The Practical Sanskrit-English Dictionary.* Rev. ed., 1965, Delhi: Motilal Banarsidass.

Babb, Lawrence
1987 *Redemptive Encounters: Three Modern Styles in the Hindu Tradition.* Delhi: Oxford University Press.

Barthes, Roland
1961 "Pour une psycho-sociologie de l'alimentation contemporaine." *Annales E.S.C.:* 977–86.

1972 *Mythologies.* New York: Hill and Wang.

Barz, Richard
1976 *The Bhakti Sect of Vallabhācārya.* Faridabad: Thomson Press (India).

Bascom, William
1951 "Yoruba Cooking." *Africa* 21:125–137.

Bhagat, M. G.
1976 *Ancient Indian Asceticism.* Delhi: Munshiram Manoharlal.

Bhaktamāla [Hindi]
1969 Nābhādāsa's (Fifth edition, with commentaries in poetry and prose by Priyadāsa Sri Bhagwān Prasād Rūpakalā). Lucknow: Teja Kumar Press.

Bharati, Agehananda
1985 "The Self in Hindu Thought and Action." In *Culture and Self: Asian and Western Perspectives.* A. J. Marsella and George DeVos (eds.). London: Tavistock Publications.

Bondurant, Joan V.
1971 *Conquest of Violence*. Berkeley: University of California Press.

Brahmachari, Prabhu Datta
1977 *Motāpan kam karné ka upāya!* [Hindi] A Way to Reduce Fatness. Calcutta: Sri Baidyanath Ayurveda Bhavan Limited.

Breckenbridge, Carol Appadurai
1986 "Food, Politics and Pilgrimage in South India, 1350–1650 A.D." In *Food, Society and Culture*. R. S. Khare and M. S. A. Rao (eds.). Durham: Carolina Academic Press.

Cantlie, Audrey
1981 "The Moral Significance of Food among Assamese Hindus." in *Culture and Morality.* Adrian C. Mayer (ed.). Delhi: Oxford University Press.

1984 *The Assamese: Religion, Caste and Sect in an Indian Village*. London: Curzon Press.

Carrithers, Michael
1985 "An Alternative Social History of the Self." In *The Category of the Person*. M. Carrithers, S. Collins, and S. Lukes (eds.). Cambridge: Cambridge University Press.

Chauhan, Ganesh Narain
1987 *Bhojan ké dvārā Chikitsā* [Hindi] "Kitchen Remedies" or "Let food be thy Medicine." Jaipur: India Book House.

Daniel, E. Valentine
1984 *Fluid Signs: Being a Person the Tamil Way.* Berkeley: University of California Press.

Davis, Marvin
1982 *Rank and Rivalry.* Cambridge: Cambridge University Press.

Douglas, Mary
1966 *Purity and Danger: An Analysis of the Concepts of Pollution and Taboo*. London: Routledge and Kegan Paul.

1970 *Natural Symbols*. New York: Vintage Books.

1972 "Deciphering a Meal." *Daedalus: Journal of the American Academy of Sciences.* Winter 1972.

Douglas, Mary (ed.)
1984 *Food in the Social Order: Studies of Food and Festivities in Three American Communities.* New York: Russell Sage Foundation.

Dumont, Louis
1980 *Homo Hierarchicus.* Complete Revised English Edition. Chicago: University of Chicago Press.

Filliozat, J.
1964 *The Classical Doctrine of Indian Medicine.* Delhi: Munshiram Manohar Lal.

Gandhi, M. K.
1957 *An Autobiography: The Story of My Experiments with Truth.* Boston: Beacon Press.

1959 *India of My Dreams.* Ahmedabad: Navjivan Publishing House.

1965 *Fasting in Satyagraha.* Ahmedabad: Navjivan Publishing House.

Hollis, Martin
1985 "Of Masks and Men." In *The Category of the Person.* M. Carrithers, S. Collins and S. Lukes (eds.). Cambridge: Cambridge University Press.

Hume, Robert Ernest
1921 *The Thirteen Principal Upanishads* (second revised edition, 1985). Delhi: Oxford University Press.

Kakar, Sudhir
1982 *Shamans, Mystics and Doctors: A Psychological Inquiry into India and its Healing Traditions.* Delhi: Oxford University Press.

Kane, Pandurang Vaman
1974 *History of Dharmasastras* (vol. 2, pts. I and II). Poona: Bhandarkar Oriental Research Institute.

Khare, R. S.
1976 *The Hindu Hearth and Home.* Delhi: Vikas Publishing House.

1976b *Culture and Reality: Essays on the Hindu System of Managing Foods.* Shimla: Indian Institute of Advanced Study.

1983 *Normative Culture and Kinship.* Delhi: Vikas Publishing House.

1984 *The Untouchable as Himself: Ideology, Identity and Pragmatism Among the Lucknow Chamars.* New York: Cambridge University Press.

Khare, R. S. and Rao, M. S. A. (eds.)
1986 *Food, Society, and Culture: Aspects in South Asian Food Systems.* Durham: Carolina Academic Press.

Kunjunni Raja, K.
1963 *Indian Theories of Meaning.* Madras: The Adyar Library and Research Center.

Leach, E. R.
1964 "Anthropological Aspects of Language: Animal Categories and Verbal Abuse." In *New Directions in the Study of Language.* (E. H. Lenneberg, ed.) Cambridge, Mass.: M.I.T. Press.

Lehrer, Adrienne
1969 "Cooking Vocabularies and the Culinary Triangle of Lévi-Strauss." *Anthropological Linguistics.* 14:155–171.

Lele, Jayant and R. Singh
1985 "The Politics of Nutrition and Food Symbolism: A Plea for the Discourse of the Unprivileged." Paper delivered at the International Conference on Food Systems and Communication Structures. Mysore, India, Jan. 2–6, Mimeographed.

Lévi-Strauss, C.
1966 "The Culinary Triangle." *New Society*, 166:937–940.

1966b *The Savage Mind.* Chicago: University of Chicago Press.

1969 *The Raw and the Cooked.* New York: Harper and Row.

Lukes, Steven
1985 "Conclusion." In *The Category of the Person.* M. Carrithers, S. Collins, and S. Lukes (eds.). Cambridge: Cambridge University Press.

Marriott, Mckim
1968 "Caste Ranking and Food Transactions, A Matrix Analysis." In *Structure and Change in Indian Society.* Milton Singer and Bernard S. Cohn (eds.), Chicago: Aldine Publishing Company.

1976 "Hindu Transactions: Diversity without Dualism." In *Transaction and Meaning.* Bruce Kapferer (ed.). Philadelphia: Institute for the Study of Human Issues.

1989 "Constructing an Indian Ethnosociology." *Contributions to Indian Sociology.* 23:1–39.

Mauss, Marcel
1985 "A Category of the Human Mind: The Notion of Self." In *The Category of the Person.* M. Carrithers, S. Collins, S. Lukes (eds.). Cambridge: Cambridge University Press.

Nichter, Mark
1986 "Modes of Food Classification and the Diet-Health Contingency: A South Indian Caste Study." In *Food, Society, and Culture*. R. S. Khare and M. S. A. Rao (eds.). Durham: Carolina Academic Press.

Nikhilananda, Swami
1963 *The Upanishads*. New York: Harper Torchbooks.

Pandey, Raj Bali
1969 *Hindu Saṁskāras*. Delhi: Motilal Banarsidass.

Prakash, Om
1961 *Food and Drinks in Ancient India*. Delhi: Munshi Ram Manohar Lal.

Raghavan, V.
1966 *The Great Integrators: The Saint-Singers of India*. Delhi: Ministry of Information and Broadcasting.

Ricoeur, Paul
1978 *The Philosophy of Paul Ricoeur*. Charles E. Regan and David Stewart (eds.). Boston: Beacon Press.

Sahlins, Marshall
1978 *Culture and Practical Reason*. Chicago: The University of Chicago Press.

Sanderson, Alexis
1985 "Purity and Power among the Brahmans of Kashmir." In *The Category of the Person*. M. Carrithers, S. Collins and S. Lukes (eds.). Cambridge: Cambridge University Press.

Satprakashananda, Swami
1965 *Methods of Knowledge*. London: George Allen and Unwin Ltd.

Toomey, Paul
1986 "Food from the Mouth of Krishna: Socio-religious Aspects of Sacred Food in Two Krishnaite Sects." In *Food, Society and Culture*. R. S. Khare and M. S. A. Rao (eds.). Durham: Carolina Academic Press.

Woodcock, George
1971 *Mohandas Gandhi*. New York: The Viking Press.

Zaehner, R. C.
1969 *The Bhagavad-Gita*. Oxford: Oxford University Press.

Zimmermann, Francis
1987 *The Jungle and the Aroma of Meats: An Ecological Theme in Hindu Medicine*. Berkeley: University of California Press.

2

You Are What You Eat: The Anomalous Status of Dog-Cookers in Hindu Mythology

*

David Gordon White

"And then he took not only the first drink of neat whiskey he ever took in his life but the drink of it that he could no more have conceived himself taking than the Brahmin can believe that that situation can conceivably arise in which he will eat dog."[1]

The Hindu lawbooks constitute a watershed on the subject of food and purity codes, as well as the status and occupations of the four castes [*varṇa*s], and the "fifth caste that is not a caste."[2] While there exist antecedents for much of what is found in these sources, it is only with the appearance of these treatises on law [*dharmaśāstra*s], ritual [*gṛhyasūtra*s, *śrautasūtra*s], and polity [*nītiśāstra*s] that treatments of these matters become truly systematized. More than this, much new material—terminology, regulations, codifications—is introduced in these sources, which generally date from the beginning of the common era.

Among the issues treated for the first time or in an original light in these sources are 1) the relationship of "checks and balances" between the Brahman and Kṣatriya varṇas; 2) classifications of food groups, according to their relative purity; 3) the system of *jāti*s, or "subcastes," as an elaboration of the varna system.

We will treat the first of these issues shortly, in the context of the myths of the rivalry between the royal sage [*rājarṣi*] Viśvāmitra and the Brahman sage [*brahmarṣi*] Vasiṣṭha. The second of these points concerns food categories which, in the time of the lawbooks, were undergoing much reevaluation. New currents of thought, both within Hinduism and without (in Buddhism and Jainism), were obliging Brahmans to "retrench" as a means to maintaining their spiritual authority. A new vogue (from the seventh century B.C. time of the Āraṇyakas and the slightly later Upaniṣads) of renunciation and asceticism seems to have incited Brahmans to assert their superiority in new ways. One of these ways consisted in the adoption of a strictly vegetarian diet, with a concomitant emphasis on the milk products used in sacrifice.[3] Historically, this shift brought about the "creation" of the third and fourth *āśrama*s, the forest-dwelling [*vanaprasthā*], and renunciant [*sannyāsa*] stages of life, of which Vasiṣṭha and Viśvāmitra were, in a sense, the mythic exemplars.

The third point concerns the beginnings of the *jāti* system which, as codified in the lawbooks, subdivided the four varṇas into a great number of subcategories. Under this system, one's *jāti* determined not only one's occupation, but also engaged one in a complex network of purity and marriage codes. Ultimately, the *jāti* system was and remains grounded in barriers to the exchange of "coded substances"[4], i.e., of foods and body fluids. In this context, we find a great amount of space devoted, in the lawbooks, to the dire consequences of the violations of such barriers. On the one hand, there are long discussions of the expiations which high caste persons must observe when these barriers have been breached. On the other, large sections of these treatises are devoted to the fallen state of those persons who commit inexpiable crimes against the purity codes.

In this latter context, laws of "karmic retribution" are brought into play, which meticulously delineate the low-caste rebirths that befall such violators. It is here that the "fifth caste that is not a caste," or the so-called "outcaste" or "Untouchable" *jātis* are discussed. Marriage or sexual intercourse—the transfer of coded substances of sexual fluids—"against the grain" [*pratiloma*][5] condemns the offending pair and its descendants to a damned earthly existence. Generally, the lowest of these *pratiloma* jātis is that of the Śvapacas or Śvapakas, the "Dog-Cookers."[6]

The balance of this study will be devoted to the truly pivotal role played by the Dog-Cooker *jāti,* the lowest of the low, which as such has constituted an antitype to all that defines the Brahman varṇa as a whole, and, most especially, to the idealized *vanaprasthin,* the forest-dwelling Brahman sage or the *brahmarṣi.* Here, we will show how the Dog-Cooker has come to stand, over a period of some 2,500 years, as the polar opposite of—yet the necessary complement to—the lofty Brahman sage. We will discuss this relationship in terms of coded substances, especially food, such as was delineated in legalistic form in the *dharmaśāstras*, but also through a close consideration of narrativizations of the same, such as appeared in the mythology of the Brāhmaṇas, epics, and Purāṇas, and a number of other sources.

Finally, we will also discuss the pivotal role played in myth by the "renegade" renunciant Kṣatriya, the *rājarṣi,* in defining this opposition. Not only the middle term between the dog and cow, Dog-Cooker and Brahman, in mythic narrativizations of the ambiguous relationship of the two, he also stands as the historical mediator between the earlier anti-brahmanic *vrātya*s ["vow-takers"] and *yati*s ["goers"], and the later tantric sects. In this light, these myths and other sources are also chronicles of a changing relationship between sanctioned brahmanic authority and unsanctioned non-Brahman renunciant power.

Classifications of Food and *Jāti* in the *Manu Smṛti*

The ca. first century A.D. *Manu Smṛti* is clearly a pivotal text in the history of Hindu attitudes toward food. In its section (5.15–18) on "Lawful and Forbidden Foods," it permits Brahmans to consume certain meats. Elsewhere, it emphasizes, on the one hand, the connection between sacrifice and the consumption of cooked meat (5.22, 30–32, 36, 39, 41–42), defending both practices; on the other, it praises abstention from meat as equal in merit to one hundred horse sacrifices (5.53, 56). And, while it states that "killing for purposes of sacrifice is not killing" (5.39), it also lauds the practice of noninjury, *ahiṃsa* (5.44–55, 58).[7]

In his major work, *Homo Hierarchicus,* Louis Dumont states that the Indian "classification of foods is essentially related to the classification of people and to relationships between human groups. It is not a primary datum resulting from a universal classification of pure and impure."[8] That is, food categories are codes for a constellation of other sorts of categories in the natural and cultural sphere. In this light, it is curious that Manu, who shows himself to be quite ambiguous on the subject of food, should at first blush be unequivocal on the subject of relationships between Brahmans and members of lower castes, in terms of physical contact in general, and food exchange in particular. This is especially the case with those *jāti*s, tribals, and other peoples whose diet was said to include the flesh of impure, necrophagic, or coprophagic animals.[9] Such persons are quite indifferently grouped together under the heading of "outcastes" by Manu and many of his contemporaries, in spite of the fact that Manu begins his enumeration of these peoples with the statement that "there is no fifth caste" (10.4).[10]

While a great number of *jātis*, with specific names, genealogies and duties, fall under the broad heading of "outcaste," two generic terms are employed throughout the post-Upaniṣadic period to designate these people in general. These are the terms *Caṇḍāla* (which has no traceable etymology) and Śvapaca. Śvapaca means "Dog Cooker," a highly pejorative characterization which draws on the strongly negative canine symbolism in post-Vedic India.[11]

Manu (10.51–56) treats these peoples in the following way:

> "But the dwellings of Caṇḍālas and Śvapacas shall be outside the village . . . and their wealth shall be dogs and donkeys. Their dress shall be the garments of the dead, (they shall eat) their food from broken dishes, black iron (shall be) their ornaments, and they must always wander from place to place. A man who fulfills a religious duty shall not seek intercourse with them; their transactions (shall be) among themselves, and their marriages with their equals . . . At night they shall not walk about in villages and in towns. By day they must go about for the purpose of their work, distinguished by marks at the king's command, and they shall carry out the corpses (of persons) who have no relatives; that is a settled rule. By the king's order, they shall always execute the criminals in accordance with the law, and they shall take for themselves the clothes, the beds, and the ornaments of (such) criminals."

While a few sources describe Śvapaca settlements as being strewn with the bones and hides of dogs, it is noteworthy that depictions of Śvapacas actually cooking dogs are nowhere to be found in Sanskrit literature. In fact, as we shall describe shortly, the only individuals whom we ever find actually stooping to cook dog are powerful sages![12] However, if Dumont is correct that food categories are in fact means for classifying people, Śvapaca is an apt name for India's outcastes since, by virtue of their location and functions in society, they are, like dogs, marginal, scavenging, coprophagic creatures.[13]

Taken together, the lawbooks and epic and Puranic sources on Caṇḍālas and Śvapacas emphasize three different facets of this group's "outcaste" situation. First, they are the product of *varṇa-saṁkara,* the mixing of castes. The product of a dangerous and sinful mixing of sexual fluids (and thus of social categories) on the part of parents of ancestors, they are condemned to birth in bodies that are *a priori* polluted and polluting. Second, they cook and eat prohibited foods; and finally, they are exposed, through their determined vocations, to polluting substances. These last two elements of the Śvapaca's situation also constitute a case of mixing, in this case of the dead and the living: both the meat they presumably eat and the corpses and excrements they dispose of are polluting, because they bear the stamp of death.[14]

It is the Brahman who is most vulnerable to pollution, and most especially to that of the Dog-Cooker, in the social intercourse that he might have with them. Here, while this vulnerability is the mark of the Brahman's elevated status and purity,[15] it is also a liability, inasmuch as the expiations he must perform are more rigorous than those prescribed for the other varṇas.[16] Here, the concomitant to those purity codes which exclude the polluting Dog-Cooker from the lower end of the social pyramid is the "self-exclusion" of the pure vegetarian and milk-drinking Brahman from the upper end.

It is here, in the delineation of this polarity of Brahman/Śvapaca as most pure/least pure, that "animals are good to think with." In this case, the animals in question are the cow and the dog. In the case of the former, it is the five pure products of the cow, the *pañcagavya* (milk, yogurt, clarified butter, dung, and urine), which define the Brahman sacrificer in his domestic setting or the *brahmarṣi* in his forest hermitage. The cow not only provides the Brahman with the purest form of nourishment, but its milk also serves in the sacrifice, and its dung and urine to purify living areas. Indeed, the animal with which the priestly *Brahman* most closely identified himself was the cow. As provider of the *pañcagavya,* the cow epitomized Brahman purity. More than this, it was from the cow that the Brahman obtained an important part of his vegetarian diet: because milk and its byproducts are "cooked" inside the cow, they are eminently suited to ingestion by the pure Brahman.[17]

In this perspective, the two poles of Indian society, the wholly pure Brahmans and the wholly impure Śvapacas or Śvapākas, are contrasted in terms of their diet: Brahmans live by the cooked milk of their pure cows, while "outcastes" live by their impure dogs. The danger of mixing the two is a leitmotif in Hindu sources, in which a dog's or "outcaste's" contact with a sacrificial vessel (containing a milk product) is an abomination for which ritual expiations must be observed by the pure Brahman sacrificer.[18]

At the opposite end of the spectrum from the Brahman, the Śvapaca, the Dog-Cooker, is identified with his dogs, the most polluting of domestic animals in post-Vedic India. So it is that we find, in scattered sources, statements to the effect that among the animals, the dog is the Caṇḍāla. As outcastes of their respective races, the dog and the Śvapaca were nearly interchangeable elements in the ideology and symbolic system of post-Vedic India.

At this point, we would do well to ask what it was, precisely, that the Śvapaca did with his dogs, to render him so defiling. While we can be quite certain that the dog served him in his hunting forays, we are faced with the question of whether the dog itself went into the Śvapaca's pot from time to time. As we have already mentioned, there are no references anywhere in the whole of Sanskrit literature to Śvapacas cooking dogs. While we know that the two are identified with one another, especially with regard to the danger that the coded substance of their saliva presents for the pure cow-milking, milk-drinking Brahman, we do not know in what way the dog played a role in the eating habits of the Śvapaca.

In the Sanskrit of these traditions, a variant rendering of the term Śvapaca is *Śvapāka*. While the two are considered to be synonymous, as compounds of the word dog (*śvan: śva-* in compounds) with derivatives of the root *pac,* "to cook", the second term may also be especially glossed as *śva-pā-ka,* from the root *pā,* "to nourish, suckle". In this reading of the term, the Śvapakas would thus be a race or people "Suckled by Dogs," "Nourished by Dogs," or even "Children of Dogs." This reading is supported, albeit indirectly, by a number of foreign sources. Since the time of Pliny at least, the ancient geographers of the western world numbered, among the fantastic races of India and Ethiopia, a group they called the *Cynamolgi,* "Dog-Milkers."[19] *Śvapāka* may thus be a synonym of *Cynamolgi,*[20] in which case this group would serve as a perfect foil to the Brahman milker of cows.

Whether this exercise in creative etymology and cross-cultural categorization serves to establish the Śvapacas/Śvapākas as Dog-Milkers or not, the polarity between Brahman and "outcaste," on the basis of the domestic animals who represent them, remains a valid one. Just as the vegetarian Brahman's *pañcagavya* are the antitype to the milk of the dog, as well as to its saliva and flesh, so the

Brahman is himself situated at the opposite end of the social continuum from the Śvapaca. We may illustrate this with a chart:

Brahman	Śvapaca
pure	impure
cow	dog
bovine milk	canine milk
"cooked" milk	canine saliva/flesh

Betwixt and Between *Śvapaca* and *Brahmarṣi:* the *Rājarṣi* Viśvāmitra

The ideological shift and its concomitant practices on the part of post-Upanisadic Brahmans brought about a certain number of social tensions. By espousing the ascetic, renunciant ideal, Brahmans were in fact following in the footsteps of groups who had previously been their adversaries, the antinomian *yati*s, *vrātya*s and others of that ilk.[21] At the same time, it would appear that in order to retain their general position of hegemony over the other castes, and over their royal patrons (who themselves had renunciant pretensions[22]) in particular, Brahmans found themselves obliged to "one-up" non-Brahman ascetics and present themselves as the ultimate exemplars of the canons of proper asceticism. It was also necessary, however, that their claim to the forest-dwelling or renunciant life be kept more or less exclusive (this proved to be an impossibility), since the now renunciant Brahmans still depended on the other castes to support them materially and clean up after them. This was particularly the case with the princely Kṣatriya caste, upon whom Brahmans had historically most depended, but who now were the most inclined to renounce the duties of their caste for an ascetic life. Thus, while themselves following the path of personal salvation, of *mokṣa,* Brahmans never ceased to exhort the rest of society to remain involved in the world, to follow their respective *svadharma*s.

It is in this context of ideological change on the part of Brahmans from a sacrificial to a renunciant model, a change which threw them into a new and quite alien environment, that we must understand the internal contradictions and ambiguities of the *Manu Smṛti.* It would seem that Manu was still trying to have it both ways, at once hearkening to the old orthodoxy of a centered, world-embracing society that turned on the great sacrifices of which Brahmans were the venerable (and well-paid) specialists;

and drawing up a manifesto of a world-renouncing ideal co-opted from others but which the Realpolitik of the day made it necessary to espouse.[23]

The turn toward the renunciant ideal generated other sorts of tensions and ambiguities in Hindu society. Renunciation implies "dying to human society" for a life in savage nature, and so it was that *ṛṣis*, *vanaprasthins*, *yogins*, *sannyāsins*, etc., came to dwell in forest hermitages or to wander alone in the wilderness. In this new situation, they came into contact with certain sorts of people of whose existence they might have only been vaguely aware back in the town or royal capital. These were the forest-dwelling *jātis,* tribes or peoples to whom they also referred as Caṇḍālas and Śvapacas.[24] Now, however—and in spite of the category formation of this period which placed the Dog-Cooker and the *brahmarṣi* in polar opposition—rather than having such subhuman creatures as their sweepers or sanitation workers, forest-dwelling Brahmans had them as their neighbors, a situation which no doubt compounded the inconveniences of the new venue of their austerities. So it is that, in the mythology of the post-Vedic age, the forest becomes the stage upon which are played out the ambiguities and contradictions that we find in Manu. The forest was also frequented by one other group of people: these were kings and princes who made forays into the wilderness in the pursuit of game, in accordance with their Kṣatriya *svadharma.*[25]

It is in this context that we are presented with a number of epic and Puranic accounts of encounters between royal hunters and Brahman hermits in the forest. The tale of Śakuntalā, daughter of Viśvāmitra, is the most celebrated of these. More to the point of this study, however, are a number of other myths of Viśvāmitra, which cast him in a pivotal role between Śvapacas and dogs, on the one hand, and *brahmarṣis* and cows, on the other.

The cycle of myths which will be the main object of this study turn around the rivalry between Viśvāmitra and another Vedic sage Vasiṣṭha, a rivalry which becomes greatly amplified in the epic and Puranic traditions. In these myths, Vasiṣṭha is the classic representative of brahmanic orthodoxy: he is a *brahmarṣi or devarṣi* who lives with his wish-fulfilling cow Nandinī in a hermitage, and who counsels Ikṣvāku princes to follow their Kṣatriya dharma and not stray into renunciant ways. Viśvāmitra, on the contrary, is a king who, after a stinging defeat at the hands of Vasiṣṭha, takes up a regime of strict asceticism, by virtue of which he becomes more powerful than even Vasiṣṭha. Power does not authority make, however, and the *rājarṣi*[26] Viśvāmitra is always cast, in epic and Puranic mythology, in heterodox roles which associate him with either renegade ascetics, Dog-Cookers, or man[-eating], ghoulish *rākṣasas*. He is, in fact, the stock mythic representative of "non-brahmanic asceticism," of an individual who exercises a brahmanic prerogative of renunciation which is properly not his own.

Two points, which qualify this dichotomy, are worth noting however. First, while he is the paragon of a sanctioned brahmanic superiority grounded in renunciant ideals, Vasiṣṭha is not a true renouncer. He is a *vanaprasthin* who lives together with his family in a hermitage, offers sacrifices, and eats the rich products of his wish-fulfilling cow. In contrast, Viśvāmitra, who attains "Brahman" or "*ṛṣi*" status by virtue of extreme austerities, is much more faithful to the post-Upanisadic ideal of *sannyāsa*. However, it must be recalled that such hard-core asceticism was originally the province of nonbrahmanic, antinomian sects—often associated with the wild, forest-dwelling Vedic god Rudra—and this is the side of Viśvāmitra's mythic persona which is constantly emphasized in his epic and Puranic conflicts with Vasiṣṭha.

This fundamental cleavage, between the *brahmarṣi* and the *rājarṣi*, constellates into a great number of other dichotomies, not the least of which is a zoological taxonomy. If Vasiṣṭha, the exemplar of brahmanic orthodoxy, is doubled by his cow, Viśvāmitra is more often associated with the dog, and therefore with those peoples who are most closely associated with dogs, the dog-cooking Śvapacas. The marginal Śvapacas are the perennial inhabitants of the Indian wilderness or wasteland, and their sphere is often placed in opposition to the paradise which is Vasiṣṭha's hermitage. This is the case even when the two spheres border upon one another. This desert wasteland motif is further expanded, in many myths, to stand for the state of the world in a period of drought or partial dissolution, a period brought on by the same sorts of human disobedience that fostered the Śvapacas as a people: this is *varṇasaṁkara,* the mixing of castes.

When they are not portrayed as dogs themselves, wandering, anti-Brahmanic ascetics are often accompanied by dogs. Here, a number of omen texts, from the sixth-century *Bṛhat Saṁhitā* and later sources,[27] underscore this connection in interesting ways. At the beginning of the section entitled "The Circle of Dogs" (*Śvacakra*),[28] Varāhamihira says:

> If a dog urinates on a man, horse, elephant, pot, saddle, milky tree, pile of bricks, parasol, pallet, seat, mortar, standard, cowrie, or a flowery or grassy site, and then passes in front of a traveller (*yātṛ*), then his (the traveller's) undertaking will be successful. If it urinates on moist cow dung, sweet foods will come to him; if on dry cow dung, then dried grain, molasses, or sweets will be obtained. Again, if the dog urinates on or kicks a poisonous or thorny tree, firewood, a stone, a dried up tree trunk, or the bones of a cremation ground, and passes in front of a traveller (*yāyin*), this portends undesirable events. Urinating on a bed of pottery vessels that are broken or intact means a blemish (*doṣa*) will befall the daughters of (the traveller's) house; on vessels (as well as sandals) in use, the pollution of the woman of the house; by urinating on a cow, a dog portends miscegenation with an outcaste (*avarṇaja*) . . . a dog suckling a calf is an evil omen."

Further omens, generally favorable, involving travellers and dogs in forest settings, are followed in this text by a long series of portents related to dogs in inhabited areas. These latter are, with but a few exceptions, extremely inauspicious. In all cases, the urinating dog is associated with a person who is defined by movement: this is the *yātṛ* or *yāyin,* the "goer" whose name identifies with those Vedic "goers" who were the *yatis*. While the dog and the sort of human it interacts with remain constant, we find a cleavage between omens issuing from the dog's passage through 1) what is clearly an auspicious "exterior" setting (*milky* tree), either the tamed forest or a hermitage; 2) an inauspicious "exterior" setting (poisonous tree), such as the wilderness or the world at the end of an age, and 3) the ordered "interior" of the household. In the first case, all omens are auspicious because the creatures involved are moving through an auspicious space suited to them; whereas in the second, it is the space itself which renders the omens inauspicious. In the third case, however, dog and wandering ascetic are entirely out of place in the domestic setting, whence the extremely dire projected result of soilure on the women of the house, and miscegenation with an "outcaste."[29]

The symbolism of a dangerous mixing of categories is entirely transparent here: canine (as in Śva-paca) excrements mixed with human (as in Brahman) eating vessels, and with the source of pure Brahman food (the cow, provider of the *pañcagavya*), is catastrophic. All of the polarities we outlined in the first part of this study are operative here: dog and cow, "outcaste" and Brahman, excrement and food, are to be held at a distance from one another. Yet, there is a pivot to possible interactions between the two poles of the orthodox system: this is the wandering ascetic, the *yati*.

The Epic and Puranic "Viśvāmitra Cycle" of Myths

Because Viśvāmitra, for all his ascetic power, himself epitomizes a mixing of caste functions, it follows that he ought to be in frequent contact with Dog-Cookers and their ilk. Viśvāmitra and the persons with whom he is associated are always on the move (*yā*), in contradistinction to Vasiṣṭha, who remains at home in his hermitage. Such an errant existence is appropriate to the true renouncer, but it also characterizes the habits of the royal hunter, the cattle thief, and the hunting or herding dog. In a way, Viśvāmitra personifies all of these.

The *locus classicus* of the origin of the rivalry of these two *ṛṣis*, as metaphor for the ambiguities inherent to the polarities we have been discussing, is found in the *Mahābhārata* (1.165.1–44 and 9.39.2, 11–29):

> Viśvāmitra, the royal son of Gādhi, becomes tired and thirsty while hunting in the wastelands (*marudhanvasu*). He comes to the hermitage of the Brahman sage Vasiṣṭha, where he sees Vasiṣṭha's wish-fulfilling cow (*kāmadhenu*), Nandinī. Viśvāmitra begs Vasiṣṭha to give her to him, but Vasiṣṭha refuses, because without a cow he, a Brahman, would be unable to perform the sacrifices proper to his station. When Viśvāmitra attempts to wrest her from him by force, she resists. Nandinī's eyes become red with fury, as she produces from her anus hordes of Pahlavas, from her excrements Śabaras and Śakas, from her foam, Yāvanas, and from her urine Puṇḍras, Kirātas, Dramaḍas, Siṁhalas, Barbaras, Daradas, and Mlecchas. These excrement-born[30] "outcaste" hordes rout the army of Viśvāmitra. After his defeat, a chastened Viśvāmitra decides that the greatest power in the world is not that of princely (*kṣatra*) dominance, but the power of *brahman* proper to the priestly (*brāhmaṇa*) caste. He then performs austerities of such intensity that he accedes to Brahman-hood (*brāhmaṇatvam avāpa*).

Well before the time of this epic narrative, it was a mythic commonplace to cast Viśvāmitra as the sole *ṛṣi* who had usurped his elevated Brahman status, a status to which Vasiṣṭha and the other *ṛṣi*s were born. Viśvāmitra, born a prince, and thereby only entitled to accede to the status of royal sage (*rājarṣi*), appropriates through his intense austerities the powers of a divine or Brahman sage (*devarṣi* or *brahmarṣi*). Although he wrests for himself the Brahman sage's power, he can never embody the latter's sanctioned authority, which is a matter of Brahman birth. In a sense, this struggle between Viśvāmitra and Vasiṣṭha mirrors the social upheavals, following the seventh century B.C., which occasioned the coopting, by princes, of priestly prerogatives in matters of sacred knowledge and ascetic practice. We find ample evidence for this in the Upaniṣads.

Another version of this rivalry, between the *brahmarṣi* Vasiṣṭha and the *rājarsi* Viśvāmitra, grows out of a Vedic tradition according to which the two feud over the sacrifices of a certain Sudās,[31] with their rivalry escalating into bloodshed as Sudās kills Vasiṣṭha's one hundred and one sons. This myth is greatly expanded in a baroque *Mahābhārata* account, in which it is Sudās' grandson, the Ikṣvāku king Kalmāṣapāda who, having killed a great quantity of game, is wandering about, tired and thirsty in the forest:

> Walking on a forest path, Kalmāṣapāda meets Śakti, the eldest of Vasiṣṭha's one hundred sons. Śakti, as is proper for a Brahman, insists that the king yield to him on the path, and Kalmāṣapāda belabours him with his whip. Śakti then curses the king to become a man-eating *rākṣasa*. Viśvāmitra, in his ongoing feud with Vasiṣṭha, causes Kalmāṣapāda to become possessed by a *rākṣasa* named Kiṁkara. Possessed, Kalmāṣapāda attempts to feed human flesh to a hungry Brahman, who curses him to become a man-eater a second time.[32] The conjoined curses take effect, and Kalmāṣapāda, at Viśvāmitra's urging, eats Śakti and all of Vasiṣṭha's sons.
>
> Vasiṣṭha learns of Viśvāmitra's role, but rather than trying to avenge himself, attempts to take his own life. When he fails, he returns home to his hermitage. On the way, he meets Śakti's widow, who is pregnant with Vasiṣṭha's future grandson, Parāśara. At this point, they

> are accosted by the still possessed Kalmāṣapāda. He is only stopped from devouring them by Vasiṣṭha's enunciation of the mantra *huṃ*. Vasiṣṭha then releases Kalmāṣapāda from his twelve-year curse. Kalmāṣapāda recognizes Vasiṣṭha to be his family priest, honors him, and requests that Vasiṣṭha father a son for him, which Vasiṣṭha does.[33]

A variant mythological explanation for Viśvāmitra's ambiguous (and thereby dangerous) status is indicative of the symbols which the orthodox ideology deployed in its portrayal of its nemesis, the non-ruling renunciant *rājarṣi*. In the *Mahābhārata,* Viśvāmitra is said to have been born from a ball of *caru* (boiled rice and barley) into which his Brahman "father" Ṛcīka had placed the energy of the supreme *brahman,* the essence of Brahman-hood. This ball of food was swallowed by a Kṣatriya princess named Satyavatī. Technically, this makes Viśvāmitra the issue of a mixing of castes (*varṇasaṁkara*), by the logic of which he would himself be an "outcaste" by birth.[34]

If the textual tradition does not emphasize such a strong reading of this myth, it nevertheless throws Viśvāmitra together with "outcastes" whenever possible. In the classical origin of his rivalry with Vasiṣṭha related above, the army of king Viśvāmitra is routed by an army of outcastes which issues from Nandinī's excrements: although they are his opponents, their role, of warriors, is structurally congruent with that of Viśvāmitra himself. In many myths, it is in a great wasteland or desert region stricken with drought that the ambiguous sage encounters his "outcastes." Perennially, the wilderness is the mythological place, or "non-place" of the Śvapaca: it is the undefined space which lies outside the limits of the royal capital town, or priestly hermitage, or between two such centers.[35]

A primal myth which unites the wasteland theme with the origins of the "outcaste" races, the *rājarṣi* Viśvāmitra, a "renunciant" Indra, and the symbolism of the dog, is the legend of Śunaḥśepa:[36]

> Hariścandra, king of the Ikṣvākus, has 100 wives but no sons. On the advice of the sage Narada (or of Vasiṣṭha, in later variants), he pleads with Varuṇa, the god of Law and Order, to grant him a son. Varuṇa acquiesces, on the condition that the son born to him be immediately sacrificed to himself. A son is born, to whom the name Rohita is given. Hariścandra withholds him from Varuṇa each time the god

demands his due. This occurs five times in a period encompassing Rohita's youth.

Before Varuṇa returns for a sixth time, Rohita runs away into the forest. Back in his capital, Hariścandra suffers Varuṇa's punishments. This god of the waters and of binding contracts distends the king's belly with dropsy. In the forest, Rohita is approached each year, over a period of five years, by Indra who has put on the guise of a wandering Brahman ascetic. In this form, Indra counsels Rohita to live the same wandering life as he.

In the sixth year of his forest exile, Rohita comes upon a Brahman named Ajīgarta who is starving in the wilderness with his wife and three sons, Śunapuccha, Śunaḥśepa, and Śunolāṅgūla ("Dog-Tail," "Dog-Penis" and "Dog-Hindquarters"). Rohita offers the Brahman 100 cows for one of his sons, who would thus replace him in his father's contractual sacrifice to Varuṇa. Ajīgarta agrees, but refuses to give up his eldest: his wife refuses to give up her youngest. So, by process of elimination, the middle son, Śunaḥśepa, is chosen.

Varuṇa accepts this surrogate victim, allowing that a Brahman is a worthy substitute for a Kṣatriya victim. Hariścandra decides to combine this sacrifice with his own anointment and royal consecration. In the sacrifice, the sacrificial priests are Viśvāmitra, Jamadagni, Vasiṣṭha, and Ayasya. None but Śunaḥśepa's father, Ajīgarta, will kill the boy; and as Ajīgarta advances on him with the sacrificial knife, Śunaḥśepa begins to sing prayers to the Vedic gods. With his last hymn, to Uṣas, the Dawn, his three sacrificial bonds fall from his body and Hariścandra is loosed from his affliction of dropsy. Śunaḥśepa then himself completes Hariścandra's sacrifice with the "rapid-pressing" hymn which has just been revealed to him.

The sacrifice completed, the sacrificial officiant Viśvāmitra now offers to adopt Śunaḥśepa as the eldest of his 101 sons. Śunaḥśepa accepts, reviling his father as a *śūdra* [the lowest caste in India prior to the conclusion of this myth] when the latter tries to claim him back. Viśvāmitra then announces the adoption of the boy to his sons, and gives Śunaḥśepa the new name of Devarāta ("God-Given").[37] Of

> Viśvāmitra's 101 sons, Madhucchanda, the middlemost, and his fifty younger brothers accept Devarāta as their elder, and are blessed by Viśvāmitra. Madhucchanda's fifty elder brothers refuse, however, and are thus cursed by Viśvāmitra with the words, "May your descendants obtain the ends (*antān*) as their lot."
>
> These brothers and their descendants became the Andhras, Pulindas and Mūtibas, who live at the outer limits (*udantya*) [of "India"]. Viśvāmitra is said to be the founder of most of the Dāsya ("non-Aryan," base, "outcaste") races.

Perhaps the most elaborate of all epic and Puranic myths concerning Viśvāmitra's ambiguous situation is that which places him in a Śvapaca village in a time of drought and in a general situation of *āpaddharma* ["the dharma of thinking on one's feet"]. Manu discusses *āpaddharma* with explicit reference to Viśvāmitra's situation, stating that when it is a question of life and death, a Brahman may break nearly all the canons of purity and propriety: "By . . . accepting gifts from despicable (men) Brahmans (in distress) commit no sin . . . He who, when in danger of losing his life, accepts food from any person whatsoever, is no more tainted by sin than the sky by mud" (10.103–04). Here he illustrates this tenet with the examples of Ajīgarta, who was ready to slay his son Śunaḥśepa to save himself from starvation; Bharadvāja, who took cows from a low-caste carpenter when he was starving with his sons in a lonely forest; and Vāmadeva and Viśvāmitra, who took dog meat to avoid starvation, the latter accepting his from the hand of a Caṇḍāla (10.105–08).

Manu does not cite the case of the god Indra himself who is, in many ways, the Vedic antecedent of the epic and Puranic Viśvāmitra, and who continues to be associated with dubious forms of renunciation throughout post-Vedic mythology. Indra himself confesses to having "cooked the entrails of a dog" in a time of distress [RV 4.18.13], and is thereby the divine "founder" of this mythic theme. An epic treatment of this motif, of a god/sage eating dog in a time of distress, is found in the post-second-century A.D. didactic portion of the *Mahābhārata*. Here, Yudhiṣṭhira asks the slowly dying Bhīṣma the way in which a king ought to rule "in times when all living on earth has become *dāsyu*-fied (slave-like)," and when "time has arrived at a low point."[38] In answer to his question, Bhīṣma relates to him the story of Viśvāmitra in the village of the Dog-Cookers:[39]

Once, at the twilight of the Treta and Dvāpara ages, and according to the ordinances of destiny, there came to pass a terrible drought of twelve years' duration. It was the approach of the end of an age, and the thousand-eyed Indra sent no rain . . . Abandoned were sacrifices and sacred studies; gone were the *vaṣaṭ* formula and the auspicious ceremony. Agriculture and herding had fallen into neglect, buying and selling had ceased, associations and assemblies were dissolved, and the great festivals had completely disappeared. The Earth was heaped up with bones and skeletons, with creatures and men in great confusion crying, "Alas, alas!" The greatest cities were deserted, and towns and houses burnt down. Cows, sheep, and water buffalo fought one another for food. The twice-born were slain, and their princely protectors laid low. In that dangerous time in which *dharma* had wasted away, those who were dying, afflicted with hunger, ate one another. The seers, having forsaken their rules of conduct, left their divine fires unattended and abandoned their hermitages.

Under these circumstances, the venerable seer Viśvāmitra, homeless and hungry, wandered about. One day, he chanced upon a settlement of Śvapacas, of those injurers and killers of living creatures, who were living in a certain forest. The settlement was scattered with broken pots, spread with heaps of dog hides, and piled with the bones and skulls of swine and asses. The clothing of the dead and garlands which had been stripped from them lay strewn about. Their hut temples were hung with iron bells and surrounded by packs of dogs.[40]

The great sage Viśvāmitra, overcome by hunger, entered that place, but in his begging, he found nothing at all to eat, neither meat nor grain nor fruit nor any other food. And thinking "Oh, what misery has befallen me!" he fell to the ground.

The muni saw in the house of a Caṇḍāla a broad piece of stringy meat from a dog which had been slain with a spear that very day. He then thought to himself, "There is truly no other available way to save my life at this point. In times of distress, theft from one's equal or inferior is permissible.

Theft is not a sin when that which is taken belongs to outcastes: I shall therefore take that food."

Having made up his mind, Viśvāmitra fell asleep. Then, seeing that it was the dead of night and that all was asleep in the Caṇḍāla settlement, Viśvāmitra slowly rose and went into the Caṇḍāla hut. There, an ugly, phlegmy-eyed Caṇḍāla, who had been lying as if he were asleep, said with a broken, rough, and cracked voice, "Who is pawing at my stringy meat? While the Caṇḍāla settlement is asleep, I am awake, and not sleeping. Away with you!" Such were his cruel words.

The sage quickly answered, "I am Viśvāmitra." The Caṇḍāla, hearing the words of that great seer whose soul had been purified, tripped up from his pallet and drew himself to his feet. With tears welling up in his eyes and hands folded in great respect, he said to Viśvāmitra, "O Brahmin! What is it that you wish to accomplish tonight?"

Viśvāmitra then sweetly spoke to the Mātaṅga, "I am starved, at my last gasp. I shall take that dog's hindquarters. My vital breaths are leaving me, and hunger is destroying my memory. Therefore, aware of my *svadharma,* I shall take that dog's hindquarters. The dharma of famine is one that corrupts. So I shall take that dog's hindquarters. Fire (Agni) is the mouth and priest of the gods, and therefore pure and clean. Just as he, that Brahman, is an eater of everything, in the same way will (eating this dog's hindquarters) be righteous in my case."

Having heard him, the Caṇḍāla said, "O great sage, hear my words. The wise say that the dog is the vilest of all game. Of the body, the vilest portion is indeed the broad hindquarters. The act you have resolved upon, particularly the taking of that which is proper to Candalahood, of that which is not to be eaten, is a perversion. O sage, seek another means by which to stay alive. O great muni, let not the desire for meat be the ruination of your vows. You should know that this path is a forbidden one. The intermingling of castes ought not to be practiced. Do not allow yourself, you who are the greatest knower of dharma, to be sundered from dharma."

> So addressed, Viśvāmitra, afflicted with hunger, responded once again: "Life is better than death. One should follow one's dharma in life. I am alive and desirous of food: I shall indeed eat food."
>
> The Śvapaca spoke: "I really do not dare give it to you. Nor can I allow my own food to be taken. We two would both be stained with our innate pollution for that, if I were the giver, and you, O twice-born, the receiver."
>
> Viśvāmitra spoke: "After today, when I have performed this sinful act, I shall lead an exceedingly pure life. Possessed of a cleansed soul, I shall hasten back to the righteous path. Speak truly, O guru! Is this a pure or a defiling act?"
>
> The Śvapaca spoke: "One must be true to oneself in matters of this world. You know what stain lies in this. He who would consider dog meat to be proper food would, I think, find nothing repugnant in this world."
>
> Having spoken to Viśvāmitra, the Mātaṅga fell silent. Possessed of consummate understanding, Viśvāmitra then took the dog's hindquarters. The great muni clung to the five-limbed (dog), in order that he might survive. Together with his wife, the great muni ritually prepared it. Then he went into the forest. At that very moment, Indra sent rain.[41] Revived, all creatures and plants came to life. And the great Viśvāmitra, with all stain burned away by long austerities, attained the highest and most wondrous of powers.
>
> [Bhīsṃa then summarizes]: "Thus one who is expert and high-souled and a knower of solutions should, through every possible means, elevate his low-spirited self. Applying one's intellect, one should always strive for survival. Man thereby obtains a pure life and enjoys great prosperity. Therefore, he who is without fault and in possession of his faculties ought to maintain a firm conviction regarding *dharma* and *adharma* in this world."[42]

A much abridged version of this didactic tale is found in the *Skanda Purāṇa* [6.90.4–22, 54], which explains one of Agni's periodic flights from the world and from the sacrificial altar through his aversion to the dog meat which Viśvāmitra had offered into his mouth on this occasion. Such would indeed have been an outrage for this Brahman god, the "mouth of the sacrifice" whose favorite oblation would have been "raw" *soma* ritually prepared with the "cooked" milk of the cow.[43]

The myth of Viśvāmitra in the Śvapaca village is linked to a great number of other similar accounts through which may be termed "homeopathic curses."[44] The first of these establishes a connection to the Śunaḥśepa myth. In the *Mahābhārata,* it is said that after Viśvāmitra had cursed his fifty eldest sons to Śvapaca-hood for their refusal to accept Śunaḥśepa, he praised Indra: this god, pleased, released Viśvāmitra from an earlier curse.[45] This curse was one placed on Viśvāmitra by the sons of Vasiṣṭha (those killed by Sudās, or by Sudās' grandson, Kalmāṣapāda, with the blessing of Viśvāmitra) that he would one day eat dog meat. After his protracted negotiations in the Śvapaca village, Viśvāmitra cooks, if not eats, dog meat.

Yet another such curse is found in the Śunaḥśepa myth, in which the fifty elder brothers of Madhucchanda, are cursed to obtain the ends (*antān*) as their lot. Because they desire that Śunaḥśepa be placed at the lower, and not the upper, end of his descent, they are placed by their father upon or beyond the end (*udantya*) of the world. In the *Rāmāyaṇa* (1.61.16) version of the Śunaḥśepa myth, Viśvāmitra's elder sons reject what they see as a usurpation of their primogeniture on the following terms: "We regard (accepting Śunaḥśepa as our elder) to be like eating dog meat (*śvamāṅsam iva bhojana*)." Viśvāmitra obliges them with a curse, by which they suffer that very lot (to be Dog-Eaters, i.e., Śvapacas) on earth for a thousand years.

Vasiṣṭha places a similar curse on a prince named Satyavrata who, after having ravished a Brahman girl, has been exiled by his father to live in the forest like a Śvapaca. There, during a drought,[46] this antinomian Kṣatriya kills one of Vasiṣṭha's cows[47] to save Viśvāmitra's wife and son Galava from starvation. Vasiṣṭha punishes Satyavrata for this heinous sin of bovicide by cursing him to become a Dog-Cooker in essence, rather than merely suffering a Dog-Cooker existence: he also changes Satyavrata's name to Triśaṅku ("Triple Sting"). This chain of curses is brought full circle when Triśaṅku, after having undergone severe austerities, enlists the help of Viśvāmitra to elevate him to or beyond his former station. When Vasiṣṭha's sons hear of this Kṣatriya conspiracy, they curse Viśvāmitra to eat dog meat—which, as we have seen, he does. But Viśvāmitra pronounces a countercurse upon Vasiṣṭha's one hundred sons at this time: they are to be reborn for seven hundred lifetimes as the "outcaste" (Mṛtapā) race of the Muṣṭikas. He then kills them with the irresistible heat of his yogic austerities, and his curse is immediately realized.[48] The *Harivaṁśa* version of this myth leads into a discussion of the Ikṣvāku Satyavrata's descendants: his son is none other than the Hariścandra of the Śunaḥśepa legend, at the end of which this entire cycle of curses "began." Angry at Hariścandra for having colluded in the attempted sacrifice of Śunaḥśepa, Viśvāmitra causes him to undergo myriad torments, which include becoming a Śvapaca and a carrion-feeding dog.[49]

The myths of the Viśvāmitra cycle constitute a set of dramatic explanations for the origins and existence of the fallen or exiled races of Dog-Cookers on the periphery of society and human categories. They thus provide an alternative to the more common legalistic explanations of marginalization through miscegenation. In the myths, *varṇasaṁkara,* caste mixing, occurs on an alimentary or ethical level, rather than a sexual level. That is, the individuals who become "outcastes," even the founders of the "outcaste" races, fall into their unhappy situation by overstepping the prerogatives of their social situation. In these cases, either their crime itself or its punishment, the fruition of a Brahman's curse, generally involves cooking or eating impure or forbidden food. Because the eating of either canine, bovine, or human flesh are abominations, the eater—whether the eating be the cause or the result of his punishment—is automatically, even ontologically, denigrated to the status of an "outcaste" Dog-Cooker. We will illustrate the "mytho-logic" of this cause-and-effect scenario with a table:

source	*crime*	*impure food*	*outcaste group produced*
Mbh 1.165	Viśvāmitra tries to steal Vasiṣṭha's cow Nandinī		all outcastes, produced from Nandinī's excrements
Mbh 1.166	Kalmāṣapāda whips Śakti on the forest path (Śakti curses Kalmāṣapada to become		

idem.	a man-eater; Viśvāmitra causes him to be possessed by a rākṣasa)	Kalmāṣapāda serves *human flesh* to a Brahman, who curses him again	
idem.	Kalmāṣapāda eats Śakti and Vasiṣṭha's 99 other sons at Viśvāmitra's instigation.	*human flesh*	
AB 7.13–18	Viśvāmitra's elder sons refuse Śunaḥśepa ("Dog Penis") as their elder.	Śunaḥśepa, offered as sacrifice to Varuṇa	all outcaste races
DP 7.16–18	Hariścandra approves of the sacrifice of Śunaḥśepa	the Brahman Śunaḥśepa: *human flesh*	Hariścandra is forced by Viśvāmitra to become a Śvapaca
Rām 1.61.16	Viśvāmitra's elder sons say accepting Śunaḥśepa would be like eating dog	*dog flesh*	Śvapacas
Hariv 9–10	Satyavrata kills Vasiṣṭha's cow to feed Viśvāmitra's wife and son.	by serving *cow flesh,* Satyavrata is condemned to become the Dog-Cooker Triśaṅku.	Satyavrata becomes a Śvapaca
Rām 1.58	Viśvāmitra helps the Śvapaca Triśaṅku to gain an atmospheric station	Vasiṣṭha's sons curse Viśvāmitra to eat *dog flesh*	Śvapaca (when "Śvapaca" Viśvāmitra takes dog meat in the Śvapaca village: MBh 12.139)

MBh 12.139; SP 6.90	Viśvāmitra sacrifices dog into the mouth of fire (Agni); Agni absconds.	*dog flesh*	
Rām 1.58	Vasiṣṭha's sons curse Viśvāmitra to eat dog flesh	Viśvāmitra effects a countercurse on Vasiṣṭha's sons, to become Dog-Cookers: *dog flesh*.	Vasiṣṭha's sons become Muṣṭikas

It should be noted here that the only individual who is truly immune to these series of homeopathic curses is the *rājarṣi* Viśvāmitra. Apart from his foray into the Śvapaca village, from which, even in Manu [10.108], he comes out smelling like a rose, he is never really touched by the maledictions of Vasiṣṭha's sons. He is moreover supported by Indra in most of his escapades. The same holds more or less for those whom Viśvāmitra protects: Śunaḥśepa, Triśaṅku, and Mātaṅga are spared from the maledictions of Vasiṣṭha and his sons. On the other hand, Vasiṣṭha's sons are completely undone in their dealings with Viśvāmitra, having their curses backfire, being transformed into Dog-Cookers, or being eaten by a *rākṣasa*-possessed king.

Viśvāmitra's power, it should be recalled, is born of the severe austerities (*tapas*) he practiced after having fallen to Vasiṣṭha's wish-fulfilling cow. Alongside the motif of the culinary origins of untouchability, this is the most important theme of this myth cycle: that the power of the renouncer is greater than that of the orthodox Brahman. Vasiṣṭha, who lives in his hermitage with his cows and who uses their products in his sacrifices, is the paragon of a pre-Upanisadic order which, as these myths clearly show in their evolution, is on the wane in the epic and Puranic periods.

Heterodox Subversions of Orthodox Codes Concerning Food and Marginality

The myths of the Viśvāmitra cycle were both catalysts for and reflections of a change in the semiotics and rhetorical uses of renunciation and coded substances which had been ongoing for more than a millennium. In the light of these myths, the wandering, renunciant ascetic is identified with the wilderness, the "doomsday" time of cosmic dissolution, "outcaste" Dog-Cookers and their dogs. It would appear that this mythic cycle routinized, in effect, the medieval code for an entire symbol system, such that, in later sources, it sufficed to invoke but one element in the code for all of its facets to come into play. More than this, this cluster of elements comes to take on a positive, albeit antinomian, valence in many sources. This is not to say that the dog or "outcaste" are ever portrayed as clearly superior to the cow or Brahman in any conventional pre-Tantric source (although the myth of Viśvāmitra in the Śvapaca village is a near miss, even if set in a time of *āpaddharma*). However, in certain contexts, they are accorded a certain modicum of respect and authenticity.

In a number of sources, mainly of Śaiva or tantric origins, the emphasis clearly shifts from a concern for purity codes grounded in caste and food distinctions, to a manipulation, even a subversion, of the same codes, in the service of a heterodox, "heretical" system of values. We have already alluded to the fact that Viśvāmitra stands, in the Puranic myths, as the exemplar of the marginal, dangerous renunciant *yati*s and *vrātya*s of Vedic tradition, in contradistinction to the orthodox, forest-dwelling *ṛṣi,* epitomized by Vasiṣṭha. A number of works, most importantly the recent *Brudershaft und Würfelspiel* of Harry Falk, have drawn important ties between these ancient antiBrahmanic sects and dogs, on the one hand, and with Rudra, the wild Vedic god of the forest, on the other.[50]

It is indeed possible to generate a history of these ascetics, in their myriad associations with both Rudra and Indra, both through mythic, historical, and legal sources. While space does not permit us here to undertake such a reconstruction, we may nevertheless point out certain key sources in which dogs, food, and purity are brought together in ways supportive of our approach.

An *udgītha* [Sāmavedic chant] of the *Chāndogya Upaniṣad* [1.12.1–6] entitled "The Circle of the Dogs" describes how Baka Dālbhya, a starving Vedic sage reduced to eating the leavings of low-caste peoples, chances upon a circle of dogs who perform a mock ritual and bark out a mock liturgy, as a means to obtaining food. Here, the dogs in question may well have been *vrātya*s performing a heterodox rite.[51]

Another direct link in this system of heterodox associations may be found in a number of practices associated with the Śaivite god Mallāri/Mailār/Khaṇḍoba/Mārtaṇḍa Bhairava of Maharastra. In a number of fascinating articles, Günther-Dietz Sontheimer describes how modern-day observances of the Dasarā festival in this region of western India replicate the practices of the *vrātyas* and *yatis* of the Vedic age.[52] In this region, Mallāri is himself closely identified with Mārtaṇḍa Bhairava, who is accompanied, in legend, by seven hundred dogs. These dogs are his devotees, who were first transformed by Mallāri/Martaṇḍa Bhairava from tigers to humans, and then instructed by him to behave like dogs.[53] On the ninth day of the Dasarā festival, the *Vaggayyas*, the "tiger dogs" of Mailār/Mallāri/Khaṇḍoba/Mārtaṇḍa Bhairava,

> . . . act and bark like dogs when pilgrims arrive . . . Formerly . . . they would run to their [begging] bowls, would howl and bark and quarrel amongst each other, and lie flat on the floor to eat like dogs . . . If food is offered into the bowls, they will fight like dogs trying to tear food from each other's mouth.[54]

This practice is attested in a number of nineteenth-century gazetteers and books; it is mentioned much earlier, in the context of the Mallāri temple at Ujjain, in Ānandagiri's 14th-15th century *Śaṅkara Vijaya*.[55] The Śaṅkara of Ānandagiri's work is, of course, the great ninth-century Hindu philosopher and missionary of orthodox Advaita Vedānta. A number of other hagiographies of Śaṅkara[56] pit this figure against the Kāpālikas, medieval India's most antinomian Saivite sect, a group known for their terrible practices and doctrines. In these accounts, the Kāpālikas often resort to violence in their attempt to best Śaṅkara in debate. Clearly heirs to the Vedic *vrātyas*, the Kāpālikas were devotees of the god Bhairava mentioned above, as well as being tantric ascetics often accompanied by dogs. Initiation into the Kāpālika sect required the murder of a Brahman and the use of his skull (*kapāla*] as a begging bowl for a period of twelve years of wandering. Bhairava himself, whose vehicle is the dog, is the divine model for this great vow [*mahāvrata*] in a number of Purāṇas.[57]

As heinous a crime as Brahmanicide is bovicide, which also figures in Tantric symbol manipulation. Thus we find, in the fifteenth-century *Haṭhayogapradīpikā* of Svātmarāma, the description of a purely metaphorical consumption of cow flesh:

> "(The yogin) should always eat the flesh of a cow (*gomānśa*) and drink strong liquor. Him I consider to be well-born, whereas those who do otherwise are the ruin of

their families. By the word *go* (cow), the tongue is intended. Its entry (into the cavity) in the palate is *gomāṅsa-bhakṣaṇa* (eating the flesh of a cow). This indeed destroys the (five) great sins."[58]

Here, the term for one of the five great sins is employed for a quite common hathayogic practice, a practice which allows the yogin to drink the "nectar" oozing from his cranial vault, and thereby attain immortality. Once again, it is an antinomian metaphor, one of consuming a prohibited form of food, that a Saivite source employs to designate a path to freedom.

Among the many antinomian positions taken by the tantrikas, the elevation of the outcaste Caṇḍāla and rejection of Brahman purity codes also figure prominently. Here as well, symbol manipulation is brought to the fore, this time as a means to realizing freedom from all bondage, especially bondage that takes the form of dualist distinctions between "pure" and "impure." Thus, the *Vīrāvalītantra* enjoins the tantric practitioner to "eat that which the common man detests and, being revolting, is censored and prohibited by the scriptures."[59] This the Kāpālikas practiced in a form of devotionalism[60] that included cannibalism, coprophagy, and indulgence in the *pañca-makāra,* the "Five Ms" or tantric sacraments. Clearly a heterodox subversion of the *pañcagavya,*[61] the five pure products of the Brahman's cow, the *pañca-makāras* consist of the use of flesh, fish, wine, parched grain, and sexual intercourse as means to supernatural powers [*siddhis*] and bodily liberation [*jīvanmukti*]. In the practice of this final sacrament, the "outcaste" Ḍombī or Śvapacī is most prized as a sexual partner, in part due to the energy latent in her extremely defiling uterine blood.[62]

Conclusion

With the tantric Kāpālikas and their anti-*pañcagavya* sacraments and other reversals of food and purity codes, we come to the endpoint of the evolution of heterodox subversions of the food and purity codes first broached in the lawbooks and later narrativized in the epic and Puranic mythology of Viśvāmitra.

In the course of some two thousand years of textual treatments of these matters, we find a clear shift in the uses of "orthodox" rhetoric on the subject of caste, purity, and licit and illicit foods, a shift we may attribute to changing values, as well as to "hostile takeovers" of orthodox sources by heterodox sectarian editors.[63]

Here, we summarize the primary features of this evolution:

1) In the orthodox treatises on ritual, law, and statecraft, there is a sharp ideological separation of the polarities of Brahman and "Dog-Cooker," cow's milk and canine bodily secretions (saliva, excrements, milk), Brahman sacrificer and non-Brahman renouncer, with the latter being associated with the gods Indra and Rudra.

2) Epic myths introduce the figure of the Kṣatriya renouncer [*rājarṣi*], who stands as both a foil to the forest-dwelling, sacrificing Brahman sage [*brahmarṣi*] and as a mediating element between the Brahman and his cow, on the one hand, and the Dog-Cooker and his dogs, on the other. The *rājarṣi* Viśvāmitra doubles for the god Indra, while the *brahmarṣi* Vasiṣṭha embodies the orthodoxy of the old Vedic god Varuṇa. As such, Viśvāmitra, like the Vedic Indra before him, cooks dog in a time of distress.

3) In the epic sources, but even more so in the Purāṇic myths, the antinomian non-brahmanic renouncer comes to gain the upper hand over the Brahman sacrificer and forest-dweller. At this point, the role of the Dog-Cooker becomes a secondary one: what is highlighted is the reversal of the relative status and power of the renouncer vis à vis the sacrificer. This is symbolically portrayed in myths in which orthodox Brahmans are forced to eat dog (Vasiṣṭha's sons in the Triśaṅku myth) or in which Kṣatriya renouncers and Untouchables kill and eat cow (Triśaṅku) or Brahman flesh (Kalmāṣapāda) with impunity.

4) These reversals become routinized and even prescriptive in various heterodox Śaiva sources, which manipulate the symbolic substances of the old orthodox codes by exalting the dog (the canine behavior of Mallāri's *Vaggayya* devotees) and Dog-Cooker and doing violence to the Brahman (the Kāpālika *mahāvrata*) and his cow (*gomāṅsa-bhakṣaṇa* in yoga).

Stated in other terms, the myriad myths of food and status anomaly we have treated here may be seen as so many commentaries on the single Vedic allusion [4.18.13] to Indra's cooking of dog in a time of distress. In discussing the *meaning* of this act, by transposing it upon the *rājarṣi* Viśvāmitra, the epic and later sources injected the element of *rhetoric* into their treatments: these narrative treatments of the matter were also responding to the highly tendentious proscriptive language of the lawbooks. The tantras co-opted the antiorthodox rhetoric of the myths of Viśvāmitra and combined these with the prescriptive spirit of the lawbooks. The way to the tantric goal of power was to be found in the explicit reversal of orthodox theory and practice. This was carried to its logical ends in the slaying of Brahmans and the eating of cows by tantric "dogs."

We should not assume, for all this, that rhetoric was, in the medieval period, a one-way affair. On the contrary, the brahmanic orthodoxy proved itself capable of generating equally trenchant rhetoric concerning its tantric rivals. A stunning orthodox rebuttal to the tantric reversals we have been discussing is the baroque account of the short rule (936–37 A.D.) of Cakravarman, king of Kashmir, related in Kalhaṇa's *Rājataraṁgiṇī*. Here, we find ourselves in the presence of an account which is structured after what can only be characterized as the paroxysm of an unnatural mixing of coded substances.

> After winning his throne through a series of alliances and a decisive battle, Cakravarman becomes debauched by a pair of Śvapacī or Ḍombī dancing girls. These quickly render the king their sexual plaything, whilst they and their family take over the royal court. Śvapaca ministers will only appoint to royal office those nobles who will eat leavings (*ucchiṣṭha*) from the Śvapacī courtesans' plates. These same ministers delight in wearing the Śvapacīs' menses-stained undergarments in court. They also enter and thereby defile temples reserved for the higher castes.
>
> Cakravarman commits a series of outrages of his own, in addition to his sexual abominations. He violates a fasting Brahman woman, performs mock penances for his sins, and treacherously slays certain of his allies. His betrayed allies turn against him: one night, while Cakravarman is relieving himself in the Śvapacī's toilet, assassins set upon him. They stab him to death in his lover's impure arms and crush his knees with stones. The story ends with the chilling line, "In the night, that king who had been consumed by Śvapākas was killed by those murderers like a dog in shit."[64]

It should be noted that all of Cakravarman's and the Śvapacīs' abominations involve body fluids. In their union with the king, it is the mingling of sexual fluids which runs counter to nature; in the court, it is the saliva in the leavings of their food which violates the purity of the nobles forced to eat such horrors; they defile brahmanic temples with their presence; the menstrual blood worn into court by the Śvapaca ministers is so powerful and polluting as to stain the entire kingdom. It is the uterine blood of the same Ḍombīs that was so highly prized by the Tantrics we have discussed.

In his chronicle, Kalhaṇa manages to string together every sort of "coded substance abuse" in such a way as to shift the key metaphor from one register to another until Cakravarman's entire kingdom is polluted, as it were, with the excrements of a dog. If a Śvapacī eats dog, as her name would indicate, then her saliva and sexual fluids would carry with them the pollution proper to canine flesh. This is transmitted into the person of the king through sexual debauchery, making him an "outcaste," and to his entire court through *ucchiṣṭha* food and menses-stained garments. In the end, worse than being an eater of dog-flesh, Cakravarman has been "consumed by dogs," and meets his end in a mire of canine excrement. This episodic "Śvapacization" of Kashmir through Ḍombīs who are the sexual partners of tantrics would indicate that Kalhaṇa's intention is to lay all blame at the door of antinomian sectarianism.

Throughout this study, we have been emphasizing the radical separation, on the level of narrative, and through the use of rhetorical and prescriptive language, of cow and dog, Brahman and Dog-Cooker, and *brahmarṣi* and *rājarṣi*. Whether the source is brahmanic and legalistic, or tantric and antinomian, the insistence on opposition (even if the values of the poles of opposition are reversed) remains constant. We could, however, also turn this statement around and say that the Brahman legalists and the tantric antinomians were in fact speaking the same language, employing as they did the same classificatory system to describe their opposition.

Even more important than this, we could talk about the common *tone* of expression on both sides. If nothing else, we may safely say that the language of all of these narrativizations of food and purity codes and status anomaly is *passionate* language. Viśvāmitra, Vasiṣṭha, and their minions are constantly furious, murderously furious, at one another, as are Cakravarman and his assassins. The passion of these narratives betrays the importance of the matters being allegorized in them. The grounds for such passion are clear. In Hindu India, eating is not merely a means to nourishment, nor is it solely a matter of "politics." Here, because "you are what you eat" in a very concrete sense, eating is tantamount to making a statement of ontological authenticity and ethical worth. A Dog-Cooker is not a human being in the eyes of Manu; a royal Dog-Cooker [Cakravarman] on the throne condemns every Brahman in his kingdom to eternal pollution, even damnation.

In this light, we may see that the impulse behind the food and purity codes with which Hindu India has been grappling for over two millennia is nothing more or less than an existential one, of finding a standard for meaning in authentic being. Partaking of the "cooked" milk of the cow, cooking and eating dog, eating like a dog, forcing others to eat dog, eating cow, and eating milk-drinking Brahmans all stand as so many rhetorical expressions for the tensions inherent to the processes of pollution, purification, and redemption in a hierarchical society.[65] Both the cows of the brahmanic orthodoxy and the dogs of India's "outcaste" society and the renunciant, tantric, heterodoxy have had their say in a number of different ways. And the dialogue—between Vasiṣṭha and Viśvāmitra, and Viśvāmitra and the Śvapacas, some of whom are Viśvāmitra's or Vasiṣṭha's fallen sons—goes on.

Notes

1. William Faulkner, *Absalam, Absalom* (New York: The Modern Library, 1964), p. 258.

2. *Manu Smṛti* 10.4: *Pañcamaḥ punarvarṇo nāsti*. In his commentary, Kullūka Bhaṭṭa explains this by stating that just as a mule is neither a horse nor an ass, so a Caṇḍāla is of neither of parents' castes: *Sankīrṇajātīnām tvaśvataravānmātāpitṛjātivyatiriktajātyantaratvānna varṇatvam:* Gopala Sastri Nene, 535; Buhler, 402.

3. Dumont 1966, 192–93.

4. Marriott 1974, 109–114. Marriott argues (111–112) that Indians are, rather than individuals, "dividuals," i.e., divisible, unbounded aggregates who "absorb heterogenous material influences" and "also give out from themselves particles of their own coded substances—essences, residues, or other active influences—which may then reproduce in others something of the nature of the persons in whom they have originated . . . What are here called "transformations" within actors consists also of transactions among parts of actors, while "transactions" among actors may constitute transformations of the actors transacting and sometimes of the system of transactions. Thus transformations and transactions may be understood as a single set of processes, considered in two ways, internally and externally."

5. *Manu Smṛti* 10.25–31, with Buhler's notes on the commentaries of Kullūka Bhaṭṭa and others, 407–9.

6. *Manu Smṛti* (10.19) gives a precise genealogy of the Śvapaca ("the son of a Kṣattr by an Ugra female is called a Śvapaca." Compare *Mahābhārata* 13.48.21: "From the Caṇḍālas spring a race called the Śvapacas, who are guardians of the dead (*mṛtapās*)." Verse 28 of the same chapter has the Śvapaca being born from a Caṇḍāla on a Niṣāda woman.

7. A didactic passage in the *Mahābhārata* [3.199.10–12] roughly contemporaneous with the *Manu Smṛti,* makes a similarly ambiguous statement on eating meat: "Even now, the old hermits rule in the matter of eating meat: 'He who always eats only after having offered to deities and ancestors according to the ordinance and with faith does not incur guilt by eating the remainder'." Compare Manu 4.213.

8. Dumont 1966, 180–81. Dumont discusses the dynamic between the Sanskrit terms *pakva* ("cooked") and *apakva* ("uncooked"), and the Hindi *pakkā* and *kaccā,* prime units in the modern north Indian classification of foods, on 179–89. Dumont's material has been greatly expanded and corrected over the past two decades, with the net result being an increased understanding of the complexity of the relationships existing between these and other terms in the social sphere. See, for example, R. S. Khare 1976, chap. 1, "Folk Categories of Hindu Foods," 1–27; and Charles Malamoud, "Cuire le monde," in Malamoud 1989, 68–70.

9. *Manu Smṛti* 4.205–222, especially 4.216: [Let him never eat food given] by trainers of hunting dogs . . . " Compare 3.239–41: "A Caṇḍāla, a village pig, a cock, a dog, a menstruating woman, and a eunuch must not look at brahmins while they eat. A . . . dog [makes rites useless] by casting his eye on them, a low-caste man by touching them."

10. See above, note 2. The term "outcaste" is covered by a great number of Sanskrit terms in this period. Pāṇini (2.4.10) uses the term *niravasita śūdra,* whom Patañjali identifies, in his *Mahābhāṣya* (1.475), as the Pulkasas, Pulindas, Caṇḍālas and Mṛtapās, of which all, with the exception of "Caṇḍālas," are "tribal" or "ethnic" names. *Antyāvasāyin* is a term employed in *Manu Smṛti* (10.39) and the *Mārkaṇḍeya Purāṇa* (25.34–36). Manu also uses *bāhya* and *bāhyavāsina* as general terms. *Avarṇaja* and *antarāla* are used in the same sense in the *Bṛhat Saṁhitā* (89.1.*kha*) and Kauṭilya's *Arthaśāstra,* respectively. This latter term has the meaning "intermediate space." The *Mahābhārata* employs the terms *hīnavarṇa* and *bahirgrāma* in addition to those found in Manu. See Sharma 1980, 139, 226, 229–31, 291.

11. A brief discussion of the "fall" of the dog in the post-Vedic period may be found in White 1986, 242–44.

12. *Manu Smṛti* (10.105–8) alludes to two such cases.

13. Marriott 1976, 133, in the general context of his discussion of code and substance, offers a case which, while limited to intracaste relationships between Brahmans, illustrates this point very well. Feast encounters

among sixty men, all potentially hosts and guests, in Kishan Garhi, "yield ranked categorizations of the actors as "refined men" (those who are feeders but not fed), "men" (those who are sometimes feeders, sometimes fed), "their own men" (neither feeders nor fed), and "dogs" (fed but not feeders)."

14. Ibid., 128: "The bodily-substance codes of these low castes are necessarily expected to become the most unselectively heterogeneous, their powers diluted and restricted, their temperaments gross and animal-like. As removers of what the higher castes conceive as "pollution," the lowest among them are masters of negative transformations—of destruction by contrast with the Brahman's creation."

15. Dumont 1966, 269: "The purity opposition is thus the *necessary* ideological form of the ideal hierarchical typology."

16. See, for example, *Manu Smṛti* 5.82–83,99.

17. Already in the *Ṛg Veda,* the "raw cow" is said to hold "cooked milk" (RV 1.62.9); cf. *Taittirīya Saṁhitā* (6.5.6.4) and *Śatapatha Brāhmaṇa* 2.2.4.15. These themes are discussed by Varenne 1982, 117; and Malamoud (1989), 52, note 51.

18. The ideological polarity of Brahman (and cow, and dairy products) versus "outcaste" or "Untouchable" is clearly stated in Dumont 1966, 77–78. The epic commonplace, "as revolting as a sacrificial vessel that has been licked by a dog," is found in *Mbh* 1.127.7; 3.253.19; 3.275.13, etc.

19. Pliny, *Naturalis Historia* 7.21. Indian Dog-Milkers are also mentioned in Aelianus, (*De natura animalium* 16.31), who is probably following Ctesias.

20. On the theory that Ctesias' term for the Dog-Men of India, i.e., Kalústrioi is itself derived from a Persian or Sanskrit term for Dog-Milker, *sa-dauzštr* or *śva-duhitṛ,* see Marquart 1913, 207–209.

21. The *yatis* came to know a checkered career through the history of Brahmanic literature. They are referred to in the *Atharva Veda* (2.5.3) and the *Āśvalāyana Śrauta Sūtra* (6.3.1) without censure. In the *Aitareya Brāhmaṇa* (7.28.1), it is related that Indra has been excluded from a soma sacrifice for having killed Vṛtra, mistreated Viśvarūpa, and thrown the *Arurmaghas* or *yatis* to the *śālavṛkas* ("house-wolves," werewolves?). This is repeated in the *Jaiminīya Brāhmaṇa* 1.185, *Tāṇḍya Mahābrāhmaṇa* 8.14, and *Taittirīya Saṁhitā* 2.4.9.2; 6.2.7.5. Certain brahmanic sources and commentators identify the *yatis* with non-Aryan peoples, antibrahmanical sects, and evil *sannyāsis.* The *Vrātyas* ("vow-takers"), while clearly an antinomian sect in the Vedic period, are referred to as both the products of miscegenation and of a rejection of brahmanic rites, in both Manu (10.20) and the *Mahābhārata* 13.49.9. Recently, an excellent study which, among other things, relates the Vedic *vrātyas* to dogs, is Harry Falk, *Bruderschaft und Würfelspiel* (Freiburg: Hedwig Falk, 1986).

22. There is ample material in the Upaniṣads to support the argument that it was in fact Kṣatriyas who became strong exponents of the renunciant ideal. See, for example, *Chāndogya Upaniṣad* 5.11–5.24, in which a king, Aśvapati Kaikeya, instructs five Brahman householders on the universal soul. This passage concludes, "And therefore, if one who knows this should offer leavings to a Caṇḍāla, it would be offered to the universal soul." Elsewhere, the teachings of the Buddha, himself a royal renouncer, emphasized *ahiṁsa* and other renunciant ideals. The great war which is the subject of the *Mahābhārata* is said to have been caused by *varṇasaṁkāra,* a mixing of castes that occurred not so much on the level of sexual union as it did in the form of princes renouncing their kingdoms for a forest life and Brahmans taking up arms in battle.

23. An enormous quantity of scholarship has been produced on this subject. Excellent examples are Dumont 1966, Appendix B, "Le renoncement dans les religions de l'Inde," 324–50; Heestermann 1964, 1–31; Bailey 1985, 9–99; and Olivelle 1981, 75–83.

24. In fact, the same terms, Caṇḍāla and Śvapaca, were applied globally to the "outcaste" sweepers of India who lived beyond the periphery of the towns they serviced, to the forest-dwelling tribes with which renunciants, sages, and hunting kings came into contact, and to foreign peoples (such as the Bactrian Greeks, called Yāvanas) who invaded and conquered much of north India from the third century B.C. onward.

25. Kings may also have gone into the forest in the context of rites of initiation or of consecration, both of their persons and of new royal territories. Such "ritual exile" is discussed in Falk 1973, 1–15; and Shulman 1986, 214–302.

26. The dichotomy between *rājarṣi* and *brahmarṣi* is spelled out with direct reference to Viśvāmitra and Vasiṣṭha in *Rāmāyaṇa* (1.17.35) and *Mahābhārata* 1.65.34 (in the D4 or Kumbakoanan version of the critical edition). A three-tiered ranking of *brahmarṣis, devarṣis* and *rājarṣis* is made in *Viṣṇu Purāṇa* 3.6.21. Vasiṣṭha, who is the paragon of orthodoxy in the myths which pit him against Viśvāmitra, is nevertheless cast as the son of a prostitute: *Mahābhārata* (D4) 13.53.13–19, 38. Another *ṛṣi,* Parāśara, is said in the same source to be the son of a Śvapāka. As for Viśvāmitra, his original encounter with Vasiṣṭha occurs, according to the *Rāmāyaṇa* (Bāla Khaṇḍa 51–65), in the context of a circuit of the earth: this may be interpreted as a royal rite of conquest, or as a form of ritual exile.

27. Apart from the *Bṛhat Saṁhitā,* such omen texts are also found in the 12th-century *Manasollāsa* (2.13.824–32) and the 14th-century *Śārṅgadhara Paddhati* 86.1–120.

28. *Bṛhat Saṁhitā* 89.1.*ka-kha* and 45.46.

29. Cf. *Bṛhat Saṁhitā (89.8) and Śārṅgadhara Paddhati* 86.106–7.

30. While urine and dung are two of the five pure products of the cow, their juxtaposition with Nandinī's "foam" (*pheṇa*) and the fact that it is "outcastes" which are produced from these excretions, leads us to surmise that the emphasis here is excremental, with the "dead" and polluting excretions of the cow corresponding to dead cows, of which outcastes are the disposers.

31. Sāyana's commentary on *Ṛg Veda* 3.53.15ff, *Jaiminīya Brāhmaṇa* 2.392, and *Bṛhaddevatā* 6.28–34.

32. This pattern, of being twice cursed by a Brahman, is found in other myths of this cycle, particularly that of Triśaṅku. The first curse renders its victim a potential *rākṣasa,* Śvapaca, etc., while the second consummates the transformation, changing the victim's ontological status.

33. *Mahābhārata* 1.166.1–1.168.25.

34. This account is found in *MBh* 13.4.1–47; *Viṣṇu Purāṇa* 4.7.12–36; *Vāyu Purāṇa* 2.29.63–88; *Brahmāṇḍa Purāṇa* 3.66.35–36; and *Bhāgavata Purāṇa* 9.15.3–13. In none of these accounts is the explicit conclusion made that this "mixing" renders Viśvāmitra an "outcaste." A variant of this myth involves Jamadagni's wife Reṇukā, whom Paraśurāma slays at his father's instigation and whom he then restores to life: *Mahābhārata* 3.116.1–18. A Tamil variant has Paraśurāma restore his mother's head upon the trunk of an "outcaste" woman, and vice versa. The former becomes the goddess Māriyammaṉ, and the latter the goddess Ěllammaṉ: both are "composite figures uniting Brahmin and outcaste elements" [Shulman 1980, 265].

35. An etymology suggested for the term *araṇya* ("forest") is "other", or "foreign" (from *araṇa*): Charles Malamoud, "Village et forêt dans l'idéologie de l'Inde brahmanique," in Malamoud 1989, 95–96 and notes.

36. The earliest versions are those found in *Aitareya Brāhmaṇa* (7.13–18) and *Śāṅkhāyana Śrauta Sūtra* 15.17–27. Later renditions of the same myth are *Mahābhārata* 13.3.6–8; *Rāmāyaṇa* 1.60.5–1.61.27; *Bhāgavata Purāṇa* 9.7.7–23 and 9.16.30–34; and *Devībhāgavata Purāṇa* 6.12.37–6.13.30; 7.14.25–7.17.46. Numerous ritual sources recommend the recitation of the Śunaḥśepa legend in the context of the rite of royal consecration (*rājasūya*). Among these are: *Taittirīya Brāhmaṇa* 1.7.10.6; *Āpastamba Śrauta Sūtra* 18.19.10–14; *Taittirīya Saṁhitā* 5.2.1.3; *Kātyāyana Śrauta Sūtra* 15.6.1–7; *Hiraṇyakeśi Śrauta Sūtra* 13.6.38; *Baudhāyana Śrauta Sūtra* 12.15–16 and 109.10–110.1; and *Āśvalāyana Śrauta Sūtra* 9.4.9–16.

37. Śunaḥśepa is related to Viśvāmitra by marriage, according to the *Mahābhārata,* which states that he is the son of the same Ṛcīka (13.3.6) who married Satyavatī, the sister of Viśvāmitra (9.15.5). He is also called the son of Ṛcīka in *Rāmāyaṇa* 1.60.9–11.

38. *MBh* 12.139.6.

39. *MBh* 12.139.13–63, 77–94.

40. Bāṇa presents a description of a Caṇḍāla settlement, quite similar to that of this account, in his *Kādambarī,* vol. 2 [*Uttarabhāga*], 267–69, as does "Vālmīki" in *Yoga Vasiṣṭha* 5.45.5–20; 5.48.1–12.

41. Another myth, also set in a time of *āppaddharma* and drought, casts the seven *ṛṣis*, including Vasiṣṭha and Viśvāmitra, together with Indra, who is disguised as a foreign ascetic named Śunaḥsakha ["Friend of Dogs"] or Śunomukha ["Dog-Face"]. The myth revolves around a decision to eat the corpse of a prince named Śaibya: *Mahābhārata* 13.94.5–13.95.81; *Skanda Purāṇa* 6.32.1–100. Similarly, in the *Rāmāyaṇa* (1.60.5–1.61.27) version of the Śunaḥśepa myth, Indra (rather than the usual Varuṇa) releases Śunaḥśepa from his fetters. He also creates the tension in this myth of marginality by urging Rohita, the son of Hariścandra, to follow the way of the renouncer.

42. This (*Mahābhārata*) text bears out a statement made above regarding the interchangeability of terms applied to India's "outcastes" in this period and the use of Śvapaca as a general theme. In this account Viśamitra's interlocutor is referred to as a Caṇḍāla, a Śvapaca, a Śvapāka, a Mātaṅga, and an Antavāsana; but Śvapaca is the term employed in the major dialogue portion of the text.

43. Malamoud 1989, 54–56. The necessity of having milk as an adjunct to the soma offered in sacrifice is found, for example, in the myth of Saramā and the Paṇis [*Ṛg Veda* 10.108.1–11]. Indra cannot battle Vṛta without first having drunk *soma.* The cows of Bṛhaspati having been stolen by the Paṇis, who are in collusion with Vala, the soma sacrifice cannot be offered. When Saramā finds the cows, the soma can be prepared.

44. I am borrowing this term from Wendy O'Flaherty 1981, 22, 24, 375, and passim.

45. *Mahābhārata* 13.3.8, 14. The two are also connected in the *Devībhāgavata Purāṇa,* which justaposes the myth of Viśvāmitra in the Śvapaca village (7.13.9–27) with its account of Śunaḥśepa (7.14.25–7.17.29).

46. This is presumably the same drought as that suffered by Viśvāmitra in the Śvapaca village in our core myth: such may be deduced from the insertion of the Śvapaca village myth (*Devībhāgavata Purāṇa* 7.13.9–27) into that of Satyavrata-Triśaṅku (7.10.1–7.14.24) version of the latter. It is also stated in the *Harivaṁśa* version of the Satyavrata-Triśaṅku myth (9.88–10.20) that Satyavrata chose a boon from Viśvāmitra. "The *muni,* having caused rain to fall in that kingdom in which a fearsome drought had continued for twelve years, performed a sacrifice for him. Viśvāmitra was the rival of both Vasiṣṭha and the gods" (10.19–20).

Mātaṅga is another "outcaste" elevated by Viśvāmitra to an atmospheric level: *Mahābhārata* 13.27.7–39 and 13.29.22–13.30.13.

47. A compendium of Puranic myths in which cows are killed, cooked, or eaten in times of drought is found in O'Flaherty 1976, 291–302.

48. *Rāmāyana* 1.58.14–20: The Muṣṭikas are described in this passage as "a shameless people who live solely on dog meat." Viśvāmitra does in fact convey the Śvapaca Triśaṅku to heaven, but the gods, led by Indra(!), refuse to brook the presence of such a vile creature in their midst. Viśvāmitra then creates a "separate heaven" for Triśaṅku (*Skanda Purāṇa* 6.6.5–18; 6.7.1–19).

49. *Devībhāgavata Purāṇa* 7.16.56–59; 7.17.45–7.18.58; and *Mārkaṇḍeya Purāṇa* 7.1–69; 8.1–270.

50. Rudra's close connections with dogs and their low-caste masters is given in explicit detail in *Kāṭhaka Saṁhitā* 17.13, *Maitrāyanī Saṁhitā* 2.9.4.5, and *Kapiṣṭhala Saṁhitā* 27.3.

51. Falk 1986, 40 and note 108.

52. Sontheimer 1981, 1–27, especially 2–9, and 1984, 155–70, especially 157, 165–66.

53. Sontheimer 1981, 6 and notes 9 and 11; and 1984, 166, citing the *Mallāri Māhātmya,* purportedly a portion of the *Brahmāṇḍa Purāṇa,* [re-] written by a certain Ramdas in 1857, and the *Mārtaṇḍa Vijaya* of Gangadhara.

54. Sontheimer 1981, 8.

55. *Śaṅkara Vijaya* 29. The Mallāri temple in Ujjain is mentioned in Monier-Williams 1891, 1974, 243, 366; and the 1884 *Dharwar Gazetteer,* cited in Sontheimer 1981, 7.

56. *Śaṅkara Digvijaya* 6.29–35 and 11.1–42; *Śaṅkara Vijaya* of Ānandagiri, 23; and *Gorakṣasiddhāntasaṁgraha,* 16–17. Translations of the latter two of these three texts may be found in Lorenzen 1972, 32–36.

57. *Viṣṇu Smṛti* 1.1–6, 15; *Yājñavalkya Smṛti* 3.243; *Baudhāyana Dharmaśastra* 2.1.2–3, etc. The origin myth of this practice, first performed by the god Bhairava himself, is found in *Skanda Purāṇa* 4.1.31.1–157; *Vāmana Purāṇa* 2.17–55; 3.1–51; 4.1; *Varāha Purāṇa* 97.1–27; *Kūrma Purāṇa* 2.31.3–73; *Śiva Purāṇa* 3.8.1–66; 3.9.1–71. These myths are translated and analyzed in O'Flaherty 1981, 277–86; and Kramrish 1981, 250–65.

58. *Haṭhayogapradīpikā* 3.47–48. The Sanskrit passages and commentaries are on 88–90, the English translation on 45–46.

59. This passage from the *Vīrāvalītantra* is quoted by Abhinavagupta in his *Tantrāloka* vol. 3, 269, cited and translated in Dyczkowski 1988, 145. An excellent general discussion of tantric subversion of brahmanic purity codes is Sanderson 1985: 190–216. On Tantric egalitarianism and anti-Brahmanism, see Dasgupta 1976, 51–61.

60. Lorenzen (1972, 16–17, 56–57, 85–87) calls this "Kāpālika bhakti."

61. Dogs are fed milk on holidays to Bhairava, according to certain devotional manuals. I have seen such feeding practiced, by a self-professed "Kāpālika," at the Śmaśāna Bhairava temple on Maṇikarṇikā Ghāṭ in Benares.

62. Cf. Marriott 1976, 130: "... Practicing maximal, symmetrical transactions, are the blood-sacrificing Tantrik cults: the more extreme of these would reverse the usual asymmetries of exchange, and confuse all substance-codes, making untenable any further distinctions of high and low... Among worshippers of the Devī, those who follow the cult of Durga may stand less far right than the worshippers of Kālī and her servant, Bhairava. Animal-sacrificing *śākta* cultists more often make transactions in gross bodily substances... Balanced at the center, but swinging pendulum-like toward both right and left in its mythology, is the ambiguous cult of Śiva, the "erotic ascetic." The classical praise of the Ḍombī in tantric intercourse is found in *Caryāgīti* 10.

63. Here, we are mainly referring to the Saivite and tantric [mainly Kāpālika and Pāśupata] reworking of earlier Puranic mythology, in which the orthodox myth is reversed in favor of a more antinomian reading. On the history of these co-optations, see Hazra 1975, 201–10.

64. *Rājataraṃgiṇī* 5.354–413.

65. These terms form a part of Kenneth Burke's massive study of rhetoric. Burke's system is outlined in Foss, Foss and Trapp 1985, 156–83. See also Burke's *A Rhetoric of Motives* (Berkeley: University of California Press, 1969) and *Permanence and Change: An Anatomy of Purpose,* 3d ed. (Berkeley: University of California Press, 1984).

References

Primary Sources

De natura animalium of Aelianus. Translated by A. F. Schofield. Loeb Classical Library, nos. 446, 448, 449. Cambridge: Harvard University Press, 1959–71.

Aitareya Brāhmaṇa. Translated by Arthur Berriedale Keith. Harvard Oriental Series, vol. 25. Cambridge: Harvard University Press, 1920.

Āpastamba Śrauta Sūtra. With the commentary of Rudradatta. Edited by Richard Garbe. 3 vols. Calcutta: Baptist Mission Press, 1885–1903.

Arthaśāstra of Kauṭilya. 3d ed. Edited by R. Shama Shastry. Government Oriental Library Series: Bibliotheca Sanskrita, no. 54. Mysore: 1929.

Āśvalāyana Śrauta Sūtra. With the commentary of Garganārāyaṇa. Anandasrama Sanskrit Series. Poona: 1917.

Atharva Veda. 2 vols. Translated by William Dwight Whitney. Revised and edited by Charles Rockwell Lanman. Harvard Oriental Series, vols. 7–8. Cambridge: Harvard University Press, 1905.

Baudhāyana Śrauta Sūtra. Edited by W. Caland. 3 vols. Calcutta: Bibliotheca Indica, 1904–24.

Bhāgavata Purāṇa. Edited and translated by C. L. Goswami and M. A. Sastri. Gorakhpur: Gita Press, 1971.

Brahmāṇḍa Purāṇa of Vyāsa. Edited by J. L. Shastri. Varanasi: Motilal Banarsidass, 1973.

Bṛhaddevatā of Śaunaka. Edited and translated by Arthur A. Macdonnell. 2 vols. Harvard Oriental Series, nos. 5–6. Cambridge: Harvard University Press, 1904.

Bṛhat Saṁhitā of Varāhamihira. Edited and translated by M. Ramakrishna Bhat, 2 vols. Delhi: Motilal Banarsidass, 1981–82.

Caryāgīti. Edited and translated by Per Kværne, *An Anthology of Buddhist Tantric Songs*. Bangkok: White Orchid Press, 1986.

Chāndogya Upaniṣad. In R. H. Hume, *The Thirteen Principal Upanisads*. Oxford: Clarendon Press, 1971; 2d revised edition.

Devībhāgavata Purāṇa. Varanasi: 1970.

Gorakṣasiddhāntasaṁgraha. Edited by Gopinath Kaviraj, Princess of Wales Sarasvati Bhavana Texts, no. 18. Benares: Vidya Vilas Press, 1925.

Haṭhayogapradīpikā of Svātmarāma. Edited with translation by Tookaram Tatya Adyar, Madras: The Theosophical Society, 1975.

Jaiminīya Brāhmaṇa. Edited by Lokesh Chandra and Raghu Vira. Sarasvati Vihara Grantha Series, no. 31. Nagpur: 1955.

Kādambarī of Bānabhatta. 2 vols. Edited and translated by Sri Mohandev Pant Delhi: 1977.

Kapiṣṭhala-Kathā Saṁhitā. Edited by Raghu Vira. Lahore: 1932.

Kāṭhaka Saṁhitā. 3 vols. Edited by Leopold von Schroeder. Leipzig: F. A. Brockhaus, 1901.

Kātyāyana Śrauta Sūtra. With the commentary of Karkācārya. Edited by Madanmohan Pathak. Varanasi: 1904.

Kūrma Purāṇa. Edited by A. S. Gupta. Varanasi: All-India Kashiraj Trust, 1967.

Mahābhārata. The Mahābhārata Text as Constituted in its Critical Edition, 5 vols. Edited by R. N. Dandekar. Poona: Bhandarkar Oriental Research Institute, 1970–76.

Mahābhāṣya of Patañjali. 10 vols. With Bhāṣyapradīpa commentary of Kaujata. Edited by M. S. Narasimhachariar. Publications de l'Institut Francaise d'Indologie, no. 51. Pondicherry: 1973–83.

Mahānirvāṇa Tantra, with the commentary of Hariharānanda Bharati. Edited by Arthur Avalon, Madras: 1929; reprinted Delhi: Motilal Banarsidass, 1977.

Maitrāyanī Saṁhitā, 4 vols. Edited by Leopold von Schroeder. Leipzig: 1881–86.

Manasollāsa of Bhulokamalla Someśvara, 3 vols. Edited by G. K. Srigondekar. Baroda: Oriental Institute, 1967.

Manu Smṛti, with the commentary of Kullūka Bhaṭṭa. Edited with introduction by Pandit Gopala Sastri Nene. Kashi Sanskrit Series, no. 114. Varanasi: Chowkhamba Sanskrit Series Office, 1970.

———. *The Laws of Manu*. Edited and translated by Georg Bühler, Sacred Books of the East, vol. 25. Oxford: Oxford University Press, 1886; reprint New Delhi: Motilal Banarsidass, 1979.

Mārkaṇḍeya Purāṇa. 2 vols. Edited and translated by F. Eden Pargiter. Calcutta: Baptist Mission Press, 1888–1904.

Pliny the Elder. *Naturalis Historia*. 10 vols. Translated by H. Rackham. Loeb Classical Library. Cambridge: Harvard University Press, 1938–63.

Rājataraṁgiṇī of Kalhaṇa. Edited by Raghunath Singh. Varanasi: 1973.

———. *Kalhaṇa's Rājataraṅgiṇī: A Chronicle of the Kings of Kashmir*. Translated with notes by Marcus Aurelius Stein. Delhi: Motilal Banarsidass, 1979; reprint of the 1900 edition.

Rāmāyaṇa of Vālmīki, 7 vols. Edited by G. H. Bhatt. et al. Baroda: Oriental Institute, 1960–75.

Ṛg Veda. With the commentary of Sāyaṇa. Edited by F. Max Müller. 2d. ed. London: Henry Frowde, 1890–92; reprint Varanasi: Chowkhamba Sanskrit Series, 1966.

Śaṅkara Digvijaya of Mādhavācārya. Srirangam: Vilasa, 1972.

Śaṅkara-Vijaya of Ānandagiri. Edited by Jayanarayana Tarkapanchanana. Calcutta: 1868; reprint, Osnabruck: Biblio Verlag, 1982.

Śāṅkhāyana Śrauta Sūtra. Edited by A. Hillebrandt. Calcutta: Bibliotheca Indica, 1888–99.

Śārṅgadhara Paddhati, 2 vols. Edited by Peter Peterson. Bombay: Central Book Depot, 1888.

Śatapatha Brāhmaṇa. Edited by Albrecht Weber. Berlin-London 1855; reprint Varanasi: Motilal Banarsidass, 1964.

Śiva Purāṇa. With an introduction by Puspendra Kumar. Edited by Nag Sharan Singh. Delhi: Nag Publishers, 1981.

Skanda Purāṇa. 3 vols. Edited by Nag Sharan Singh. Delhi: Nag Publishers, 1984.

Taittirīya Saṁhitā. With the commentary by Mādhava. Calcutta: Bibliotheca Indica, 1860.

Vāmana Purāṇa. Edited by A. S. Gupta. Varanasi: All-India Kashiraj Trust, 1968.

Varāha Purāṇa. Calcutta: Bibliotheca Indica, 1893.

Viṣṇu Purāṇa, with the commentary of Śrīdhara. Calcutta: 1972.

Viṣṇu Smṛti, with the commentary of Nandapaṇḍita. 2 vols. Edited by V. Krishnamacharya. Adyar Library Series, no. 93. Madras: 1964.

Yājñavalkya Smṛti, with the commentary of Vijñāneśvara. Edited by N. R. Acharya. 5th ed. Bombay: Nirnaya Sagara Press, 1949.

Yoga Vasiṣṭha of Vālmīki. *Laghu Yogavasiṣṭha* of Vālmīki. 2 vols. Edited by Srikrsnapanta Sastri. Varanasi: Acyuta Granthamala-Karyalaya, 1976–77.

Secondary Sources

Bailey, Greg

1985 "Materials for the Study of Ancient Indian Ideologies: *Pravṛtti* and *Nivṛtti*." *Pubblicazione di Indologica Taurinensia,* 19:1–90.

Dasgupta, Shashibhushan

1976 *Obscure Religious Cults*. Calcutta: reprint of 3d (1969) edition.

Dumont, Louis.

1966 *Homo hierarchicus: Le systeme des castes et ses implications*. Paris: Gallimard.

Dyczkowski, Mark S. G.

1988 *The Canon of the Śaivāgama and the Kubjikā Tantras of the Western Kaula Tradition.* Albany, N.Y.: SUNY Press.

Falk, Harry
1986 *Bruderschaft und Würfelspiel.* Freiburg: Hedwig Falk.

Falk, Nancy
1973 "Wilderness and Kingship in Ancient South Asia." In *History of Religions* 13 (1973), no. 1, pp. 1–15.

Foss, Sonja K., Foss, Karen A. and Trapp, Robert
1985 *Contemporary Perspectives on Rhetoric.* Prospect Heights, Ill.: Waveland Press.

Hazra, R. C.
1975 *Studies in the Puranic Rites and Customs.* 2d ed. Delhi: Motilal Banarsidass.

Heestermann, Jan
1964 "Brahman, Ritual and Renouncer." In *Wiener Zeitschrift für die Kunde Süd- und Ost Asiens* 8:1–31.

Kane, Pandurang Vamana
1941 *History of Dharmaśāstra,* 5 vols. Poona: Bhandarkar Oriental Research Institute, 1941.

Khare, R. S.
1976 *Culture and Reality: Essays on the Hindu System of Managing Foods.* Simla: Indian Institute of Advanced Study.

Kramrish, Stella
1981 *The Presence of Śiva.* Princeton: Princeton University Press.

Lorenzen, David N.
1972 *The Kāpālikas and Kālamukhas: Two Lost Śaivite Sects.* New Delhi: Thomson Press, 1972.

Malamoud, Charles
1989 *Cuire le monde: rite et pensée dans l'Inde ancienne.* Paris: Editions de la Découverte.

Marquart, Joseph
1913 *Die Benin-Sammlung des Reichsmuseum für Völkerkunde in Leiden.* Veoffentlichen des Reichsmuseum für Völkerkunde in Leiden, sér. 2, no. 7. Leiden: Brill.

Marriott, McKim
1976 "Hindu Transaction: Diversity Without Dualism." 109–42. In *Transaction and Meaning: Directions in the Anthropology of Exchange and Symbolic Behavior,* edited by Bruce Kapferer. Philadelphia: Institute for the Study of Human Issues.

Monier-Williams, Monier
1974 *Religious Thought and Life in India: Vedism, Brahmanism and Hinduism,* 4th ed. (London: J. Murray, 1891; reprint ed. New Delhi: Motilal Banarsidass).

O'Flaherty, Wendy Doniger
1976 *The Origins of Evil in Hindu Mythology.* Berkeley: University of California Press.

——— 1981 *Śiva: The Erotic Ascetic.* London, New York: Oxford University Press.

Olivelle, Patrick
1981 "A Definition of World Renunciation." In *Wiener Zeitschrift für die Kunde Südasiens und Archiv für indische Philosophie* 19:75–83.

Sanderson, Alexis
1985 "Purity and Power among the Brahmins of Kashmir." In *The Category of the Person: Anthropology, philosophy, history,* ed. Michael Carrithers, Steven Collins, and Steven Lukes. Cambridge: Cambridge University Press, 90–216.

Sharma, Ram Sharan
1980 *Śūdras in Ancient India.* Delhi, Motilal Banarsidass.

Shulman, David Dean
1986 *The King and the Clown in South Indian Myth and Poetry.* Princeton: Princeton University Press.

——— 1980 *Tamil Temple Myths: Sacrifice and Divine Marriage in the South Indian Saiva Tradition.* Princeton: Princeton University Press.

Sontheimer, Günther Dietz
1981 "Dasarā at Devaraguḍḍa: Ritual and Play in the Cult of Mailār/Khaṇḍobā." *South Asian Digest of Regional Writing* 10:1–27.

——— 1984 "The Mallāri-Khaṇḍobā Myth as Reflected in Folk Art and Ritual." *Anthropos* 79:155–170.

Varenne, Jean
1982 *Cosmogonies védiques.* Milan: Arché.

Weller, Friedrich
1956 "Die Legende von Śunaḥśepa im *Aitareya Brāhmaṇa* und *Śānkhāyana Śrauta Sūtra." Berichte über die verhandlungen der Sachsischen Akademie der Wissenschaften zu Leipzig, philologische-historische Klasse* [Berlin] 102(2):8–21.

White, David
1986 "Śunaḥśepa Unbound." *Revue de l'Histoire des Religions* 203(3):227–62.

3

Sharing the Divine Feast: Evolution of Food Metaphor in Marathi Sant Poetry[1]

*

Vidyut Aklujkar

Profusion of food imagery is a striking feature of Marathi Sant poetry.[2] As early as the thirteenth century, we find an extended metaphor of feast employed by Jñānadeva[3] (1275–1296) to communicate his experience of yogic bliss. In the works of other eminent saints belonging to this tradition, Nāmadeva, Ekanātha, and Tukārāma, we come across a lot more than a stray metaphor of feast. Food metaphor assumes a wide range of applications in their Bhakti poems. Long, detailed descriptions of feasts; lists of distinguished dinner guests; poetic menu cards with mouth-watering delicacies; accounts of divine and mortal serving squads; and certificates of satisfaction given by the assembled guests are employed at every imaginable context of worship, or bhakti. In addition, anecdotes focused on food are narrated with considerable frequency by Nāmadeva and Ekanātha to illustrate concepts such as the grace of God and the importance of selfless worship. This chapter explores the dynamics of popularity of food in Marathi sant literature. It will discuss the possible reasons behind the choice of the food imagery by Marathi sants, explore its semanticity, and try to delineate the gradual shift of emphasis in its use from personal to social realms.

Before proceeding to discuss the evolution of the food metaphor in Marathi sant poetry, perhaps a few words on the general status of food in the Bhakti movement and in the broader area of Hinduism are in order. From the Vedic times, the use of food in sacrifices and other rituals to appease Gods was common in India. There is a hymn in praise of food, Anna-stuti, in the Maṇḍala of the Ṛg Veda (Ṛg Veda, 1.187). In the *Puruṣa sūkta,* (Ṛg Veda, 10.90:6), some cow products, butter and clarified butter, are mentioned as foods offered in the primeval cosmic sacrifice. Later on, in the classical Hindu rituals, the fivefold cow products assume greater purificatory significance.[4] The Brāhmaṇas describe the importance of food in various words.[5] Many rules of personal and preparational purity were laid down for the ritual preparation and consumption of food in the Gṛhysa-sūtra and other such works. Even a text on grammar such as the Kāśikā vṛtti on Pāṇinī mentions the slothful eating habit as a distinguishing mark for the Ionians. For example, this text remarks, *Śayānā bhuñjate yavanāḥ* (Kāśikā 3.2.12). Indians in general show an overwhelming preoccupation with rules, regulations, taboos, and rituals concerned with food. Maybe this is why the wise philosopher of the Upaniṣads identified food with the cosmic principle, Brahman.[6]

Although the Bhakti movement stemmed as a movement of protest against the rigid ritualism of the manifold of Hindu traditions, it retained in principle all that was good in the old tradition in some form or another. Thus, even as the Bhakta poets raised an outcry against the ritualistic rules of worship and purity/pollution stipulations in food preparation as an offering to God, they recognized a heartfelt desire on the part of the common man to offer whatever he or she has to God. So any offering of food made in the right spirit was always given a legitimate place in Bhakti tradition. In the Song of the Lord, the *Bhagavad Gītā,* Lord Krishna assures Arjuna, his best disciple and friend, as follows: "I accept and relish anything given to me in the spirit of worship by a person; be it a leaf, a bud, a fruit, or a drink" (Gītā 9:26). In this spirit, till this day in India, food made for human consumption is first offered to God to be blessed by Him and, after this symbolic gesture (called *naivedya*), is to be consumed by Bhaktas as blessed by God and as a sacred leftover (called *prasāda*) from His plate. As we scan Marathi Sant poetry, we shall note various interpretations of *naivedya,* the symbolic offering of food to God and explore the semanticity of *prasāda,* the sacred leftover.

In the context of Bhakti literature, full treatment of the subject of food should deal with the Bhakta's poetic treatment of feasting as well as fasting. Similarly, other issues related to food such as the concept of Bhikṣā (the begged alms) for which Sant Rāmadāsa (1608–1681 A.D.) devotes a whole chapter of treatise Dāsabodha are worthy of note. But that is beyond the scope of this chapter. Therefore, I choose to leave the fascinating issues of fasting and other food consumption practices to some later date and focus for the time being only on the metaphor and other images of feasting in poetic repertoire of the above-mentioned poets.

The period under consideration falls roughly between the thirteenth and the seventeenth centuries. The sant poets of this period in Maharashtra are the four illustrious siblings: Nivṛttī, Jñānadeva, Sopāna, and Muktābā.ī, along with Nāmadeva, Janābā.ī, Ekanātha, Tukārāma, Cokhā meḷā, and a host of others. For brevity's sake, I shall concentrate mostly on the four cornerstones of the Sant edifice, Jñānadeva, Nāmadeva, Ekanātha, and Tukārāma. I use the word cornerstones, but Sant Bahiṇābā.ī[7] puts it better when she says:

> With the grace of the sants, this edifice is accomplished.
> Jñānadeva laid the foundation of this temple,
> Nāmadeva expanded the courtyard of it,
> Ekanātha was the pillar of strength, and
> Tukārāma was the pinnacle.

I will touch upon the historical background, the mystical-philosophical makeup, and poetic vision of each sant so as to delineate the rationale behind the food imagery in the works of these major poets.

Jñānadeva: The Bliss of Bhakti Yoga

The pioneer of Marathi sant tradition, Jñānadeva, was the second of the four siblings from Aḷandī, who were ostracized by the orthodoxy as offspring of an ascetic turned householder. Only after their purification were these children recognized as great sants. Jñānadeva, the most famous of all, established the budding vernacular Marathi as a vehicle for expressing sophisticated philosophical ideas, which was so far only a monopoly of Sanskrit. One of his works called *Jñānadevī* or *Jñāneshwarī* is profoundly philosophical and elegantly poetic commentary on the *Bhagavad Gītā*. Another inspiring poem called *Amṛtānubhava* describes the experience of Nātha yogic bliss and bodily immortality. Several of his *abhaṅgas*, are composed as poetic offerings to God Viṭhobā of Paṇḍharapūra. His philosophy is a synthesis of the elite Sanskrit tradition of Advaita Vedanta, the mystic pan-Indian tradition of the Nātha pantha, and the local tradition of bhakti of Viṭhobā. This synthesis is reflected in the following metaphor of feast he employs to his own yogic bliss. He opens the *abhaṅga* with reference to the four cosmic elements and then moves on to describe the inner space where the feast takes place:[8]

> The earth is the place mat,[9] the sky, the dish on it, the water and the light are the all-pervading nectar. In this feast forever, the brilliance shines through all the doors of Brahman. The good diner feasts and is appeased; it is the *paramahaṁsa*[10] yogi who is thus pacified.
>
> The rice is the moonlight all around in the sky/void of which is poured good butter. The special blue *śāka*[11] is indeed well done, add[12] to that the sour and hot love.
>
> Both Gangā and Yamunā [merge] in the third sea, thus, a special *khīra*[13] is cooked. With the brilliance of Brahman, the *sānjorī* is sugared and only the diner can experience its sweetness.
>
> Iḍā is the *Ghāri,*[14] Piṅgaḷā is the stuffing [lit, the raw sugar], and the third [i.e., the Suṣumnā] is the oil between the two.
>
> Due to the tasty Suṣumnā, the turyā state is furnished, and is ready to enjoy the feast day and night.
>
> The moon is the cool, soaked *āmbawaḍā,* the sun is the crisp *kuruwaḍā.* Along with these two, the states of mind are the *mānḍe,* so focus on the feast and enjoy the dinner.
>
> The purified [fried][15] *pāpaḍa* is the hand [fig., the blessing] of the Guru on the head. Therefore, the initiated is stamped/branded by him.
>
> He (the Guru) is blessed with the flavor of good taste, so when he preaches, the fruit of immortality is enjoyed.
>
> Having left over the evil passion, then make the *śevā* and the *kurwaḍaī* enjoyable.
>
> Having tasted the sweet *lāḍū,* near the feet of the Guru, then the King of the yogins dines with relish.
>
> With the grace of the Guru, when this feast is enjoyed pervading the elements, and the space, the sound rises in the sky as the bliss begins to grow from within.
>
> If I try to describe it by using the simile of the six flavors, [I cannot, for] nothing is as sweet as the essence of Brahman.

> When the dinner is thus concluded with the Yogurt-rice,[16] the hot[17] love is also present there. [He] dined on the nectar, rinsed his mouth with the nectar, and then rested on the supportless bed.
>
> The mind is colored with the color of the *tāṁbūla,* where is the new *abhaṅga* going to go?[18]
>
> The pure fragrance of the camphor and musk is united with the sweetness of the raw sugar. The idol of flowers is worshipped with flowers, and the offering made is of golden flowers.
>
> Thus was the manifold feast accomplished, served by the father/yogin Nivṛtti. Says Jñānadeva, I ate to my heart's content. Father Viṭṭhala, the groom of Goddess Rakhumā, has made me happy.

Here the feast metaphor captures a spontaneous poetic expression of an intensely personal experience of bliss, attained by Jñānadeva after his teacher/brother Nivṛtti blessed him. All the elements of Jñāndeva's metaphysical makeup are present in this account. We find traces of his Nātha-yogic heritage in the mention of the three *nāḍīs* or channels of consciousness (Iḍā, Piṅgaḷā and Suṣumnā), the sun and the moon and the states of mind, the two rivers merging in the third sea, and finally, the *nāda* or the sound in the inner sky. The spiritual master, the Guru, is important both in the Nātha sect and the Sant tradition; hence, he is mentioned here with reverence. The teacher Nivṛttinātha, who was in fact his elder brother, is referred to here as the father since he aids the spiritual rebirth, as it were, of the aspirant. Finally, we also find the whole mystic experience linked with the grace of the God of Paṇḍharapūra, Viṭṭhala, and Viṭhobā.

The choice of food metaphor in the context of bliss hails from a long tradition going back to the Upaniṣads, where the experience of bliss was linked with the enjoyment of food.[19] In the immediate Nātha yogic tradition[20] too, Gorakha-nātha often describes his blissful experience as drinking the milk of the heavenly cow which he has tied within his own back yard.[21] Nivṛttinātha, Gorakhanātha's grand-disciple and Jñāndeva's teacher, uses the classical metaphors of the enjoyment of the nectar, or the milk of the female tortoise, or of the Kāmadhenu,[22] to describe the bliss.[23] But Jñānadeva goes further than that. He is the first sant to employ the more mundane details of *khīra, ghāri, sānjorī, āṁbavaḍā, pāpaḍa,* and *tāmbūla* to capture this elusive mystic experience. In his extension of the metaphor of a feast, he paved a way for the later sants to follow. By going beyond the conventional and employing more tangible metaphors, he made available for a wider audience the poetic expression of an experience, so far the monopoly of the chosen few.[24]

Nāmadeva: The God's Pal

Both Jñānadeva (1275–1296) and Nāmadeva (1270–1350) were contemporaries and had achieved fame in their childhood, but their personalities and their poetic sensitivities are quite distinct. Jñānadeva was a child prodigy who could write an original exposition of the Gītā at the tender age of fifteen. Nāmadeva was a child bhakta who could make God eat off his hands. As we move from Jñānadeva to Nāmadeva, we witness a curious reversal in the roles of the diner and the host. Jñānadeva describes the joy of the divine feast as it is served to him by Lord Viṭhobā while Nāmadeva's earliest memory recorded in his *abhaṅgas* (poems) is that of serving the God and making Him eat the food of the mortals. In Jñāndeva's expression of the divine feast, there is an unmistakable flavor of Nātha yogi's bliss, and his ecstatic experience stays entirely personal. With Nāmadeva, the divine feast, wherever it occurs, is always shared. The main companion is the God Viṭhobā, but often other sants are also invited to join the feast.[25] Sometimes, Nāmadeva gives us an "eyewitness" account of feasts shared by God with his earlier Bhaktas such as Sudāmā.[26] Sudāmā's story from the Bhāgavata purāṇa holds a special fascination for the Marathi sants like Nāmadeva because it shows Krishṇa, the Lord of Dwārakā, a high and mighty king, fondly gobbling up a handful of parched rice brought to his palace as a humble gift in self-conscious embarrassment by his childhood friend Sudāmā, who is a poor Brahman. It is an encounter between royal wealth and priestly poverty. Nāmadeva is sparing in describing the royal feast given by Lord Krishṇa in honor of his visiting friend, but when it comes to the humble gift to God given by the poor man, he mentions the eagerness in God's acceptance of it, and in particular Krishṇa's unwillingness to share it even with his queen Rakhumā-bāī and other gods, such as Brahmā, who stand behind with outstretched hands. The moral is, that it is not the value of the gift but the sentiment of bhakti which makes it priceless and fit to be enjoyed by the Lord. The bhakta shares the food with God, but even other gods are unworthy of sharing the mutual enjoyment. We notice in the accounts of Nāmadeva seeds of the concepts developed further by the later sants.

This transition of attitudes from personal to mutual enjoyment of food in the respective poems of Jñānadeva to Nāmadeva is better understood when we take into account the anecdotes about Nāmadeva's childhood entreaties with God. Nāmadeva was never content with the customary symbolic offering of food, *naivedya,* to the temple idol of the God. It is said that he would wait in the temple until God actually cleaned the whole plate and belched with satisfaction. This incident is narrated quite humorously in a couple of *abhaṅgas* in the section called "The life-account of Nāmadeva" (Nāmadeva *caritra*)[27] found at the beginning of the *Nāmadeva Gāthā.* We are told that when Nāmadeva first returns after thus feeding Viṭhobā, his mother demands to have the plate back so that the blessed leftover can be eaten by the rest of the family members. Instead, Nāmadeva hands her an empty plate. She scolds him, saying, "Was there no food for you here at home? Why did you finish off the food offered to God?" Nāmadeva tries to clear his name by saying, "I didn't eat it. You sent me to give it to Viṭhobā, which I did. *He* ate it." Of course the mother refuses to believe him. His skeptical father says, "Let us not discuss it any further. I shall go with him tomorrow to see for myself." So the father accompanies the boy to the temple and hides in the dark while Nāmadeva again pleads with the idol of God Viṭhobā to finish the food so he can take the plate home. Viṭhobā complies with his wishes. Then the astounded father comes forward to talk to Viṭhobā. Viṭhobā tells him in hushed tones not to spread the word, to keep it all in the family.

This incident is a key to our understanding various interpretations of the divine feast found in Nāmadeva's poetry. He is an eternal child. His relationship with God moves from that of a child-parent relationship to the special friendship between childhood buddies. As a child, Nāmadeva often calls for his divine mother, Viṭhā.ī or Viṭhābā.ī,[28] to feed him. But sharing his food with God becomes an ecstatic expression of his worship through friendship, or *sakhya-Bhakti.* Throughout Nāmadeva's *abhaṅgas,* we find repeated references to sharing a common feast with God. There are many variations on the theme. Sometimes he refers to the childhood incidents of the temple idol of God drinking up the bowl of milk or eating the *naivedya* off his plate. Sometimes Viṭhobā and Nāmadeva as adults share a common plate of food, cooked and served by Viṭhobā's consort Rakhumā.ī or Rukmini.[29] Sometimes

Nāmadeva imagines himself to be one of God's cowherd friends from the Krishna incarnation and describes the exploits of sharing the dairy food stolen from the milkmaids.[30]

The dream goes on. Nāmadeva is God's companion, sharing the divine feast daily. Food becomes a symbol of Bhakti itself, the food for soul, and the enjoyment of Bhakti is like the satisfaction of a filled belly. The Bhakta and the God share a feast, but all creatures can share in this enjoyment. Nāmadeva's ecstasy expands across time to encompass all of God's incarnations, and across space to include all beings as manifestations of God. In another well-known incident, enjoyed especially by Indian children, Nāmadeva is in the kitchen and his dinner is ready, while a dog comes and snatches away a roṭī.[31] Bhakta Nāmadeva runs after the dog, not to chase him away or punish or curse him, but to give him some ghee[32] to eat with his roṭī, so that it is not a dry meal. An *abhaṅgas*[33] describing this incident is as follows:

> With a bowl of ghee in his hand, Nāma ran after the dog, saying, "God, take some ghee with it. Why eat a dry roṭī?" Then the dog smiled and asked, "Nāma, how did you recognize me?" He answered, "I was taught by Visobā Khecara[34] to see God in all beings."

The dog who was the God shares food with Bhakta Nāmādeva, whose sense of oneness with God and all his manifestations extends to a cosmic identity.

Within these parameters of Nāmadeva's personality, we can better appreciate the place of food imagery in his poetry. The joy of a full belly or the sense of well-being that comes when the mother feeds the child is one of the central themes in Nāmadeva's relationship with God. However, it is not the only theme in his poems. I cannot agree with Vaudeville when she remarks about the "*prem-bhakti*" of Maharashtrian sants, "But the relationship always remains that of a child to his father or mother, bridal symbolism is nearly unknown in Maharashtrian Bhakti."[35] Contrary to Vaudeville's conclusion, filial worship or *vātsalya-bhakti* is not the only prominent relationship expressed in the Maharashtrian sant poetry. As we shall see in this chapter, *sakhya-bhakti* or friendly worship, is another favorite mode of worship in which they often indulge. In the mood of separation, Nāmadeva calls God to feed the starving baby. But in the mood of union, he often describes the feasts shared with God since he visualizes God as his eternal friend, his *sakhā*, his *jīvalaga*.[36]

The novelty of Nāmadeva's use of food imagery in the context of his friendly worship is better revealed in the Tīrthāvaḷī *abhaṅgas* attributed to Nāmadeva.[37] The context of these *abhaṅgas* is of Nāmadeva's pilgrimage with Jñānadeva to sacred places away from Paṇḍharapūra and the reception given to him by God Viṭhobā on his subsequent return from a long trip. The mood on these *abhaṅgas* is quite different from the usual mood of servitude, *dāsya* or *vinaya,* common in the bhakti of the latter-day northern sants such as Sūradās and Tulsīdās. In the northern bhakti poetry, or even in Nāmadeva's own poems in another mood, there is a description of the devotee's longing for God. However, in the mood of friendly worship, a bold Nāmadeva describes how Viṭhobā Himself was lonely for Nāmadeva when he went away for a pilgrimage and how God was happy to see his devotee return to him. Normally we find that the devotee desires to share God's leftover food as the sacred *prasāda*. But here, Viṭhobā tells Nāmadeva how He missed Nāma daily at dinnertime.[38] Later, when they sit down to enjoy a feast, God wants to eat Nāmadeva's leftover, his *ucchiṣṭa*. Only the sacred leftover is to be shared by the devotees; but the leftover of an individual is considered polluted for anyone else to share it. Therefore, the God's wish is quite unheard of anywhere else. Of course, an outcry issues from the Brahmans gathered to witness the feast. God then explains to them His reasons for this unusual desire. God Has become *one* with Nāmadeva and, therefore, the roles of God and the devotee as they are usually known are reversed in this case. Further in these *abhaṅgas* Nāmadeva describes the feast as God serves it to the sants and that the message is that since the sants are the bosom friends of the Lord, they share food with each other, without the usual protocol.[39]

Ekanātha: The Brotherhood of Sants

Sant Ekanātha (1533–1599), who appeared more than two hundred years later than Nāmadeva, carried further this message of equality by using the metaphor of sharing the divine feast with an added dimension of actual social practice. Ekanātha was a Brahman by birth and a well-read pandit by profession. Following Jñānadeva, he had brought the traditional knowledge from Sanskrit to Marathi. His erudite scholarship is evident in his prolific writings. Yet in the true spirit of Bhakti, he practiced and preached the message of equality regardless of caste or creed. He often uses the metaphor of sharing the divine feast to bring home this message. He describes the pastoral life of Krishna in great detail, dwelling at length on the favorite games of Krishna and his friends. Even in common games such as hide-and-seek, Ekanātha finds a metaphysical meaning. In a section called Communal Meals (*kālā*), he describes the communal meals of Krishna and his friends on the banks of Yamunā.[40] For Ekanātha, this is not just a poetic description, there is an obvious message that follows from God's practice. Krishna comes from an affluent home, so he brings good food from home for his noonday meal, but his friends are from humble homes, and whatever they bring tied in their soiled napkins is day-old food of the rustics.[41] Ekanātha's Krishna never eats alone. He makes everyone open his *shidori,* the bag lunch, and makes them all put it together in a big pile. Then the friends feed each other and share the mixture of all tastes. Sometimes they engage in mock quarrels as to who should have the honor of taking the first morsel. Sometimes they accuse Krishna of being mischievous and gobbling up their food. Krishna often must break up their friendly quarrels by sharing his food with them. The gods in heaven become envious of this innocent joy of the cowherds, and they wish to share it. So the gods assume the forms of fish in Yamunā and wait in the hope of sharing the crumbs (*ucchiṣṭa*) when the cowherds come to wash their hands in the river. But Krishna anticipates their plan and scares his friends away from the river by telling them stories about a ghost in the river. So they resume their play by simply wiping their hands on their bottoms. The cunning gods are thus deprived of sharing the leftover (*ucchiṣṭa*) which is freely available to those who are Krishna's friendly devotees. Ekanātha considers himself blessed enough to partake the sacred leftovers from the feast of the cowherds served by God Himself.[42]

The moral of this story is in line with Nāmadeva's account of Sudāmā. Ekanātha wanted to break the barriers of caste and shake the Brahman orthodoxy which had remained obstinate for centuries in spite of repeated attempts by sants like Nāmadeva to shake it. Therefore, he used anecdotes of Krishna's communal meals, *gopāḷa-kālā,* as a model for the Maharashtrian community and advocated the actual sharing of food in society. This practice earned him the wrath of the orthodoxy and cost him the loss of his status, but apparently, he could not care less.[43]

Ekanātha uses other anecdotes focused on food to celebrate the greatness of a true *bhakta* regardless of his low caste. For this purpose, Nāmadeva had used an older example of Sudāmā from the pan-Indian Bhāgavata tradition, but Ekanātha uses Cokhā Meḷā, an example from the tradition of sants in Maharashtra. A prominent episode tells about the purification of the heavenly nectar which takes place in Cokhā's house.[44] Cokhā Meḷā (thirteenth century) was a great sant who was born a mahār, an untouchable. If we read his own *abhaṅgas,* we find that he is acutely aware of his low status in the society as a mahār and of the fact that he always has to subsist on the leftovers of society.[45] But Ekanātha has elevated him to a glorious status in his *abhaṅgas* by using the concept of "leftover" *in reverse* in addition to the motif of purification of *amṛta.* We are told that *Amṛta,* the nectar of immortality which is possessed by gods in heaven, has gone stale. It is no longer tasty. The king of gods in heaven, Indra, asks the sage Nārada where it can be purified again. Nārada points to Paṇḍharapūra, a city on the earth, where the great sant Cokhā Meḷā lives. Indra appears to Cokhā's door when Cokhā has fasted for three days in the name of God and is about to break his fast by serving the food to God. Indra joins the feast, and also wonders whether his *amṛta* could be restored to its original taste. God Viṭhobā, who is chief guest at Cokhā's breakfast, asks Cokhā to restore Indra's *amṛta.* Cokhā sniffs at the *amṛta* in Indra's hands and declares that it is no comparison to the nectar of the Name, *Nāmāmṛta,* that he serves. He purifies Indra's *amṛta* by chanting the name of God Viṭhobā. The social overtones of this episode are unmistakable. Ekanātha's sympathies with the deprived classes are genuine[46] and, even in the limited context of food, he finds novel ways to bring home the message of equality.

Tukārāma: The Solidarity of Bhakti

A spiritual successor of Nāmadeva and Ekanātha is Tukārāma (1598–1649). He was a humble shopkeeper of Dehu and a towering saint who left an indelible imprint on the masses with his outspoken *abhaṅgas* and inspiring conduct. Unlike Jñānadeva and Ekanātha, he had no formal training in yoga nor knowledge of Sanskrit, and he did not claim to be a great poet.[47] All he had was great faith in the Name of God and a Socratic sense of wisdom.[48] Tukārāma was truly a poet of the masses, with a rough diction and a sharp wit which exposed evils in the society and extolled virtues of simple *bhakti*.

Following Ekanātha, Tukārāma devotes a considerable number of *abhaṅgas* to the topic of communal meal of Krishna,[49] and preaches the message of brotherhood through these stories. He also uses other well-known stories from the *Bhāgavata purāṇa* about Krishna's eating to bring out the cosmic reality of the familiar God Viṭhobā and stress the importance of *bhakti*. Often Tukārāma's interpretation of the older accounts is quite unique. Take, for instance, the fire-eating episode.[50] While the cowherds are playing on the banks of Yamunā, a fire breaks out and threatens to engulf them. They get sacred, but Krishna tells them to shut their eyes and rescues them by consuming the whole fire in his mouth. Unlike the *Bhāgavata* account, in Tukārāma's account the cowherds open their eyes in time to notice this miracle. They marvel at the fact that the fire did not burn their friend anywhere. Tukārāma, as one of them, sums up the story for us.[51] He says to the wonder-struck cowherds, "Why do you marvel at this? No wonder Krishna can work such miracles; after all, he is nourished by eating our food, our *shidories*." The idea is that the food offered by the devotees with real love strengthens God. In a sense it is the devotees that make the God what he is. Although the episode narrated by Tukārāma is well known within the larger Bhakti tradition, the anthropocentric interpretation he gives it is his own, and it stems out of his acceptance of the mode of *Sakhya Bhakti,* or friendly worship in which the devotee is equal in status with the God.

We have seen now the evolution of the metaphor of feast through the works of four sants. What started with Jñānadeva as an ecstatic expression of personal yogic bliss with a tinge of qualified worship, *saguṇa-bhakti,* has evolved into an expression of full-fledged friendly worship, *sakhya-bhakti,* with Nāmadeva, and assumed the significance of a widespread social movement in the hands of Ekanātha and Tukārāma. In this evolution, we saw related symbols and concepts, such as *naivedya,* and *prasāda,* undergo a sea change. The concept of *naivedya,* which was a symbolic offering of food in the larger Bhakti tradition, was interpreted literally by the child-bhakta Nāmadeva and used effectively to convey the appreciation by God of the bhakta's child-like innocence. The concept of the sacred leftover, *prasāda,* has undergone a significant change from being God's leftover food desired and consumed by the devotee to being the devotee's humble leftover *ucchiṣṭa,* desired and shared by God himself. Other concepts, such as the nectar of immortality, *amṛta,* also have undergone similar transformations in the context of this evolution, as we saw above.

The popularity of food imagery in Marathi sant poetry is not confined to the metaphor of divine feast, although it certainly claims the place of honor. The Maharashtrian love of food spills into many more poetic vessels. Consider, for example, the device of "name dropping" used cunningly by the sants in their Vinaya (entreaty) poems. All sants in India indulge from time to time in the pastime of producing standard lists of earlier devotees in their poetic entreaties. They use this device either to sing God's glories as the savior of great devotees or, more effectively, in the tongue-in-cheek manner to remind Him of His earlier acts of salvation of sinners and to boast of being a greater sinner and claim a place in that list for themselves. When northern saints like Sūradās engage in this, the list includes devotees such as Prahlāda, Dhruva, or Bali, or famous sinners such as King Ajāmila, the elephant (gaja), the courtesan (gaṇikā), the hunter (vyādha), and the vulture (gīdha). Usually, it is only a matter of convincing God that the devotee who is the name dropper is, in fact, a greater sinner than the ones whom God had saved earlier. However, when the Marathi sants produce such lists, they do not go the *Vinaya* route to convince God that their claim for the title of a "sinner" is greater than those before them. More often than not, the Marathi sants focus on food and relate the tales of God's sharing humble food at the hands of different devotees. For example, Nāmadeva recalls, "He ate mere leaves at his sister's (Draupadī's) house. He gobbled up dry rice flakes brought to Him by Sudāmā. He ate the broken rice offered by poor Vidura until He had His fill, and He also became a doorkeeper at the door of Baḷī. No one knows why He does this. Says Nāmadeva, maybe He is really crazy for his *bhaktas.*" Sant Janābā.ī, an inspired poetess who was a maidservant in Nāmadeva's family, relates the tale of cooking pot, *thālīpāka,* in order to glorify God. This is a tale of Draupadī, the wronged heroine of the Mahābhārata, feeding her friend/soul-brother Krishna who appears at her forest dwelling at an odd hour and demands food. In the hospitable tradition of an Indian housewife, Draupadī manages to offer Krishna the only item of food available to her then, a little leaf of vegetable stuck to her cooking pot, and with that, Krishna is full.[52] Note that instead of God fulfilling the desire of the devotee, the devotee is the donor, and God, the recipient in this exchange. Elsewhere, too, Janābā.ī portrays God as a child who comes to her on the sly and asks for food.[53] Sāvatā the gardener, another great Bhakta, sees God in the onion, radish, garlic, and hot pepper in his soil.[54] Ekanātha relates in several *abhaṅgas* how God ate humble food, such as the berries given by Śabarī, who had first tasted them for sourness, thereby unconsciously making them *ucciṣṭa,* "the leftover" from her plate which is otherwise considered polluted. In the Rāma incarnation, the incident of Śabarī, and in the Krishna incarnation, the communal meals of the cowherds are cited by Ekanātha as examples of God's partiality to food offered with love, even if it is *ucchiṣṭa,* the mundane leftover.[55] This, in turn, speaks of God's hunger for love.[56] Just like the devotee who is eternally hungry for God, God Himself is hungry for real love and is sated only on a steady diet of these. This reminder of the mutual dependence of God and devotees is what sets the Marathi sants apart from the other sants in the Bhakti tradition. It is in keeping with their notion of equality in their "friendly worship" or *sakhya-bhakti.* Tukārāma sums up his life experience by saying:

> My heart is content with God, now the world tastes bitter. But the belches issuing from my inside are the joyous ones of the sound "Harihara."[57] He pierces all the rest, thus is his nourishment. Hence, Tukā says, once you enjoy him, you are no longer hungry.[58]

By now, we have seen reversals in the usual relationship of the host and the guest, the sacred and the polluting leftover, the role of God and the devotee. We are preparing ourselves to experience a complete flux, a loss of identity, or in other words, an expansion of identity, which promises to be more than just a linguistic reversal. Indeed, it is the ultimate merging of the diner, the dish, and the dinner, the great experience of cosmic unity which is captured first in the metaphor of the divine feast by Jñānadeva, as we saw above, and is also expressed by the later-day sant poet Ekanātha.[59]

The feast is unending. But the discussion must now conclude. In passing, I would like to share a few points: In the hands of the northern Bhakti poets such as Sūradāsa, food appears in certain descriptions of household dinners of Krishna's childhood and in incidents such as His famous theft of butter. But nowhere does it occupy such a central place as in the Marathi sant poetry. What are the reasons for this all-pervasive love for food imagery in this poetry? Such popularity of food imagery and anecdotes centered on food may be due to the fact that the sants were mainly addressing the masses. Therefore they chose the imagery which can be appreciated by men and women, young and old, all alike. Perhaps it was the proverbial bitter pill of advice coated with sugar. Because, although they talk about the mouth-watering feasts of devotees and God, they do not forget to warn the fickle of heart that the reward of Bhakti, of selfless worship, is like the bread atop a stake. Only the brave souls can attempt and win it.[60] But ultimately it reveals their major social concern of teaching the eternal values of equality and brotherhood to the masses. Their goal was to share one's own food, mundane or spiritual, with everyone else. Hence, they deliberately picked or composed stories that focused on such a sharing. The Bhakti movement in Maharashtra in its poetic utterance was thus a collective experience of a divine feast, where everyone was welcome, everyone was seated in a circle without protocol, where no food was polluting, nobody an untouchable, and no one left without having his fill.

Abbreviations

M: Molsworth's Marathi English Dictionary.

SSG: Sakala santa gāthā (gāthā pancaka) in five volumes. Ed. Dhere and Kamat. The number after SSG in my notes denotes the volume number.

Notes

1. An earlier draft of this paper was read at the Association for Asian Studies Conference in Washington, D.C., in March 1989.

2. Historically, "sant" denotes poet-saints of India, belonging to the Bhakti tradition and falling into two distinct, though related groups: one from Maharashtra and the other from the North. For more on the term, see *The Sants: Studies in a Devotional Tradition of India,* edited by Schomer and McLeod, 1987.

3. Also known as Jñāneshwara/(Dnyāneshwar) or Gyānabā. I use the name which occurs in his works and follow the standard transliteration. Words, such as Krishna or Marathi, that have become part of English are not transliterated.

4. Basham 1959, 319.

5. *Annam vā āyatanam* (Śatapatha Brāhmaṇa 7.5.1.20), *Annam prāṇāḥ* (Taittrīyạ Brāhmaṇa 3.2.3.4.)

6. *Annam Brahmeti vyajānāt* (Taittrīya Upaniṣad 3.2.)

7. *Bahiṇābā.īcā Gāthā,* 1956, 66; *abhaṅga* 229.

8. I give a somewhat literal translation of SSG 1:95; *abhaṅga* 159. Underlined words in it are names of dishes unless otherwise specified.

9. Āḍaṇī means the wooden rectangle on which a dinner plate is kept in front of the diner who is sitting on a similar support.

10. The individual, one with the cosmic principle.

11. Cooked vegetable preparation.

12. The original shifts from past tense descriptions to imperative prescription. I have retained this trait in translating.

13. A liquid preparation of three ingredients—milk, sugar, and rice/wheat/sago/etc. This refers to the three channels of consciousness in the Nātha-yoga.

14. A wheaten cake stuffed and fried.

15. The pun on the word "pavitra" allows the poet to bring in the literal frying meaning of the *papaḍ,* and also the holiness of the blessing from the Guru.

16. Usually the last dish in a well-prepared Maharashtrian dinner, which is often accompanied by a hot pickle.

17. Twice in this poem Jñānadeva refers to love as "*tikhe*" and "*tikhaṭa,*" meaning spicy hot, sharp. The bliss of Brahman is sweet; but the love of a personal god is pungent, perhaps because, unlike the former, the latter is flavored with the pangs of separation.

18. I am not sure about the accuracy of the text here. The word *abhaṅga,* which means "unbroken," is also the name of the poetic form in which these sants composed their sayings.

19. *Annam brahmeti vyajānāt,* Taittirīya Upaniṣhad 3.2; *rasaṁ hi evāyaṁ labdhvā ānandībhavati, Ibid,* 2.7.

20. The chain of teachers in the Nātha yogic tradition of Jñānadeva is given as follows: Macchindranātha, Gorakhanātha, Gahinīnātha, Nivṛttinātha, and Jñānadeva. SSG 1:21, *abhaṅga* 135.

21. yāhi dhena kā dūha ju mīṭhā pīvai gorakh hanana baiṭhā. For more on Gorakhanātha's interpretation of the cow and the milk, see V. Aklujkar, "In Search of the Unholy Cow," *Religious Traditions,* vol. 12, 1989.

22. The wish-fulfilling cow of mythology.

23. SSG 2:2, *abhaṅga* 106; p. 27, *abhaṅga* 175; p. 39, *abhaṅga* 251, etc.

24. Perhaps it is another instance of the spirit to transmit the elitist philosophy into the vernacular which prompted Jñānadeva to write a commentary on the Gītā in Marathi and compose his poetic work in the language of the people.

25. For example, see *abhaṅga* 664 in the *Tīrthāvaḷī abhaṅgas,* SSG 2:179.

26. See *abhaṅgas* 2173–4. SSG 2:602.

27. Dhere (1970) is doubtful as to the authorship of the Nāmadeva *caritra.* Although it is written in an autobiographical form, Dhere finds strong reasons against attributing it to original Nāmadeva. Inamdar (1970) agrees with Dhere that some references in certain *abhaṅgas* are anachronistic, but he believes that the whole account need not be of a later date. He considers only such anachronistic *abhaṅgas* as of a later authorship. Whichever way the dispute is resolved, the incidents related in the *caritra* are quite well known and form a vital part of the personality of Nāmadeva as it was known in Maharashtra and projected in Gujarat and Punjab, within his lifetime.

28. The feminine form of "Viṭhobā," fondly employed by Nāmadeva and other sants as an expression of vātsalya Bhakti, a child's mode of worship.

29. *Tīrthāvaḷī abhaṅgas,* 639–646. SSG 2:164–170.

30. SSG 2:397. *abhaṅga* 1528. This is a graphic description of the famous butter thief surrounded by his friends, such as Pendyā who talks with a lisp and Nāma who is the eyewitness. When Krishna cannot reach the pot of butter hung high, he stacks the wooden seats high and brings down the pot. Pendyā smacks on his bottom and shouts with joy. Krishna scolds him for shouting and balances the lump of butter in his hands. As the gopi comes after them, he throws a shower of milk in her eyes and runs along with his friends. The verses are written in a child's lisping words and are quite realistic in reflecting children's pranks.

31. A round tortilla-like unleavened wheat bread made daily.

32. Clarified butter.

33. SSG 2:53, *abhaṅga* 153.

34. The guru of Nāmadeva. For more on his identity, see Dhere, *Chakrapāṇī* 1977; Vaudeville "Maharastrian Santism" 215–228 in Schomer and McLeod, 1987.

35. Schomer and McLeod, 1987,29; I shall not dwell on bridal symbolism except to point out that it is quite prominent in Jñānadeva's and Ekanātha's "virāṅī" (*virahiṇī*) *abhaṅgas.*

36. Kurvāḷonī māthā ghāsa ghālī mukhī, taṁva lakṣmīpati tanmaya hota . mhaṇe jivalagā bole sukha goṣṭī, ārta āhe poṭī bahu divasāṁce. SSG 2:166, *abhaṅga* 641.

37. Dhere (1970, 31) and Ajganvkar (1941, 6) argue against attributing the authorship of these *abhaṅgas* to Nāmadeva, but Inamdar (1970,167) has argued convincingly about the authenticity of the tradition.

38. "Anudinī bhojana karitā udakapāna, tevhā āṭhavaṇa hoya tujhī" SSG.2: p. 166. *abhaṅga* 642.

39. Avghe santa jana āmuce sāṁgātī, jevūṁ ekā paṁtī sarīse āmhī, mhaṇonī sakaḷāṁ pācārileṁ deveṁ kavatuka aghaven pāhatī dvija. SSG 2:179, *abhaṅga* 663.

40. SSG 3:65–76, *abhaṅga* 240–269.

41. "Śiḷyā viṭakyā bhākarī dahī bhāta loṇī, meḷavonī meḷā karī cakrapāṇi SSG.3:65, *abhaṅga* 240.

42. SSG 4:65, *abhaṅga* 241. Śriharī vāḍhīle, gopāḷa jevīle, ucchiṣṭa sevile ekā janārdanīm.

43. Accounts of incidents in Ekanātha's life support this hypothesis. In one account (Dandekar 1974), Ekanātha invites all the Untouchables of Paiṭhaṇa to the ritual meal of śrāddha, the feast for the ancestors' spirits, that is served in his house. The Brahman priests, infuriated by this conduct, refuse to come to his house for the feast and refuse to bless him. The story goes on to relate how Ekanātha served the feast in the name of the absent Brahmans anyway and how it was heartily consumed by the manes of the very same Brahmans.

44. SSG 3:690–692, *abhaṅga* 3680–3687.

45. Johāra māya bāpa johāra, tumacyā maharācā mī mahāra, bahū bhukelā jhaloṁ, tumacyā uṣṭyāsāṭhī āloṁ. SSG 5:148, *abhaṅga* 9.

46. This is also noted by Eleanor Zelliot in 'Eknāth's Bharuds' in Schomer and McLeod 1987, 91–109.

47. He often cites the compelling inspiration he receives from God as an excuse for his urge to compose *abhaṅgas.* SSG 4:460, *abhaṅga* 3064.

48. Tradition relates another common element between the lives of Socrates and Tukārāma, both had to put up with the nagging of an unsympathetic wife.

49. SSG 4:552–562, *abhaṅga* 3502–3549.

50. *Bhāgavata purāṇa,* 10:19, 1–16. Ekanātha, Sūrdāsa, and many others have narrated this incident, each in a different manner.

51. SSG 4:551, *abhaṅga* 3498. Kaisīre Kānhobā evaḍhī giḷiyelī āgī, na dekhoṁ poḷalā tuja toṁḍī koṭheṁ aṁgīm. tukā mhaṇe kāṁ re tumhī karitā navala, āmacī sidorī khāto, tyāce ālem baḷa.

52. SSG 4:756–759, Thālīpāka *abhaṅgas* 321–333.

53. SSG 2:718, *abhaṅgas* 121, Koṇe eke divaśī viṭho gelā janīpāśī. haḷūca māgato khāyāsī kāya deū bā mī tusī? hātī dharuna nelā āta vāḍhī pañcāmṛta bhāta. prema sukhācā ḍhekara dilā, janī mhaṇe viṭho dhālā.

54. Kāndā muḷā bhājī, avaghī viṭhā.ī majhī. lasūṇa miracī kothimbirī avaghā jhāla mājhā harī. SSG 5:145, *abhaṅga* 3.

55. SSG 4:527, *abhaṅga* 2909–2912; p. 528, *abhaṅga* 2913; p. 531, *abhaṅga* 2934; p. 542, *abhaṅga* 3002, etc.

56. A popular Marathi proverb is: Deva bhāvācā bhukelā. "God is hungry for real love."

57. A name for Vithoba pointing to the unity of Hari, Viśṇu, and Hara, Śiva. This amalgam of Śaiva and Vaiśṇava sects is another unique aspect of the saguṇa bhakti tradition of Maharashtra.

58. SSG 4:45, *abhaṅga* 293.

59. SSG 4:570, *abhaṅga* 3156.

60. SSG 4:448, *abhaṅgas* 2973. Bhakti to kaṭhiṇa, suḷāvarila poḷī, nivaḍe to baḷī, viraḷā śūra.

References

Ajgavkar, J. R.
1927 *Santa Shiromaṇī Śrī Nāmadeva Mahārājā āṇi Tyānce Samakālīna Santa*. Pune. Latest edition 1941.

Aklujkar, Vidyut
1989 "Unholy Cow." In *Religious Traditions*. No. 12, 1989. The Faculty of Religious Studies, McGill University and The Department of Religious Studies, University of Sydney.

Bahiṇābā.i
1956 *Bahiṇābā.īcā Gāthā*. Pune: Citrashala Prakashan. Second edition.

Basham, A. L.
1959 *The Wonder that Was India*. New York: Grove Press.

Bhāgavatam
1954 *Śrīmad-Bhāgavata-Mahāpurāṇa* Gita Press: Gorakhpur.

Dandekar, G. N.
1974 *Shri Santa Ekanātha Majestic Prakashan*. Bombay: Girganv [2nd edition 1980].

Dhere, R. C. and Ashok Prabhakara Kamat
1970 *Śrī Nāmadeva: eka vijaya yātra*. Pune: Visvakarmā Sāhityālaya.

Dhere, R. C.
1977 *Cakrapāṇī*. Pune: Vishvakarmā Sahityālaya.

——— (Editor)

1985 *Sakala santa gāthā (gāthā pancaka)*. A compendium of major Marathi sants' works based on the Sakhare tradition of manuscripts. Volumes 1–5. Pune. First ed. 1908.

Inamdar, Hemant Vishnu
1970 *Santa Nāmadeva*. (Namdev: The Saint-poet of Maharashtra). Pune: Kesari Prakashan.

Jñānadeva
1976 *Amṛtānubhava,* published as the *Jñāneshwara Janma śatābdi smṛti grantha,* by Itihāsācārya vi. ka. Dhule: Rajwade Saṁsodhana Manḍaḷa.

Molsworth, James Thompson
1975 *Marathi-English Dictionary*. [First edition 1831, corrected reprint with preface by Dr. N. G. Kalelkar.] Pune: Shubhada-Saraswat.

Śatapatha Brāhmaṇa. *Śukla-yajurvede Śatapatha-brāhmaṇam.* Varanasi:
Chowkhamba Sanskrit Series. vol. 86, 1964.

Schomer, Karine and W. H. McLeod (Editors)
1987 *The Sants: Studies in a Devotional Tradition in India*. New Delhi: Motilal Banarsidass.

Tattirīya Brāhmaṇa.
1958 *Tattirīya Brāhmaṇam*. Ed. V. G. Anandāśrama-Apte. Sanskṛta-granthāāvalī. Pune. Vol. 37.

Tattiriya Upanisad.
1958 *Eighteen Principal Upaniṣads*. V. P. Limaye and Vadekar, R.D., Editors. Gandhi Memorial Edition.

Vaudeville, Charlotte
1987 "The Shaiva-Vaishnava Synthesis in Maharastrian Santism." In *The Sants: Studies in a Devotional Tradition in India*. Karine Schomer and W. H. McLeod (eds.). New Delhi: Motilal Banarsidass.

Zelliot, Eleanor

1987 "Eknath's *Bharuds:* The Sants as a Link Between Cultures." In *The Sants: Studies in a Devotional Tradition in India*. Karine Schomer and W. H. McLeod (eds.). New Delhi: Motilal Banarsidass.

Zelliot, Eleanor and Maxine Berntsen (Editors)
1988 *The Experience of Hinduism: Essays on Religion in Maharashtra*. Albany: State University of New York Press.

4

Mountain of Food, Mountain of Love: Ritual Inversion in the Annakūṭa Feast at Mount Govardhan

Paul M. Toomey

"So, you are going to conduct field research at Mount Govardhan?" a person knowledgeable in the ways of Braj asked, "Well, you ought to find plenty to eat *there*." I was later reminded of this comment when I had settled into the field situation and began to realize how important food is: both as the main commodity of the pilgrimage culture and as a communicator of social and religious messages. Large food displays and feasts, and a generally more elaborate cuisine than is described for social and domestic life elsewhere in North India (Khare 1976; Mayer 1960), are characteristic of pilgrimage centers like Govardhan. Local Brahman priests (*paṇḍās*) are skilled confectioners. One of *paṇḍās'* chief tasks is to advise pilgrims on offerings to be made in the local temple and to arrange and cook charitable feasts (*bhaṇḍārā*) for them. In Braj, males serve as professional cooks in sweet shops and temples and at feasts and other festive occasions as well. It is difficult to convey to a Western audience the joy and interest which food sparks in these surroundings. Giving and receiving invitations to feasts during peak pilgrimage periods connotes friendship among Brahman families. The size of feasts and the cost of their ingredients are a constant topic of conversation in the Brahman neighborhood (*mohallā*).[1] The reason for this is not simply that in the absence of consumer goods found in more industrialized sectors of Indian society, the largess of pilgrimage-related occupations is concentrated in food;[2] rather, Brahman epicurism springs from another, deeper cultural source: from an ideal of personhood know as *mastrāma*.

A *mastrāma* is a person who is *mast* (happy, lusty, proud, carefree, intoxicated); he enjoys a carefree lifestyle with a sense of physical and emotional well-being (*mastī*). For the *mastrāma,* four elements are essential to living the good life: eating tasty foods (*bhoga*), engaging in song and prayer (*bhajana*), drinking large amounts of *bhang* (an intoxicating beverage made from milk and the extract of cannibas leaves), and wrestling (*kuśtī*). Lynch (1990) tells us, instructively, that this ideal is a sensible and a sensual symbol—which is thought about and felt by *paṇḍās* in Braj and which has its origins in a tradition of good living that runs contrapuntally to the ascetic one in Sanskrit classical tradition. This ideal gains meaning from the *bhakti* notion that Krishna is manifest in the phenomenal world, that he is *saguṇa* (with form) rather than *nirguṇa* (without form). I would add to Lynch's discussion by saying that, in my opinion, the hypersensuality of the *mastrāma* ideal approximates a kind of inverse yoga. In a corporeally based religious system like this, divinity's presence is not experienced by suppressing the senses, but, rather, by activating and in some cases overloading them.[3] Unsurprisingly, this focus on sensual enjoyment leads to a conception of Krishna and his worshipers as connoisseurs (*rasikas*). It also helps explain why *Brajvāsī* Brahmans are so fond of bragging about their ability to consume large amounts of food and *bhang*.[4] In one extreme case I know, pet names of all the children in a *paṇḍā* family are based on names of local sweets.

For reasons which will become clear later in the paper, Mount Govardhan is host to several large food festivals each year. On festival days, the hillside is draped with row after row of viands; pilgrims turn out in droves to view the displays. Tourist photographs and Nathdwara-style cloth paintings, sold in Mathura, show Govardhan ubiquitously flanked by decorative food arrangements. "Why all this food?" one might ask. "Isn't it there simply to assuage rapacious *paṇḍās*?" By examining one large food festival, *Annakūṭa* (the Mountain of Food)—or *Govardhan Pūjā*, as it is sometimes known—this chapter will attempt to explain the significance, for Hindus, of this tendency towards gastro-hyperbolism.[5] This festival is closely associated with Govardhan in the Hindu calendar. The practice of making large offerings to Krishna has firm roots in Vaishnava cosmology and ritual.[6] A metonymy is established in *Annakūṭa* between the food offering itself and the way Krishna experiences his own blissful nature (*rasa*) through the emotions of devotees he brings into existence.[7] *Annakūṭa,* then, is best understood as a ritual or performance that enacts for viewers the theory of grace on which Krishna religious experience is based (Toomey 1990).

Annakūṭa can also be considered a reversal ritual. Such rituals, and, for that matter, the entire category of inversive symbolic forms, have been a focus of recent investigation in fields as far-ranging as anthropology, literary criticism, and art history (Babcock 1978). In many cultures, reversal rituals accompany season changes and other periods of transition, as, for example, do the Western Mardi Gras (DaMatta 1984) and *Holī* in Hindu North India (Marriott 1966). These rituals have been variously described by anthropologists, as "reversal rituals" (Turner 1969), "dramas of conflict" (Norbeck 1967), or "rituals of rebellion" (Gluckman 1969). Reversal rituals are marked by mockery, mimicry, and the ridiculing of one category of person or conception of the universe by another. They exhibit what Leach (1984) alludes to as "a systematic inversion of signs, a playing of everyday life from front to back." In this analysis, I shall depart both from the earlier functionalist view that these rituals are a form of cultural catharsis and from Victor Turner's notion that such rituals produce a feeling of "communitas" out of the collapse of logical categories (Turner 1969). I take, instead, a more interpretive approach to the problem, emphasizing the ritual's "metacommunicative" effects and reflexive value for members of Vaishnava society. By "interpretive," I mean that the interpreter, whether an anthropologist or an actor in a drama, has to go outside the text (a text can be a sentence, a story, a parade, a ritual) to understand its unstated or metacommunicative messages. Two interpreters with different backgrounds and understandings of a context might well arrive at different conclusions about the same situation or event.[8] This is more likely to be true of festivals, where interpreters are confronted with a confusing mass of performances all taking place at the same time.

My approach here follows a general trend in anthropology where it is not only the analyses which have opened up—in the sense of providing multiple perspectives—but the very subject matter itself which has changed. Anthropologists have increasingly turned their attentions to subject matter which is paradoxical, and hence susceptible of interpretation at several simultaneous levels.[9] In the past, anthropologists saw the logic of inversive symbolism as underscoring the moral correctness of social order. In this analysis, I shall argue instead that *Annakūṭa* plays across two systems of differences which operate in the Braj religious system. With respect to religious form, the rite comments on the full array of images in Vaishnava worship: seen and unseen images, as well as formally consecrated icons (that is, anthropomorphic images of Krishna either scultped (*mūrti*) or painted), and their opposite, images found in nature, like Mount Govardhan. *Annakūṭa* decenters or dislocates, oftentimes in an inverse manner, the visual orientations and much of the protocol reserved for worship of temple icons. On the social level, the rite aims at what Fernandez (1984), in another context, refers to as "transcendent humanization," a horizontal leveling of society. In the Govardhan context, transcendent humanization is brought about by sharing *prasāda*—food which is first transformed into Krishna's body and which signifies for devotees the love between Krishna and human beings of all ranks. In Braj mythology the miraculous transformation of ordinary food into Krishna's body takes place in the Govardhan myth. *Annakūṭa* re-creates this mythic event for pilgrims in festive time. By referring to the Govardhan myth, with all its naturalistic implications, and by incorporating archaic and folk ritual elements, *Annakūṭa* effectively transgresses rules of iconic ritual. A paradoxical middle ground is created in this ritual between the world of divinized nature (described in the myth) and the temple's structured ritual environment. This accounts for the easy transference in the ritual of human, animal, and vegetable forms. Opposing processes and assumptions, thrown up in the ritual's contradictory images, simultaneously justify multiple, even mutually exclusive interpretations. Folk and sectarian sources offer different interpretations of the feast. But, in general, *Annakūṭa* is best understood as a metacommentary on the relations of high to low, human to subhuman, divine to human, normal to abnormal. *Bhakti's* social ideal (the belief that all men are equal in their love of Krishna) gives unified shape to this metacommentary. Of course, this social ideal is occluded and only imperfectly realized in the everyday world of social reality.

This chapter describes *Annakūṭa*, as it is celebrated in popular and sectarian temples around Govardhan hill. In cases cited here all ritual specialists are Brahman priests.[11] This chapter opens with a discussion of the Braj pilgrimage setting and the Govardhan myth. This is followed by analysis of inversive and mediatory symbolism in the rite. The chapter's next section considers the actual food offerings: their variety and amounts, their manner of cooking and display by priests, and their distribution afterward to the public. The chapter's final section relates *Annakūṭa's* egalitarian social message and nonhierarchical ritual food practices to the "encompassing hierarchical order of Hindu society" (Dumont 1980). I conclude by comparing the approach used in this paper with that of several other recent studies of sects in South Asia.

Festive Menus in Krishna's Landscape of Memory

Leach's (1984) concluding remarks to a collection of essays by anthropologists on text and performance raise two basic points from which one could work in this account of Govardhan's pilgrimage setting. His first is that place should be added as a middle term in the relational link between myth and ritual (a link long recognized in anthropology since the time of Robertson-Smith); his second, that in their studies of festivals, anthropologists ought to give more attention to crowd behavior. On the first, Leach writes:

> It is not just that "places" serve to remind us of stories that are associated with them; in certain respects, the places only exist (in the sense that they are identified by name) *because* they have stories identified with them. But once they acquire this story-based existence, the landscape acquires the power of "telling the story." (Leach 1984, 356)

Much of what Leach says is true of Braj, the "pastureland" of Krishna's youth, where countless stories have been written and rewritten across and onto the region's sacred groves (*banas*), ponds (*kuṇḍas*), and hills (*pahāṛ*), and where pilgrims come to revel in the memories this landscape evokes. Pilgrimage in Mathura District, some ninety miles south of Delhi, operates on a subtle theory of memory: one in which the landscape is transformed into a living text (or, more correctly perhaps, a series of overlapping texts). Pilgrims express love for Krishna through the fourfold devotion (through name, form, sports, and abode: *nāma, rūpa, līlā, dhāma*). They visit *dhāma,* places where Krishna is reported to have sported in Braj; recall episodes of *līlā* in song, chanting, poetry, and oral recitation (*nama*); and worship Krishna's visual images (*rūpa*) in nature (e.g., bodies of water, trees, creepers, mountains), and in temples, paintings, and performances, such as *rāsa-līlā*.

Braj places are arranged in a 168-mile circular concourse, the *caurāsī kosa parikramā* (Growse 1883; Entwistle 1987). Myths and legends, culled from the expansive corpus of Vaishnava texts, are physically referenced on the region's sacred map. When pilgrims visit a particular site they seek to awaken in themselves an emotional memory of the *līlā* they believe took place there.[12] Of course, it is equally true that in Hindu thought and ritual places can be visited or events reexperienced, entirely on a mental plane—as they are in meditation or when a devotee listens to an account of *līlā*. Pilgrims frequently visit pilgrimage places one at a time (on festival days, for instance), but many also make *bana yātrā,* a journey round the entire Braj concourse which lasts up to forty days (Lynch 1988).

It ought to be clear by this point that Krishna worship has a firm grounding in sensual experience. Devotees participate in memories of Krishna's eternal *līlā* through a sophisticated and theatrical worship system which is characterized by synesthesia: the playing off of one sense, say sound, against such others as sight or taste. Rituals frequently put devotees in a "fused" sensual state where several senses, operating together, create an immediate and emotional perception of Krishna's presence. This process finds its most public expression in festivals—which brings us back to Leach's second point, concerning the festive behavior of crowds. For Leach, festivals combine aspects of tourism and pilgrimage in that they appeal to pilgrims' secular-commercial interests, as well as to their ecstatic-religious inclinations. He concludes, "It is because pilgrims gain satisfaction from what they see and hear, and from what they themselves perform, that such affairs are perpetuated." In Braj—and Leach's Kataragama—pilgrims are participants rather than spectators, unlike Western tourists who passively take in the spectacles at Disney World or the historical wax museum. Regrettably, anthropologists have not always been successful in capturing, at the level of the crowd, the infectious psychologism of festivals; this may be attributed, in part, to a lack of available theoretical models for doing so.

The crowd ethos takes over at Braj festivals. Masses of pilgrims, undifferentiated by caste or class, pour into sleepy Braj towns on festival days. Except for *Holī,* which is celebrated each spring, Braj's best known festivals take place in monsoon season, roughly from June to October (*cāturmāsa*), when "all the gods sleep in Braj." Towns and temples are renowned for the pomp and pagentry of their festivals: Mathura for Krishna's birthday (*Janmāṣṭamī*), Brindāban's many temples for their "swing festivals" (*Haryālī Tīj*), Barsānā for Radha's birthday (*Radhāṣṭamī*), Govardhan for its large festivals at the start and finish of rainy season. On festival days temple images and precincts are sedulously decorated and lit, food offerings and displays varied and sumptuous, and the atmosphere heightened by special songs (*rasiyā*), dances, and performances of *rāsa-līlā*. Festivals are highlights of the Braj pilgrimage year. Throughout the proceedings temple entrances are thronged by pilgrims who come to see the displays and enjoy the street performances.

In Braj folklore, local deities and festivals are signified by special foods; such dainties thus become "emblems" of the occasion at hand (Ferro-Luzzi 1977). Interestingly, Hindus believe that ingesting *prasāda* like this stirs pleasant memories of pilgrimage. This explains why, when they visit a site or attend a festival, pilgrims make certain to obtain sufficient quantities of *prasāda* to share with family and friends back home.[13] This tendency to link specific foods with Braj pilgrimage places finds its most elaborate expression in guidebooks of *Pushṭi Mārga Sampradāyȧ*. Guidebooks plot a gastro-topography of the region. This lends a smorgasbord-like effect to the sect's travels and enables pilgrims to apprehend (through various kinds of cross-sensory practices set out in these texts) memories of Krishna's earthy drama.

Myth, Ritual, and Place at Mount Govardhan

Mount Govardhan (literally "mountain of cow dung wealth") is a small hill only five miles long and one hundred feet high located in Braj's southwest corner. Pilgrimage here began in the sixteenth century, when Vallabhacarya and Caitanya, saintly preceptors of the *Pushṭi Mārga* and *Gauḍīya Vaishnava Sampradāyas,* established centers at opposite ends of the hill, in Jatipura and Radhakund respectively. Myths about the hill appear in the earliest texts which deal with Krishna's life in the region (Vaudeville 1976). Briefly recounted, in the Govardhan myth the boy Krishna persuades the Braj cowherds to make their annual offerings of harvest grains and pulses (*Annakūṭa*) to Mount Govardhan, instead of to Indra. Once the food is mountainously piled in front of the hill, Krishna miraculously splits in two: in his first identity he jumps into the hill, saying "I am Govardhan; Govardhan is me," and sucks in the food through a crack in the hill (known locally as *mukhāravinda,* "lotus mouth"); in the meantime, his alter ego remains stationed at the side of the hill, alongside other cowherds waiting to enjoy the bounteous feast. Afterward, angry Indra punishes the locals with rain. Sliding into his persona as "mountain holder" (*Giridhārī* or *Govardhananāthjī*), Krishna shelters locals from the torrential downpour by lifting the hill aloft on his fingertip.

Though *Giridhārī* is perhaps Krishna's most beloved image, my concern here is more with the myth's edible portions. The *Annakūṭa* episode in the myth is defined by a three-way metonymy, which links Krishna, the hill, and the *Annakūṭa* offering. As we shall see, this three-way image crops up repeatedly in the *Annakūṭa* celebration itself. Pictographs of *Annakūṭa,* sold throughout Braj (Figure 4.1), show this metonymy clearly. Krishna appears in two places at once in the illustration: Standing within a square niche inside the hill, and outside, kneeling to the left of the hill with his hands folded in prayer. To a certain degree this iconography can be said to reflect the processual formation of food ritual and the love relationship it signifies: the gift of food-love moves in a circle, from the cowherds to the hill Krishna-Govardhan and back to Krishna and the cowherds once more. The food-love metonymy also substantializes the circular process underlying devotional experience: Krishna, it is believed, creates devotees through his grace (*pushṭi*) in order that he might reflexively experience through their loving feelings his own blissful and loving nature (*ānanda*).

This three-way metonymy is also key to understanding the peculiar image in Govardhan's main temple (Mukuta Mukhāravinda Mandira)—the place where locals say the hill's mouth (*mukhāravinda*) is located. This temple image is made up by two stones. *Paṇḍās* explain that one stone is standing Krishna, with impressions of Krishna's crown (*mukuṭa*) in it; the second, a low-lying stone, is said to be Mount Govardhan, replete with the imprint of a mouth. In this temple the distinction between natural and iconic models of worship—rigidly adhered to in temples housing consecrated images—is blurred; here the image is treated half like a temple icon and half not. Unlike regular icons—which require tending by *pujārī* who dress and feed by the image at regular intervals throughout the day (Toomey 1986)—Mukuta Mukharavinda's stones are left unadorned for most of the day so that pilgrims can enter the temple and feed them directly with their own hands. *Paṇḍas* explain that, because the hill is Krishna in his "self-manifested" form (*svayaṃbhū*), no attention to priestly codes of purity and pollution is necessary to ensure the stones' continued sanctity. At four o'clock each afternoon, stones are dressed in the iconic fashion, as mirror images, with identical faces, costumes and jewelry (Figure 4.2). Thus, when the stones are rendered iconically, the two stones are seen as one (Eliade 1965).

I conclude this first section with a few remarks made by one of my *paṇḍā* informants at Govardhan. His comments should help pull together some of the complex ideas discussed thus far in the paper:

> Krishna is Govardhan, the hill is Krishna. We call him Krishna, Govardhan, Krishna-Govardhan: they all mean the same thing. Krishna's love for us is unending, vast as a mountain. He shows us this love by giving us the mountain of food you see in the temple today. The idea behind *Annakūṭa* is to offer all this goodness—the food and the love we put into it by saving for the feast in the neighborhood and cooking it for three days or more—back to Krishna, so he will make his love and our world continue to increase and grow. To keep these things—money, food, or love—to ourselves is selfish; by offering them, they multiply. At *Annakūṭa* we share everything we have with visitors to our temple. No priests or temples are mentioned in the *Govardhana-līlā,* so we consider *Annakūṭa* the freest, most spontaneous food offering there is. Like Krishna's grace, the feast just happens! On *Annakūṭa* nobody can be made to feel unloved or hungry; we make certain there is plenty of food and love to go around.[14]

Mediation, Inversion, and Other Forms of Symbolic Play in *Annakūṭa*

Annakūṭa incorporates numerous symbols, ranging from the archaic to the liminal and inversive. Eliade (1959) remarks that, in many cultures where they occur, "first fruits" festivals nearly always convey the sense of a temporary dissolution of cosmic and social order. In the following discussion, I deal first with symbols of mediation, such as those dealing with the timing of the ritual, and then with more complicated inversions: frame-switching and role and category reversals.

Symbols of Mediation

Govardhan's two major festivals occur at complementary nodes in the agricultural cycle; they are also linked, in interesting ways, to the Govardhan myth's two key segments. The first festival, *Asāḍa*

Figure 4.1. A Popular Illustration of the Govardhan Myth.

Figure 4.2. The Two Stone Images in Govardhan's Mukut Mukharavind Mandir Dressed as Mirror Images at the Time of *Sṛngār*.

Purṇimā (the "Full Moon of the Shaven Ascetics"), is celebrated at the start of the rainy season, on the full-moon day of June/July; the second, *Annakūṭa,* takes place on the first day of the bright fortnight of *Kārtika* (October-November). The two festivals stand in the relation of a vow, made at the start of rainy season when crops are planted, to a thanksgiving celebration for the bounteous crops which come at the end of this period. As regards the Govardhan myth, *Asāḍa Purṇimā* can almost certainly be identified with the onset of rain and with Krishna in his identity as mountain holder or protector from the rains; *Annakūṭa,* of course, reenacts the harvest banquet described in the myth.[15] *Annakūṭa's* auspicious properties are ensured by the fact that the feast occurs in the interval between the end of one crop rotation and the start of another.[16] Implied here is food without beginning or end: a horn of plenty resulting from a poignant moment in the continuing ecological course.

Annakūṭa occupies a similar mediating position in the Hindu calendar. Like *Dīwālī*—the pan-Indian festival of Lakshmi, the Goddess of Wealth—which it follows by a day, *Annakūṭa,* too, is associated with wealth. It will be remembered that Govardhan hill itself is regarded in most traditions as a veritable storehouse of food, wealth, and other sensory pleasures (*bhoga*). The day of the month on which *Annakūṭa* occurs is also significant: the first day of the bright half of a lunar month is that pivotal day when the waning moon begins to wax, making it an astronomical moment rife with possibilities for obtaining wealth and having one's earthly desires fulfilled.

Annakūṭa belongs to a constellation of festivals which occur at the end of rainy season and which signal a shift from the values of asceticism, deemed necessary in this season, to the ritual concerns of householders (*gṛhasta*). Hindus believe that it is inauspicious to perform life rites (*saṃskāras*) and other Vedic rituals during *cāturamāsa.* The four months of rainy season are given over, instead, to pilgrimage and other kinds of pious devotional activities, not having to do with one's status as a householder; thus, from the ritual standpoint, the entire culture undergoes a kind of enforced asceticism in this period. The procession of newly shaven ascetics, a central performance of *Asāḍa Purṇimā,* refers to an ancient custom which required ascetics not to wander about freely in this season, resting in one spot to muster the physical strength to move on after the rains. By contrast, festivals at the end of rainy season promote family and domestic values. Houses and temples undergo a "spring cleaning" on *Dhana Teras* (the "wealthy thirteenth")—

earthen pots from the old year are broken and new ones are purchased. Family solidarity is proclaimed in *Bhaiyā Doj,* a protection ritual celebrated in Mathura on the day following *Annakūṭa.* On this occasion brothers and sisters join hands and bathe together in the Jamuna. In mythology the river is Yami, sister of Yama, the Hindu god of death. Thus, females invoke the river to intercede with Yama on behalf of their brothers. Time symbols discussed throughout this section all appear to express the same idea: wealth gained from pilgrimage activities in the old year will multiply in the year to come.

Frame Switching

The way basic elements of icon worship are rearranged in *Annakūṭa* is certainly one of the ritual's more notable symbolic features. *Annakūṭa* decenters the iconic model, drawing attention away from solo icons to Govardhan hill and the food offering. Pilgrims' attention is divided in this rite between Govardhan hill, the mountainous food display in the temple courtyard, and the distant temple icon, which presides over the festivities from its niche inside the temple. The display is circular, rather than frontal or lateral, as is the case when the display is arranged with the icon at its center. At Govardhan, where the actual hill is present, it is referenced in the ritual; at other places in Braj a single Govardhan stone is substituted for the hill; when a stone is not available—outside Braj, for example—the hill and the food offering are signified by the food display's metaphoric shape. The visual focus of the rite is a huge pile of rice (around which breads and sweets, and dishes prepared from grains and vegetables, are arranged in a circle) erected in the temple courtyard or in some such public place. That the display is detachable, in a visual sense, from the temple icon, is brought home in the common practice of celebrating the ritual outside the temple altogether. When this is done, the food display is constructed at the side of Govardhan hill, and the temple icon is taken out of his sanctuary to view the display from atop a ceremoniously decorated palanquin.

At Jatipura, great fanfare attends the arrival of *Gokulnāthajī,* one of *Pushṭi Mārga's* seven prized icons, who makes a special trip to Govardhan on this occasion from his permanent residence across the river at Gokul.[17] At the time of the display, the gates of *Gokulnāthajī havelī,* which flank side of the hill, are thrown open, admitting crowds of pilgrims who come to view the proceedings and the temple itself, which is usually off limits to those outside the sect.[18] Here, the triple images of the Govardhan myth are lined up three in a row: the majestic *Gokulnāthjī* icon, at one end, faces Govardhan hill at the other, across a ten-foot-high pile of rice in the center of the temple courtyard. Pilgrims are mesmerized, not by the splendidly dressed icon, as would normally be the case, but by the mountainous food display in their midst.

Symbols of Inversion

A range of inversive symbols and behaviors is found in *Annakūṭa*. These inversions add to the ritual's overall sense of ambiguity, helping to create a ritual environment full of possibilities for symbolic transformation and multiple interpretation.

The role of *pujārī* is downplayed in *Annakūṭa*. In some cases Brahman *pujārī* dress as cowherds (*gopā*); in others still, an actual cowherd is invited into the temple to preside over the ritual. *Annakūṭa* at Jatipura's *Gokulnāthajī havelī* ends on a climactic note when a local Brahman, dressed in a *gopā* costume, dives into the rice mound, from a balcony above the courtyard. In other temples, in the act known as *lūṭnā* (the "stealing"), pilgrims are permitted to dismantle the display by rushing in and taking as much food away as they can carry. In Nāthdwārā's *Shrināthajī havelī,* only Meena and Bhil tribesmen are extended this privilege, out of respect for the help they gave Rana Raj Singh of Mewar in protecting Nāthdwārā from the Moguls. Tribals save portions of dried rice to which they attribute special magical and medicinal powers. These acts of ritual stealing refer, of course, to Krishna's identity as the mischievous "butter thief" (*mākhancor*), who snitches butter, milk, and curds from his foster mother Yashoda and from the *gopīs,* his cowmaiden consorts.

In temples all over Braj, an effigy of Krishna-Govardhan (usually with one arm raised, in his *Giridhārī* posture) is constructed out of cow dung at a place near the central food display. This same cow-dung figure is the focus of a domestic ritual performed by women on this day in homes throughout North India. Newly harvested crops, it is believed, should not be eaten until they have first been offered to this cow-dung effigy. At dusk on the day of *Govardhan Pūjā,* women and children in each household courtyard circle the figure, singing folk songs and shouting slogans, such as *"Shrī Girirāja Mahāraja kī Jai!"* (Hail to Govardhan, King of Hills!), in praise of the mighty hill. The image, surrounded on four sides by walls, has an appendage of some sort hanging between its legs; by some accounts, this is a phallus, by others a cow's tail. In any event, this hybrid image makes reference to Krishna's identity as cosmic creator. At one point in the proceedings at Govardhan's Makuta Mukhāravinda Mandira, a local cowherd leads a cow, coquettishly adorned with bells and flower garlands around its neck, into the temple precincts. Spectators sing spirited folk songs (*hīro*), as the cow prances around the food display and tramples the cow-dung effigy beneath its hoofs (Mittal 1966; Satyendra 1968). Remnants of the cow-dung effigy are saved and rolled into crackers which are attached later in the spring to the *Holī* bonfire.

Beyond lending an obviously folkish touch to *Annakūṭa,* this intrusion of elements from domestic ritual raises a number of compelling issues. To me, it is perfectly in keeping with the "genre-mixing" we find throughout this ritual. After all, *Bhakti* is known for incorporating idioms of erotic and familial love into the public sphere. This example may lead us to draw the conclusion that the community of Vaishnava worshipers shares the love of a happy family, writ large. Lest this interpretation seem too far fetched, *Pushṭi Mārgīs* refer to themselves as *"Vallabha-kula,"* Vallabha's family; and, one of the sect's prized possessions is a cow (*"Gaumātā"* or Mother Cow) which is believed to be directly descended from cows of Krishna's original herd.

The greatest source of symbolic dislocation in *Annakūṭa* comes from the display of *kaccā* foods (that is, rice, grains, and vegetables boiled in water) in the temple's open courtyard. Following DaMatta (1984, 213), "dislocation" refers to the capacity of an object to become the focus of strong allusions when it passes from one domain to another quite removed and contradictory in terms of a given social system. This same author goes on to note:

> The distance between domains calls attention to the object, transforming it. Understanding dislocation [the heart of the symbolizing process] as the critical mechanism in the transformation of objects into symbols is basic to our understanding of what a rite is. (DaMatta 1984, 213)

In contrast to most other large food festivals in Braj, where *pakkā* fare (foods cooked in or with cow products) is central, *Annakūṭa* is the sole occasion where *kaccā* food is displayed. In most ritual circumstances, rice is offered to temple deities only behind closed doors, unobserved even by *pujārī.*[19] *Annakūṭa* is the only occasion in the entire ceremonial year when *kaccā* food is offered to *Balarāma's* icon at nearby Baldev. This popular image, like most *Brajvāsīs,* considers himself a *mastrāma* and prefers *bhang* and sweets to simple boiled foods. Succinctly stated, visual display of a category of food, which is hedged with prohibition in most commensal situations and in a space which is defined as public, underscores, in ritual terms, the Govardhan myth's strongly egalitarian message.

These points are beautifully condensed in an *Annakūṭa* illustration (Figure 4.3) taken from a *Pushṭi Mārga* manual on temple ritual (Shivajī, ed. 1936). At the top of the illustration, the old *Shrināthajī havelī* stands poised on a pinnacle of Govardhan hill, looking down over the food display below. The picture's foreground and background are knitted together by cowherds and cows roaming about in the picture's middle ground. Ritual, which is normally confined to the microcosmic Braj of the *havelī's* interior (for, in this sect, temple floor plans re-create Braj topography), is here turned out-of-doors. Annakūṭa plows divinity back into nature in a vision of pastoral harmony. Absent entirely are visual references to Vallabhacarya, the sect's founder, his priestly descendants, the Goswamis, and other mainstays of the sect's iconographic repertoire. Even Krishna himself is not iconically represented: the semiotic message being that he is contained in the circle formed by the half-circles of the hill and the food display. At the center of this circle, stands a cow, suckling her calf. This is a provocative, naturalistic statement for a sect, acknowledged by itself and by other Hindus, to be the iconophiles *par excellence* of Krishna worship.

Annakūṭa Food Practices

Moving now to the level of practice, this discussion of food offerings should highlight differences between *Pushṭi Mārga's* fully iconic model of food ritual and the popular model found in Mukuta Mukhāravinda Temple. The discussion should also reveal how Brahmans try to mask disorderly elements in the ritual by continuing to make use of food categories in the display, and how they have also developed a social framework for sharing expensive foods once the display is over.

Annakūṭa in the *Pushṭi Mārga* sect is sponsored by the Gokul Goswami, who presides over the sect's house (*gaddī*). The feast is

Figure 4.3. *Annakūṭa* illustration taken from a *Pushṭi Marga* manual on temple ritual.

paid for through large donations given by the Goswami's wealthier disciples and by selling small portions of *prasāda* to his other disciples. *Annakūṭa* and other large food offerings, it is believed by members of the sect, are given to honor the temple icon. By contrast, local, or "village," *Annakūṭa* is supported through a collection in the *paṇḍā* neighborhood.

In general, *Pushṭi Mārga* has a more elaborate cuisine than is found in the local temple. Sectarian priests adhere to strict protocol when food is offered and displayed in front of the icon. *Gokulnāthajī Annakūṭa* takes twenty-one days to prepare. Cooks are imported from outside of Jatipura to assist the *haveli's* regular staff. Foods are subdivided into seven or eight categories, ranked on a sliding scale of purity. Sun-ripened fruits, rock sugar, and nuts of various kinds, which do not require cooking of any kind, are considered most pure, followed, in turn, by sweets and other dishes made with milk, and finally, by grains and vegetables. The broadest division in the sect's cuisine is between *ansakharī* (grains and vegetables cooked in milk or ghee, with no water added) and *sakharī* (food cooked in or with water) preparations. Cooks prepare time-consuming sweets first, waiting till the last day to cook more perishable boiled foods. More than fifty baskets each are offered in the *ansakharī* and *sakharī* categories. Many of the same recipes appear in both categories. An average recipe is made in eighty-pound quantities. Of course, salt and spices are never used in the sect's cooking, because these are believed to be injurious to the deity's sensitive child's palate.

Arranging the food in front of the icon takes six or seven hours to complete. Food is displayed in utensils, like earthen jugs, vine-woven baskets, and silver plates, which, it is thought, possess high ritual valences. Fruits, nuts, pickles, and preserves are placed on small silver plates in front of the deity. The icon stands in front of an enormous painted scene of Govardhan (*pichvāī*). Elsewhere in the sanctum, rows of *ansakharī* offerings are arranged. Outside the sanctuary doors, which are flanked by stalks of fresh sugar cane and festooned with hanging strings of mango leaves, a large space has been left clear. At the center of the courtyard stands a ten-foot-high mound of rice, around which two rows of earthenware jugs and three rows of baskets, all containing *sakharī* food, are arranged. There are twenty baskets in each row; foods cooked in peanut oil are placed in one row, boiled foods in another.

The sect's skill in food arrangement is unsurpassed in Hindu gastronomy. *Pushṭi Mārga Annakūṭa* is a truly harmonious display.

The mound of white rice at the center of the display sets off the autumn golds, oranges, and greens of the cooked grains and vegetables, and the various shapes of jars and baskets. With the display set in place, priests depart from the temple precincts to permit the icon time to consume the offering in private. Pilgrims are permitted to view the display between two and five o'clock in the afternoon. After the display is over, pilgrims are given leaf plates of rice, curries, and stewed vegetables. Sweets and other fried foods are returned to the *havelī* storeroom and priced according to weight and the ingredients used in their preparation. Pilgrims who want to do so can purchase sweets at fixed prices. Later the same evening, the Gokul Goswami hosts a large feast for his staff and members of his entourage. At the close of the day, large amounts of sweets are taken away by followers; the remainder is sent by mail to the Goswami's other disciples.

The celebration of *Annakūṭa* in Govardhan's Mukuta Mukhāravinda Temple is in most respects a simpler affair. Food is cooked by five *paṇḍās* in a large open space in front of temple committee headquarters. *Kaccā* and *pakkā* are the only good categories observed here. Whereas *Pushṭi Mārga* cooks prepare seven or eight different recipes for popular dishes like *khīra* (rice pudding), local cooks prepare only one. Dishes, particularly in the *pakkā* category, are made in three flavors: sweet, bland, and salty or spicy. The arrangement is completed by the waving of an oil lamp (*āratī*); at no time in the proceedings is an effort made to shield the image from public view. While the formal orientation of the sect's icon dictates a display marked by lateral symmetry, in the local display foods are arranged in circular patterns around the stone images. In fact, the temple itself has two doors, placed at right angles to each other: the first door faces the standing stone, the second, the smaller stone with the *mukhāravinda* seal. *Pakkā* foods are arranged in the sanctum according to flavor—sweets in one place, salty snacks, in another, and so on. A line of turmeric, drawn at the doors to the sanctuary, separates *pakkā* foods inside from the pile of rice and other *kaccā* offerings arranged outside on a platform in front of the temple. Offerings are placed in an assortment of aluminum and other utensils borrowed from local homes for the occasion.

Pilgrims are given *khicṛī prasāda*—a mixture of rice, lentils, and curries. Later the same afternoon, *paṇḍās* hold a neighborhood feast where fried breads, stewed vegetables, sweets, and other snacks are served. The remaining sweets are weighed and distributed on a donation basis in the neighborhood. As one *paṇḍā* observes, preference for *pakkā* food in *Annakūṭa* has grown steadily over the years:

> In the past twenty-five years or so, the trend in *Annakūṭa,* and with feasts in general, has been toward a higher percentage of *pakkā* preparations. *Kaccā* food, like lentils, curries, barley, and rice, are mainstays of the feast. The change has come about as more sweet preparations have been introduced. In earlier times, the proportion of *kaccā* to *pakkā* offerings was more balanced. But, today, *pakkā* appears to be winning out. Of course, *pakkā* food is required to help defray the cost of the feast. It is our feeling that *Annakūṭa* is a special feast for the *paṇḍā* neighborhood. Before the festival, donations are collected from local families, and the temple committee prepares the requisite amount of food for the feast. Earlier *Annakūṭa* seldom cost more than Rs. 400 or 500. Last year we spent Rs. 1,600; this year we expect to spend over Rs. 2,000. *Paṇḍās* who choose to do so are free to sell their share of *pakkā* food to visiting pilgrims, but this is not common practice.[20]

Pakkā food has undoubtedly been added in both sectarian and popular celebrations for pecuniary reasons. The strategy whereby *kaccā* is distributed to pilgrims free-of-charge but *pakkā* is reserved by priests for their own use would appear to compromise the feast's egalitarian objectives. But however true this is—and it is true from the standpoint of priests' motives—*Annakūṭa* will continue to impart its egalitarian message, as long as rice and other boiled foods are displayed outside the temple sanctuary. Priests' attempts to order foods by category takes on a paradoxical cast when this essential fact is considered. Lastly, there is a touch of irony in priests' fondness for *pakkā* over *kaccā* food which is considered exclusive in ordinary commensal situations, is rendered inclusive in the *Annakūṭa* feast; conversely, priests' commercial interests render the normally inclusive *pakkā* category exclusive. Thus, even this modification reflects the same inversive quality for which *Annakūṭa* is known.

Conclusion

A number of conclusions can be drawn from this interpretation of a major Braj festival. Parry (1974, 118) finds fault with Dumont's

(1980) notion that Hindu caste society is based on the hierarchical opposition between purity and impurity. In Parry's estimation, this model neglects those sectors of Indian society whose ideology plays down, or even repudiates, the values of hierarchy. As I have stated repeatedly throughout this chapter, Krishna *bhakti* is one such area of Indian social life. What results from *Annakūṭa* and other similar nonhierarchical rituals, like *Holī,* is not a clear alternative to hierarchy but an indeterminate system which reshuffles and mixes traditional symbolic elements and ritual logic. In *Annakūṭa,* Dumont's monolithic purity/impurity contrast is relativized, becoming in the process a single strand embedded in a dense skein of symbols. Other symbols which are called into play include: opposition between natural and iconic images and the grounding of religious experience in sensory experience. Even among Krishna worshippers, what one sect considers "pure" may not have much significance for members of other sects or for ordinary worshippers generally. The *Annakūṭa* ritual comments on this by foregrounding elite and popular traditions alike in the earthiness of the Govardhan myth.

Allowing, of course, for their radically different historical contexts, the mixing of ritual styles we find in *Annakūṭa* can possibly be compared to the breakdown of the classical doctrine of the "separation of styles" in early Christian tradition (Auerbach 1968). This doctrine depended on a strict separation into different stylistic levels all that was "high"—grandiloquent, stylized, rhetorical—from the "low," unfiltered life of the masses. Christianity posed an alternative, indeterminate decorum to this based on Christ's paradoxical fusion of divine and human elements. Auerbach (1968, 272–276) traces this "mingling of styles" in Dante's realism, in miracle plays where Christ's passion is juxtaposed to crude farce, and in Rabelais' "promiscuous intermingling of the categories of event, experience, and knowledge which demonstrates the vitalistic-dynamic triumph of the physical body and its functions." With unruly mobs in the cities and barbarians at its gates, early Christianity seized upon the crumbling decorum of the classical world to create a novel system of decorum with indeterminacy, or ambivalence, as its norm. For Auerbach, Christianity created this new system by showing that the highest sublimity was compatible with the humblest forms of sensory life. This transfiguring discovery shattered the class distinctions and symbolic order on which the classical world depended. There are similarities here with the *bhakti* resurgence in sixteenth-century India, a movement which managed to pull the Hindu masses together against the Muslim invaders that were then sweeping across North India. *Bhakti,* like early Christianity described by Auerbach, created a symbolic order which made greater use of vernacular languages and which transformed sensory images into bearers of religious ideas and sentiments.

There have been several studies of Hindu sectarian movements in recent years. The focus of Pocock's (1973) and Williams's (1984) studies is on sectarian leadership, showing how leaders accommodate, over time, values of the encompassing social order. Other studies (Bennett 1983; Cantlie 1984) take a different approach, viewing sectarian membership in isolation from the wider society. This approach tends to wrap the community and their ritual practices in Durkheimian assumptions.[21] In this interpretation of *Annakūṭa* I have tried to explain priests' actions and motivations against a background of publicly shared symbols. I have also attempted to show that sects and their followers are not easily separated from the popular tradition going on around them. Conversely, on *Annakūṭa,* the public, in the form of teeming masses of pilgrims, is thrust for a brief moment into the sectarian sphere. In doing so, the rite questions sects' ideological assumptions about love and equality. Future studies of sects need to turn their attentions away from priestly and ascetic leaders to the "outer rim" of the sect, where members' personal commitments to the sect's beliefs and practices cut across other social ties and obligations. Anthropologists cannot look only to priests and to priestly sources for understanding, but, like the *Gokulnāthajī* icon during *Annakūṭa,* should offset this tendency by looking out to the crowd, for answers to new and exciting questions.

Acknowledgments

Data on which this chapter is based were gathered from January 1979 to March 1980, during which time the author conducted anthropological fieldwork at Mount Govardhan (District Mathura, U.P.). This research was funded by a doctoral dissertation grant of the American Institute of Indian Studies. I am grateful to R. S. Khare, who has guided this paper, and others besides, with a "chef's touch." I also wish to thank Alan Entwistle, Shrivasta Goswami, John Stratton Hawley, Owen Lynch, and Charlotte Vaudeville for sharing their knowledge of Braj with me over the past several years.

Notes

1. Pilgrims contract *paṇḍās* to arrange these feasts. Giving a feast is a meritorious act associated in the Govardhan context with Krishna-Govardhan's having granted the pilgrim a boon. Before the feast, a pilgrim presents his *paṇḍā* with a specific allotment of cash; raw foodstuffs, such as sugar and flour, are sometimes presented as well. A pilgrim donor usually specifies the number of guests he wants invited to the feast. Feasts are priced according to the menu being served and the number of anticipated guests. *Paṇḍās* naturally prefer it when pilgrims leave most of the decision making about a feast in their hands. When *paṇḍās* have control of a feast they usually opt for more expensive food and fewer guests. A *paṇḍā's* closest male friends and their families are nearly always invited to feasts given by his pilgrim clients. Thus, the best index of factionalism in the neighborhood is to see who invites whom to feasts.

2. It is difficult to gauge *paṇḍās* wealth. Most *paṇḍās* live in the same simple whitewashed mud brick houses. In reality a *paṇḍā's* wealth is determined by the wealth of his pilgrim clients (*jajmāna*) and the frequency of their visits to the town. Rich *paṇḍās* have often taken me into their homes and shown me consumer goods like tape recorders and transistor radios which they keep hidden away in closets. It is perfectly in keeping with *paṇḍas'* public image as simple rustics that they hide such consumer items from pilgrims' view. Most *paṇḍās* agreed, however, that the best way to find out about a *paṇḍā's* economic status is to show up at his home at mealtimes.

3. *Bhāng* and sweets addiction go hand in hand in the *paṇḍā* community. *Paṇḍās* exhibit a high degree of tolerance for *bhāng* addiction and other similar forms of eccentric behavior. Such extreme attitudes ought, of course, to be taken into account in cultural studies of addiction now being carried out in India.

4. There is a saying around Govardhan: *"Anyaur ké nau, aur gāon ké sau"* (literally, "nine men of Anyaur [a village located on the opposite side of the hill from Jatipura] can eat more than hundreds of ordinary villagers").

5. *Annakūṭa* is one of several large food festivals held in Braj. Others include *Kunvarāu* (an engagement party for Krishna) and *Chappan Bhoga* (a wedding feast), given by members of the *Pushṭi Mārga Sampradāya; Chattīsa Vyanjana* (the "thirty-six delicacies"), found mainly in temples of the *Gaudīya* sect; and *byāurū,* a wedding feast for Radha and Krishna given in the Radhāvallabha temple at Brindāban. For similar examples of food hyberbole in Western sources, see Bakhtin (1984) on Rabelais.

6. Rām and Krishna are the main *avatāras* of Lord Vishnu. Krishna worshippers are therefore classified as Vaishnavas. This distinguishes them from Saivites and Shaktas, followers of Shiva and the goddess. The

terms of Krishna worshipper and Vaishnava are used interchangeably throughout this chapter.

7. In contrast to a metaphor, which suggests a likeness or analogy between two different objects or ideas, in a metonymy, the name of one thing is used for that of another of which it is an attribute or with which it is associated. Religious rituals are frequently full of examples of metonymies. In *Annakūṭa,* for example, Govardhan acts as a metonym for Lord Krishna because the hill is closely identified with him in Krishna mythology.

8. For example, Bennett's (1983, 1990) excellent ethnography of *Pushṭi Mārga* temples at Ujjain (M.P.) offers a more Durkheimian interpretation of this sect's *Annakūṭa* celebration than the present study does.

9. Geertz's (1973, 412–453) definition of metacommentary as a questioning, a dispute, or at least a comment on the existing order of things is now widely accepted in anthropological discourse. Much can be also be learned in this area from literary criticism. I quote from Harpham (1982, 187):

> Meaning is made through connections, by linking something with something else outside itself; it is made by establishing relations both within and outside the text, by ascribing intentionality to things that do not inherently possess it, and by seeing elements in contexts other than the ones in which they occur, by seeing one thing as another.

10. Boon (1984) remarks that, opposed to the worldview which is linear, sequential, causal, unified, and normal, there are areas of social life, such as festivals and anthropology, that are nonlinear, open, and radically plural—where everything is happening at the same time, where images are as significant as words, and where plural voices rather than monologic speech is heard.

11. Ritual inversion is a more noticeable feature in priestly traditions than in traditions where ascetics (*sādhus*) are the dominant ritual specialists. I omitted mention of *Gauḍīya* celebrations at Radhākuṇḍ for reasons of length. Members of the *Gauḍīya* sect claim Mādhavendra Purī, a twelfth-century saint, brought this ritual to Govardhan from Puri in eastern India. Rice is the main offering at Jagganath Purī and has there all the time the inclusive properties which it does here only during *Annakūṭa* festivities.

12. Braj is not without its controversies, particularly in respect of where such and such an episode in Krishna's *līlā* is thought to have taken place. Vaishnava texts are a storehouse for Deconstructionist scholars, as one tradition pulls out the rug from another over such matters. The location of the hill's mouth (*mukhāravinda*) is a very good illustration of this. In the folk tradition the mouth appears as an impression (*cinha*) in a stone in the Mukuṭa Mukhāravinda Temple, a temple located in Mānasī Gangā, a pond at the center of the hill. By contrast, *Pushṭi Mārgīs* locate

mukhāravinda at the Jatipurā end of the hill. They also say this is the same spot where the sect's prized *Shrināthjī* icon first appeared. Traditions differ on sites of many other *līlās* as well. Best known, perhaps, is the debate over where Krishna's moonlight circle dance (*mahārāsa-līlā*) took place; for *Gauḍiyas* it took place on the banks of the Jamuna at Brindāban, whereas *Pushṭi Mārgīs* say it took place at Candrasarovara (Moon Tank), a small octagon-shaped pond near the village of Parasoli.

13. *Pushṭi Mārgīs* are particularly dedicated to the practice of obtaining *prasāda* from festivals in their sect. This sect attracts an enthusiatic following in western India, especially among urban business communities in parts of Uttar Pradesh, Gujarat, Rajasthan, Malwa, and Bombay (Bennett 1983). Whenever the sect sponsors a large food display, followers who are unable to accompany their *gurus* on pilgrimage request to have leftover offerings from the display shipped to them by mail: so they can "absorb from afar the Braj *līlā* enjoyed by their fellow *satsangis*."

14. Babu Lal Sharma, Das Bisa Mohalla, Govardhan, interview, October 14, 1979.

15. In his study of crowd behavior, Canetti (1962) lists rain and the festive banquet as "crowd symbols," together with fire and the field of corn. He maintains that once a spark has been set off, these symbols tend to focus the attention of a crowd and to carry the action along.

16. These are the rainy season crop (*kharīf*), sown in July and harvested in October, and the winter crop (*rabī*), sown in the fall after monsoon has ended and harvested around *Holī,* in March or April. Monsoon crops include the following: rice, several kinds of millet, barley, corn, lentils, sorghum, peanuts, sugar cane, cotton, sweet potatoes, tomatoes, and chili peppers. Wheat, gram, mustard, peas, and carrots are winter season crops.

17. The *Gokul Gaddī* has a colorful history, which sets it apart, in many senses, from other branches of *Pushṭi Mārga*. Gokulnatha was Viṭṭhalnatha's fourth son and a grandson of Vallabhacārya. He was a prolific author and a powerful figure in the sect's early history. The practice of looking on Vallabha's male descendants as incarnations of Krishna may have started with this Goswami. Even today, his descendants and their twenty thousand followers distinguish themselves from the sect's other branches by reciting a variation of the *Brahma-saṃbandha mantra* at initiation and wearing a different form of the sect's marker (*tilaka*) on their foreheads. Worship in the *Gokulnāthajī havelī* is also slightly different. *Gokulnāthajī* is a four-armed image of Krishna, playing a flute with one arm and holding a ball of butter in another. He is gold in color, attended on both sides by female figures.

18. *Pushṭi Mārga* temples are known as *havelī,* "palaces" or "mansions," rather than *mandira*.

19. In one Braj temple *pujārīs* so fear the pollution which serving and eating rice brings that they remove the temple icon to a special eating chamber, adjacent to the main sanctum, when *kaccā* food is being offered.

20. Guri Ram Master, local schoolteacher and *paṇḍā,* interview, October 9, 1979.

21. Owen M. Lynch, personal communication.

References

Auerbach, Erich
1968 *Mimesis: The Representation of Reality in Western Literature.* Princeton: Princeton University Press.

Babcock, Barbara A., ed.
1978 *The Reversible World.* Ithaca, N.Y.: Cornell University Press.

Bakhtin, Mikhail
1984 *Rabelais and His World.* Tr. Helene Iswolsky. Bloomington, Ind.: Indiana University Press.

Bennett, Peter
1983 *Temple Organization and Worship Among the Puṣṭimārgīya-Vaiṣṇavas of Ujjain.* London: Ph.D. dissertation, School of Oriental and African Studies, University of London.

1990 "In Nanda Baba's House: The Devotional Experience in Pushṭi Mārg Temples." In *Divine Passions: The Social Construction of Emotion in India.* Owen M. Lynch, ed. 182–211. Berkeley and Los Angeles: University of California Press.

Boon, James
1984 "Folly, Bali, and Anthropology, or Satire Across Cultures." In *Text, Play, and Story: The Construction and Reconstruction of Self and Society.* Edward M. Bruner, ed. 150–177. Washington, D.C.: The American Ethnological Society.

Bruner, Edward M., ed.
1984 *Text, Play, and Story: The Construction and Reconstruction of Self and Society.* Washington, D.C.: The American Ethnological Society.

Canetti, Elias
1962 *Crowds and Power.* New York: Viking Press.

Cantlie, Audrey
1981 "The Moral Significance of Food among Assamese Hindus." In *Culture and Morality: Essays in Honour of Christoph von Furer-Haimendorf,* Adrian C. Mayer, ed. 42–62. New Delhi: Oxford University Press.

1984 *The Assamese: Religion, Caste, and Sect in an Indian Village*. London and Dublin: Curzon Press.

DaMatta, Roberto
1984 "Carnival in Multiple Planes." In *Rite, Drama, Festival, Spectacle: Rehearsals Toward a Theory of Cultural Performance*. John J. MacAloon, ed. 208–240. Philadelphia: Institute for the Study of Human Issues.

Dumont, Louis
1980 *Homo Hierarchicus: The Caste System and its Implications*. trans. Mark Sainsbury, Louis Dumont, and Basia Gulati. Chicago: University of Chicago Press.

Eliade, Mircea
1959 *Cosmos and History: The Myth of the Eternal Return*. trans. William R. Trask. New York: Harper & Row.

1965 *The Two and the One*. trans. J. M. Cohen. New York: Harper & Row.

Entwistle, A. W.
1987 *Braj: Centre of Krishna Pilgrimage*. Groningen: Egbert Forsten.

Fernandez, James
1984 "Convivial Attitudes: The Ironic Play of Tropes in an International Kayak Festival in Northern Spain." In *Text, Play, and Story: The Construction and Reconstruction of Self and Society*. Edward M. Bruner, ed. 356–364. Washington, D.C.: The American Ethnological Society.

Ferro-Luzzi, G. Eichinger
1977 Ritual as Language: The Case of South Indian Food Offerings." *Current Anthropology* 18:507–24.

Geertz, Clifford
1973 *The Interpretation of Cultures*. New York: Basic Books.

Gluckman, Max
1969 *Customs and Conflict*. Manchester: Manchester University Press.

Growse, Frederick Salmon
1883 *Mathura: A District Memoir*. 3rd edition. Allahabad: North-western Provinces and Oudh Government Press.

Harpham, Geoffrey Galt
1982 *On the Grotesque: Strategies of Contradiction in Art and Literature*. Princeton: Princeton University Press.

Khare, R. S.
1976 *The Hindu Hearth and Home*. Durham, N.C.: Carolina Academic Press.

Leach, Edmund

1984 "Conclusion: Further Remarks on the Realm of Folly." In *Text, Play, and Story: The Construction and Reconstruction of Self and Society.* Edward M. Bruner, ed. 356–364. Washington, D.C.: The American Enthnological Society.

Lynch, Owen M.

1988 Pilgrimage with Krishna, Sovereign of the Emotions." *Contributions to Indian Sociology* n.s. 22(2):171–194.

1990 "The Ideal of the *Mastrām* Among Mathura's Chaubes." In *Divine Passions: The Social Construction of Emotion in India.* Owen M. Lynch, ed. 91–116. Berkeley and Los Angeles: University of California Press.

Marriott, McKim

1966 "The Feast of Love." In *Krishna: Myths, Rites, and Attitudes.* Milton Singer, ed. 200–212. Honolulu: East-West Center Press.

Mayer, Adrian C.

1960 *Caste and Kinship in Central India.* London: Routledge and Kegan Paul.

Norbeck, Edward

1967 "African Rituals of Conflict." In *Gods and Rituals.* John Middleton, ed. 197–226. Austin: University of Texas Press.

Parry, Jonathan

1974 "Egalitarian Values in a Hierarchical Society." *South Asian Review* 7(2):95–121.

Pocock, David

1973 *Mind, Body, and Wealth.* Oxford: Basil Blackwell.

Tambiah, S. J.

1981 "A Performative Approach to Ritual." *Proceedings of the British Academy* 65. 113–169. London and Oxford: Oxford University Press.

Toomey, Paul M.

1986 "Food from the Mouth of Krishna: Socio-Religious Aspects of Food in Two Krishnaite Sects." In: *Food, Society, and Culture: Aspects in South Asian Food Systems.* R. S. Khare and M. S. A. Rao, eds. 55–83. Durham, N.C.: Carolina Academic Press.

1988 "Rediscovering Braj in the Anthropological Imagination." In *Rediscovering Braj, IAVRI Bulletin no. 14.* A Entwistle, ed. 26–32. London: International Association of the Vrindaban Research Institute, School of Oriental and African Studies, University of London.

1990 "Krishna's Consuming Passions: Food as Metaphor and Metonym for Emotion at Mount Govardhan." In *Divine Passions: The Social*

Construction of Emotion in India. Owen M. Lynch, ed. 157–181. Berkeley and Los Angeles: University of California Press.

Turner, Victor W.
1969 *The Ritual Process*. Chicago: Aldine.

Vaudeville, Charlotte
1976 "Braj Lost and Found." *Indo-Iranian Journal* 18:195–213.

1980 "The Govardhan Myth in North India." *Indo-Iranian Journal* 22:1–45.

Williams, Raymond B.
1984 *A New Face of Hinduism: The Swami Narayan Religion*. Cambridge: Cambridge University Press.

Sources in Hindi

Mittal, Prabhudayāla
1966 *Braj kā Saṃskṛtika Itihāsa*. Delhi: Rajkamal Prakashan.

Satyendra, Dr. S. N.
1968 *Braj Loka-Sāhitya*. Mathura.

Shivajī, Raghunatha, ed.
1936 *Vallabha Pushṭi Prakāsha*. Bombay: Lakshmivenkateshvar Steam Press.

5

Pañcāmirtam[1]*: God's Washings as Food*

Manuel Moreno

Introduction

Food in Hindu South Asia is a complex entity with multiple dimensions. Salient among them is that which sees food (*anna*) as an absolute, ontologically on a par with life (*prāṇa*) and God (*Brahman*). A great deal of thought is invested in traditional texts, particularly the Upaniṣads, on discerning how food and life are linked together and to God. The result is a series of mysterious identities such as "food is life," "life is God," "God is food," and "Food is the cosmos," among the most prominent (*Taittirīya Upaniṣad* III. ii. 1; iii. 1; vii. 1; Nikhilananda 1963, 272–73.) I find this cosmology of food to be a very outstanding contribution which Hinduism has made to the history of culinary thought.

There is another perspective, more akin to the taste of the Hindu logician, the physician, the jurist, or the moral philosopher, which sees food as the perfect medium to exercise the virtuosities of their respective crafts. In their hands, food becomes variously an epistemological, medical, legal, and moral tool which can be easily used, and even manipulated, to punctuate the contingencies of daily life. Thus, we find numerous types of classifications imposed on food (pure/impure, good/bad, hot/cold, boiled/fried, human/divine, food for feasting/food for fasting, and others) whose primary task would seem to bring food down from the level of an absolute to that of a relative and contingent necessity of life. Despite this process of relativization, the larger cosmological implications of food are not lost in these more concrete Hindu perspectives. This can be seen in the fact that, among all classifications related to food, the most important is that which distinguishes between "eating" and "feeding" (Khare 1982) and valorizes the latter. Perhaps the best example is provided by the biomoral injunction of the jurist Manu: "He who prepares food for himself (alone), eats nothing but sin" (Manu III, 18; Bühler 1886, 96). This reflects what seems to be an Upaniṣadic axiom, namely that giving food away is the only way of preserving it, and thus preserves life itself (*Taittirīya Upaniṣad* III, x.6; Nikhilanada 1963, 276). The fact that in Hindu culture "feeding," the giving away of food, is culturally more important than "eating" is probably responsible for more attention given to "food transactions" than to the "anthropology of eating." This may also explain the recent attention given to "gastro-politics" (Appadurai 1981), "gastro-dynamics" (Khare and Rao 1986), and "gastro-logics" (Ferro-Luzzi 1977a, 1977c), all indicative of the uses feeding plays in various contexts, like conflict, social change, and cultural semantics.[2]

These absolute and relative dimensions of food coalesce together in those special categories of food known as "food for the gods" (*naivēdya*), and "God's leftover food" (*prasād*). In this context, it is particularly important to note that gods do not eat on their own but must be fed by humans. Why humans should feed the gods, reversing thereby the principles of hierarchy, could be explained by the Upaniṣadic injunction that the first duty for the preservation of life is not to eat, but to feed others. It is readily apparent that men assume this duty by feeding the gods and being fed their leftovers.

This chapter explores some aspects of the absolute and relative dimensions of food. First, I will make some suggestions regarding food as an absolute, homologous to life, God, and the cosmos. Then, I will concentrate on a particular category of food, namely food (or foodstuffs) for the gods, either for the purpose of feeding (*naivēdya*) or bathing (*abhiṣéka*), and divine food-leavings or washings (*prasād*) for human consumption.[3] I will also review some of the meanings of this classification, as they appear in the anthropological literature, and I will add a new understanding of it, which derives from my own anthropological fieldwork among worshippers of the Tamil god Murukaṉ at Paḻaṉi.[4] This understanding revolves around the restorative use of divine food to make its consumer's body more like the body of the god, which in the case of Murukaṉ at Paḻaṉi, is conceived as a *rasam*-like mixture or concoction of sweetness and poisons. To ground this understanding in ethnographic evidence, I will give a detailed account of the handling, uses, and understandings of a particular divine foodstuff—*pañcāmirtam*—a jelly-like substance employed to bathe Murukan̲ in his winter festival at Pal̲an̲i. Once so used, this jelly is returned to the god's devotees as "divine washings" *prasād*). Very salient among Murukan̲'s winter worshippers are the members of a Tamil trading caste, the Nāṭṭukkottai Ceṭṭiyār. How the ingestion of Murukan̲'s winter washings impact in the bodies of these traders, and in their identity as a caste, is really the central aspect of this study.

God, Food, Life: The Cosmological Triangle

Efforts to understand the role of food in Hindu South Asia should naturally include its ecological, economic, and nutritional dimensions. They should also integrate fundamental cosmological aspects which food has in this civilization. One of these appears to be the axiom that food comes from God and life comes from food. This view has been profoundly articulated in the sacred texts, particularly in the *Taittirīya Upaniṣad* (II. ii.1–2; Nikhilananda 1963, 266–267), which highlights the unbroken continuity that links God with the five primordial elements; these with plants; plants with food; and food with all life. God, food, and life appear then as the essential elements of a Hindu cosmological triangle.

In this triangle, food appears to have the privilege of being a nexus where all possible concerns–cosmological, social, psychological, biological, physical–coalesce. When the Upaniṣadic text states that "life verily is food," or when the Veda declares that "food is life and therefore it should be given to others, as food is the highest offering" (Kane 1941, 755), there is an unmistakable sense of totality attached to food. It is very likely that this holistic configuration would also be found in the treatment of food in the Purāṇas, Dharmaśāstras, Darśanas, and Ayurvedic texts (see Kane 1941, Jolly 1928, Prakash 1961). With this in mind, food in Hindu South Asia should then probably be treated as that modality of social phenomena that Mauss called "total social facts," which remain "at the same time juridic, economic, religious, and even aesthetic" (1967: 76); that domain wherein "body, soul, society—everything merges" (Mauss, 1950, 302). This position comes about from the realization that social phenomena are "first social, but also, and simultaneously, physiological and psychological" (Lévi-Strauss, 1966a, 113). Nowhere does this totality seem better realized than in the domain of food.

I think it is convenient here to summarily explore the various ways in which this sense of totality could be understood. First, there is a relative sense of morphological or semantic totality which concerns only the domain of foods and foodstuffs. According to Ferro-Luzzi (1977a, 511), this is often illustrated in food combinations containing antithetical pairs (coconut/bananas as hard and soft foodstuffs), or the six tastes (sweet, sour, salty, bitter, astringent, and hot), or multiple combinations whose number (particularly five, seven, nine) stands for a possible totality of food. One also finds this sense of totality expressed in ethnographic research, as when Khare and Rao (1986, 4) refer to the study of "total food systems" in contrast to research limited food taboos and intercaste restrictions. But more importantly, beyond these restricted domains of food, one must confront that unmistakable sense of absolute totality which equates food with God and life itself.

From this absolute and holistic dimension, food in Hindu South Asia is impervious to exclusive paradigmatic, symbolic, or metaphoric handling ("good to think" ideology, as in Lévi-Strauss 1966b), as well as to exclusive syntagmatic, materialistic, or metonymic handling ("good to eat" ideology, as in Harris, 1985). Every morsel of food is in a way both a metaphor and a metonym of the whole cosmos. When one cooks (particularly if cook is a Brahman), one cooks the world (Malamoud, 1978). When one eats, one eats the world since food is the cosmos (Appadurai 1981, 496). It is clear that this holistic perspective of food should be integrated in the study of the various socioeconomic aspects of the food process–production, distribution, consumption–as has been done in the analysis of more detailed aspects, like the structure of meals (Khare, 1986a), or in the treatment of food as a medium of messages (Ferro-Luzzi, 1977a; 1977c; Madan, 1975), a ranking medium (Marriott, 1968; 1976), a moral entity (Cantlie, 1981), or medicine (Nichter, 1986; Thite 1982, Zimmerman, 1987).

Included in this absolute and holistic dimension is the sacramental quality food has in Hindu South Asia.[5] This aspect comes out more clearly when the process of agricultural production is analyzed. In a study of the cycle of rice cultivation in South India (Moreno, 1990), I sought to find out what a seed or a sapling needs in order to be transformed into food, so that it can be eaten to sustain life and bring enjoyment. According to the actions and opinions of Tamil Veḷḷāḷār farmers, the requirements include not only the technologies involved in nursery beds, plowing and watering, transplantation, weeding, harvesting, threshing, winnowing, measuring, storing, and selling, but also the distribution of human shares due to laborers and of divine shares due to the gods and goddesses, and the rituals punctuating all these various operations. More importantly, drawing homologies between human bodies and the earth as a divine body of the goddess Bhūdévī, it is clear that agriculture in India has the characteristics of bodily sacraments (*saṁskāra*) and that the farmer occupies the position of custodian of the earth's potential for "reproductive prosperity" (*śrī*).

A recurrent opinion of the Veḷḷāḷār farmers, and indeed an axiom of Tamil culture, is that the proper order of things (*ṛta, ōruṅku*) requires that food should always come in plentitude (*śrī, palan̠*), even beyond what is required to sustain life. This view has similarly been expressed by Khare, who states that "even the illiterate contemporary Hindu believes that before God creates life on earth, He takes care of the question how He is going to feed them" (1976a, 132). This notion that food comes in abundance, and when given away is "perennial," obviously informs particular types of behaviors, like indulgence (Greenough, 1983), hospitality, and feasting, as well as moderation in eating and fasting (Khare, 1976b; 1986a; Madan, 1975; Cantlie, 1981). These cosmological notions provide also a suitable context to assess other cultural and moral values associated with production and distribution of food in Hindu South Asia, such as crop abundance (and consequent contentment) and crop failure (and potential hunger). They would also lead to a better understanding of what goes on in food emergency situations, such as famines (Greenough, 1982; Torry, 1986a; 1986b), and the characteristic intrafamily distribution of hunger (Harriss, 1986).

All these cosmological features of food in Hindu South Asia—absoluteness, sacramentality, transformative exchangeability, perennial abundance—coalesce in that particular type of foodstuffs which humans give to gods (*naivédya*) and gods return to humans (*prasād*), consecrated by their powerful and graceful touch.

Food for the Gods

There are usually procedures (*upacāra, aṅga*) in temple worship (*pūjā*) (Diehl 1956; Kane 1941). Two of them are "feeding the god" (*naivédya, upāhāra*) and "bathing the god" (*snāna;* Tamil, *apiśēkam, tirumañjan̠am*). The order of their implementation may vary from temple to temple according to tradition, but in both the

Vaiṣṇava (*Pañcarātra*) and the Śaiva (*Āgama*) liturgies bathing precedes feeding the deity.

A relevant aspect of feeding and bathing the deity is that both include common ingredients and these are foodstuffs. According to Kane, "the *snāna* (bathing) of images is effected with five materials called *pañcāmṛta* (five ambrosial things), viz., milk, curds, clarified butter, honey, and sugar. The image is to be bathed with these five in the order stated, so that sugar coming last removes all effects of oiliness. After these a bath with pure water follows." (1941, 731). Breckenridge reports the presence of similar food ingredients in the worship of Viṣṇu at Tirupati. According to a pre-Vijayānagara inscription, "such offerings included rice, ghee (clarified butter), curds, milk, honey, gingelly seeds, four sorts of vegetables, tamarind, turmeric, sugar, tender coconuts, split green gram, areca nuts, betel leaves, salt, and pepper" (Breckenridge 1986, 47). The inscription is not clear as to which ingredients were for bathing and which for feeding the deity. Much later, the term *amutupaṭi* became a suffix for foodstuffs to be used in feeding the deities, and the term "may have been employed to differentiate food offerings from anointment offerings" (Breckenridge, ibid).[6] It could be said, however, that, with the exception of plain boiled rice (*cātam*), the ingredients for bathing are usually uncooked foodstuffs.

Food offerings for feeding the god (*naivédya*) change into leftovers or leavings once the divine person eats a portion of them. These divine leftovers are known and handled as consecrated or transvalued food (*prasād;* Tamil *piracātam*) containing the "qualities" (*guṇa*), blessings, or "energy-grace" (Tamil, *aruḷcakti*) of the god. The food offerings for bathing (*abhiṣéka*) the deity become washings of the god and are also referred to and handled as *prasād*. It is probable that they were given a common term (*piracātam*) in South India because they also contained a common ingredient, "boiled rice" (*cātam*). It is, however, uncommon nowadays to use boiled rice in the bathing or anointing of a deity. The only case I have witnessed is the "food bathing" (*an̲n̲apiṣékam*) of the goddess Māriyamman̲ at Paḻan̲i at the time of the year when she is supposed to get her first menses. Here the term *anna,* "food", is tantamount to *cātam,* "boiled rice." And indeed, the stone embodiment of Mariyamman̲ is covered with a huge heap of boiled rice which subsequently becomes *prasād,* "food washings," given for consumption to the sponsors of the celebration.

Although the gods of the Vaiṣṇava tradition (Viṣṇu, Krishna) as well as the Śaiva gods (Śiva, Pārvatī, Murukan̲) are all fed in their respective temples, the meaning and handling of divine leftovers varies considerably. As Breckenridge states, "The offerings of food and water take on their greatest significance in the context of Śrī Vaiṣṇava worship" (Breckenridge 1986, 30). And, indeed, the most notable Śrį Vaiṣṇava temples of South India are also well known for particular sweets and savories which are major ingredients in the presiding deity's menu. Ferro-Luzzi (1978) offers considerable information on the subject, including detailed lists of food offerings and ingredients. In general, Śiva worshippers avoid contact with the god's leftovers (known as *bhōjana,* not *prasād*), which are consumed by his priests. The worshippers of Murukaṉ (an offspring of Śiva) generally avoid contact with the god's leftovers with one exception—the *tinaimāvu prasād,* which is given to worshippers in the sixth and last daily temple worship (*irākkālam pūjā,* see appendix). Other exceptions are the foodstuffs which devotees offer the god in colorful baskets, often a bunch of bananas and a coconut (*teṅkai-paḻam*), and that later are retrieved as *prasād.* It is, however, important to note that these foodstuffs are not an integral part of the god's diet but rather a manifestation of love (*aṉpu*) and devotion (*bhakti*) on the part of his devotees. (For a list of ingredients in Murukaṉ's daily diet and bathing schedules, see appendix.)

These differences in the way divine leavings are perceived and handled in the Vaiṣṇava and Śaiva traditions are related to fundamental differences in the nature of their respective principal gods—Viṣṇu and Śiva. Viṣṇu is generally perceived as an unambiguously benevolent deity, easy to please and worship, who likes the food, the songs and the love of his many devotees (Sitapati 1969). One could say that his countenance is Apollonian. According to Khare, Viṣṇu does not actually eat (and digest) the food presented to him; it is only touched by his "halo" (Khare 1976a). Hence, his *prasād* is accessible to all devotees. Śiva, on the other hand, is a god of extremes, erotic and ascetic (O'Flaherty 1973), associated with poisons (he drank the "poison" of the primeval ocean) and with substances of "eternal life" (his semen is said to be *amṛta* "the elixir of life"). A god difficult to please, often called "mad" (Ramanujan 1973), of Dionysian countenance. He is said to eat and digest the food offerings presented to him. However, the relevant *prasād* in Śaiva temples, which is to be distributed to all devotees, is not constituted by divine leftovers but *by divine washings.* Divine leftovers are considered either too intimate or perhaps even dangerous for general distribution. Only the god's attendants have access to them. This provides a major liturgical differentiation between Vaiṣṇava and Śaiva temples, or between the Pañcarātra and Āgamic liturgical canons (Diehl 1956).[7]

Some of the washings are clearly not foodstuffs. Sandalwood paste (*cantaṉam*) and sacred ashes (*vipūti*) are the only two non-food substances[8] which are used in bathing the Śaiva gods and are, subsequently, distributed as divine washings (*prasād*). The other substances, at least in the worship of Murukaṉ and Śiva in the temples of *Paḻaṉi*, are all foodstuffs. These are gingelly oil (*tāyilam*), sacred water (*tīrttam*), a jellylike mixture (*pañcāmirtam*), milk (*pāl*), young coconut water (*iḷanīr*), curds (*tayīr*), and rosewater (*paṉṉīr*). Of these the only one to be subsequently distributed as divine washings is sacred water (*tīrttam*). Occasionally, the jellylike mixture (*pañcāmirtam*) is also distributed as divine food. I will discuss in detail one of the contexts of its distribution in the next section.

There has been more discussion on the nature, meaning, and handling of divine leftovers than of divine washings. Since both are substances which have entered in contact with the god's bodies and have parallel transformative effects, I find it convenient to equate them here to simplify the analysis. The fact that divine "leavings" and "washings" receive a common name—*prasād*—and are, in many cases handled similarly, would seem to justify this provisional equation.

The discussions about food for the gods may be divided in different classes: those which emphasize the separation of the human and divine (Babb, Ferro-Luzzi); those which stress the temporary unity of the human and divine (Yalman); those which explore the relationships of separation and unity between the human and divine (Marriott); and those which bring to the foreground the various effects that divine leftovers have in humans (Khare, Breckenridge).

While analyzing structural features of Hindu ritual in Central India, Babb found that two elements were combined, the creation of a zone of purity, which allows approaching the divine and a reciprocal transaction of foods between humans and gods. Referring to the second component, the transaction of food, Babb says: "The transaction is a reciprocal one: the worshippers give food to the god, and the food is taken back and consumed. In the initial offering, God is given superior food, whereas the worshippers receive the symbolic leftovers, or *jūṭhā*, of the God. The retrieval of the God's *jūṭhā* enables the God to be 'paid' for the past or future favors without dishonor and, at the same time, establishes a hierarchical opposition between the god and the worshippers as a group" (1970, 302–303). A similar explanation is offered by Ferro-Luzzi: "During *pūjā* the foods are first presented to the idol or symbol of the god as *naivédya* (food for the god) and then returned to the devotee as *prasād* (consecrated food). The eating of *prasād* forms just as important a part of the ritual as the offering itself, since in the Indian concept of the gift, the giver ranks higher than the receiver and a unilateral offering by the devotee would put him into a superior position with respect to the god" (Ferro-Luzzi 1978, 86).

Discussing the categories of food offerings in Sri Lanka, Yalman notes that something more than hierarchical opposition is going on in the offerings, namely, the temporary unity of the human and the divine. "How is it that in caste ideology whereby cooked food can only be given to equals or inferiors, there can be food offerings to the gods? The contradiction is more apparent than real. It is precisely because the gods are so superior to men that the symbolism of food offerings is so potent. By accepting the food cooked by men, the gods become like equals. For the duration of the offering a union is established between god and men. But as in the other rituals of unity, the offering of food by the wife to the husband, the equality is a union (sexual in the domestic case) in which the subordination of the offerer to the lord is complete" (Yalman 1969, 93).

The relationship of union (intimacy) and subordination (rank) has been more recently pursued by Marriott (1978), who, referring to food and other substantial transactions, concludes that intimacy and rank are positively correlated so that the more unequal the transacting dyad, the more likely their food transactions are to be intimate.

Going beyond Babb and Yalman, Khare (1976a) explores all the symbolic possibilities of the meaning of divine leftovers within the total conceptual food system, particularly in the Vaiṣṇava sect. Besides vertical alignments (distance/union) between humans and gods created by food offerings and the acceptance and consumption of divine leftovers, Khare points out that horizontal alignments among humans are also generated as a result. "The social function of *prasād* is mainly to produce a bond of social cohesiveness among the devotees across the caste and class differentials" (Khare 1976a, 99). This treatment of the social effects of *prasād* resembles Srinivas's (1952) constructs of vertical solidarity (here temporary union of the human and divine) and horizontal solidarity (here cohesiveness among humans).

Along similar lines, Breckenridge argues that "in India, feeding the gods is a special route by which humans feed each other" (1986, 21), and thus worship cannot be separated from its sociopolitical implications. It is precisely here where Breckenridge's contribution seems most valuable, in showing "how the sacred cuisine gets linked with political control on the one hand, and temple economy on the other" (Khare and Rao 1986, 9). Breckenridge, however, sees the problem as engrained in a larger perspective. "Historical and textual studies," she states, "as well as substantial ethnographic research show that Hindu culture in India has preserved, throughout its history, a set of core cultural assumptions concerning the link between human society, food transactions, and divinity" (Breckenridge 1986, 24). She then goes on to specify these assumptions. The first is that the interdependence of men and gods depends on ritual transactions of food between them. The second is that the distinctiveness of various groups in Hindu society as well as the relationships between such groups is "ritually constructed" in such transactions with the gods. The third, and last, is that the ritual concentration and redistribution of food is a critical mechanism for the formation of social groups and articulation of leadership.

There is abundant research which illustrates the mediating position of food between the human and divine (Babb 1970, 1975, 1983; Ferro-Luzzi 1977a, 1977b, 1977c, 1978; Khare 1976a, 1976b; Yalman 1969; Waghorne and Cutler 1985; among others). Appadurai has summarized well the general view regarding this cultural assumption on the interdependence of men and gods facilitated by food transactions: "In a very real sense, in Hindu thought, food, in its physical and moral forms, *is* the cosmos. It is thought to be the fundamental link between men and the gods. Men and gods are co-producers of food, the one by his technology and labor (the necessary conditions) and the other by providing rainfall and an auspicious ecological situation (the sufficient conditions). Men assume this cooperation by feeding the gods and eating their leftovers (*prasād*)" (1981, 496; see also Khare 1976a, 120, for similar thoughts). Research on the second assumption has been more limited. Toomey (1986) is perhaps one of the most outstanding examples, illustrating how two Krishnaite sects (Vallabhites and Bengali Vaiṣṇavas) are ritually constructed upon particular types of food transactions with lord Krishna at Mount Govardhan. Breckenridge's own study is oriented to illustrate the third assumption, namely, the definite role divine leftovers played in the political economy of south Indian temples, facilitating "a quest for power by men of rank and a quest for rank by men of power" (Breckenridge 1986, 22).

My present study on the management of divine foodstuffs aims at filling the interstices between Breckenridge's second and third assumptions. It concerns the handling of Murukaṉ's food washings by a particular group of worshippers who ingest them to regenerate certain lost qualities in their bodies, so that slowly they become more like the body of the god. The ritual constructions of these worshippers' identities and their quest for power and rank are consequences of their eating god Murukaṉ's food washings, that is of experiencing Murukaṉ as food. To understand the dynamics of this restorative process, we must turn to explore the nature of the actors involved—the god Murukaṉ and a caste of Tamil Traders—as well as that of *pañcāmirtam,* the substance used to bathe Murukaṉ.

The Divine Washings of Murukaṉ

1. The Personality of Murukaṉ

Murukaṉ, an offspring of Śiva, is the most beloved god of the Tamils. Like all the great gods of Hinduism, he has multiple biographies (Clothey 1978; Navaratnam 1978; Vanamamalai 1979). In Vedic and Upaniṣadic texts, he is known as Skanda or Kumāra, and his personality is defined by abstract principles rather than by concrete processes. He incorporates the principles of sonship, war, and energy. Hence, as firstborn son, he is *hiraṇyagarbha,* "the offspring of austerity, created prior to the waters, and dwelling, with the elements, in the cave of the heart" (*Kaṭha Upaniṣad* II:i:6; Nikhilananda 1963, 77). As a principle of war, he incorporates in himself the qualities of Indra, Agni, and Rudra as the preserver of *dharma* (*Ṛg Veda* 1:59:5; III:15:1). As a principle of energy, he is the sun, source of life and dispeller of darkness, and *soma* (often identified with the moon), the fountain of life-giving intoxication (*Śatapatha Brāhmaṇa* V:3:11). We must turn to the Epics to find full-fleshed and less abstract biographies of the god, rooted primarily in biological relationships. In these texts, particularly the Vana Parva of the *Mahābhārata* and the Bālakānda of the *Rāmāyaṇa,* physical and biological processes replace the Vedic abstract principles which define the god. The god, whose birth is painstakingly described, becomes the offspring of the unbearably hot semen of Śiva which must travel through various unfit containers to find the proper womb wherein to grow until ready to be born. The birth and development of this offspring in the Saravana lake of the Himalayas are at times portrayed in terms not unlike those used in describing alchemic processes by which gold is brought into being (Vanamamali 1979, 219). Indeed, god and gold share the common name of *gaṅgeya*. Other elaborate Sanskrit biographies of Skanda/ Kumāra are found in the *Skandapurāṉa* and in Kālidāsa's *Kumārasambhava*.

Concomitant to this Sanskritic tradition, numerous allusions are found to a god of parallel attributes but different name—Murukaṉ or Ceyōn—in early Dravidian texts, especially in the poetic corpus comprising two outstanding collections, *Eṭṭuttokai* (*The Eight Anthologies*) and *Pattuppāṭṭu* (*The Ten Idyls*). In these texts, the god is associated with the hill area (*kurinci*), one of the five traditional landscapes (*tiṇai*) into which Dravidian poetics divided the land (Ramanujan 1969). Each of these landscapes suggested a particular human emotion (*bhāva*) expressed in a particular mood (*rasam*) by means of characteristic flora and fauna, season, time of the day, food, melodies, and presiding god, among other attributes. The human emotion suggested in the hill landscape is the "union of lovers" (*puṇartal*); its flora, the *kaṭampu* and *vēṅkai* trees, as well as the jackfruit and bamboo; its fauna, the elephant, peacock, and rooster; its season, the winter and early frosts; its time, the night and dawn; its food, honey and hill millet; its melody, the *kuṟiñcippaṉ*; and its presiding god, Ceyōn, the "Red One," often also called Murukaṉ. First and foremost, the concern of these Dravidian texts seems to be to endow the god with the substantial qualities which are manifest in the hill area. Chief among these qualities is *muruku,* from which the principal name of the god—Murukaṉ—derives. *Muruku* is the quality that incorporates the properties of youth, vigor, freshness, tenderness, and, very particularly, sweetness; in other words, he embodies the essence (*rasam*) of the hills and their inhabitants.

The god's Sanskritic and Dravidian features coalesce together in the *Tirumurukāṟṟuppaṭai,* "The Guide to Murukaṉ," a sixth-century A.D. poem attributed to Nakkīrar, said to be the earliest *bhakti* poem in the Tamil language (Ramanujan 1981, 110). The poem is divided into six cantos, each one extolling a particular place where Murukaṉ has the right to reside in contentment. These places are all hills, which mark the traditional borders of the Tamil country and house nowadays temples to Murukaṉ. In each of these temples Murukaṉ is worshipped under a different manifestation, primarily as a child, a warrior, a householder, a teacher, and an ascetic. The poem's conclusion, probably a later interpolation of a Śaiva Siddhānta origin, is embedded in a spectacular image. Murukaṉ rushes down the mountain as a powerful waterfall (one of the poetic elements of the hill landscape) with such power that he uproots the trees swelling with ripe fruits, cracking the fruits open, crushing the honeycombs and the fragrant flowers, and mixing all these substances (which are symbols of Murukaṉ's worshippers) in a sweet pulp (*tēṟal*). This image is fusion with the god—a paradigm of mutuality and grace—is at the very root of the shift in sensitivity which the *bhaki* movements inaugurated in the sixth century (Ramanujan 1981).

The poem's third canto praises Murukaṉ's residence at Tiruvāvinaṅkuṭi the present-day Paḻaṉi, whose Hill Temple is the most popular and most often visited temple in Tamilnadu.[9] Murukaṉ resides there as an ascetic (*āṇṭavar*), without the company of his two wives, Devasena and Vaḷḷi. The history of the temple and the properties of the hill are discussed in the *Paḻaṉittalappurāṇam* (PTP), written by Balasubrahmaniya Kavirayar in 1628 (Kavirayar 1903). The best-known passage of this book deals with the origin of the name Paḻaṉi, deriving it from the (Tamil) expression *paḻam* ṉi, "you are the fruit." The holy Śaiva family, Śiva and Pārvatī and their offspring Gaṇeśa and Murukaṉ, was living at Mount Kailaś in the Himalayas. Śiva promised a beautiful pomegranate, given to him by the sage Nārada, to whichever of his sons could go around the world in a moment. The clever Gaṇeśa went around his father, the lord who pervades the universe, and won the contest. The younger Murukaṉ set out for the world of men on a peacock. When he returned, he understood what had happened and left alone for the South. He chose to dwell as a great lord at Tiruvāvinaṅkuṭi. Soon Śiva became lonesome for his son and went down south with Pārvatī. Śiva then told Murukaṉ: "You who are forever a child and yet a man, is a pomegranate, a fruit? You are the fruit (*paḻam nī*)!" Murukaṉ bowed to his father, and Śiva agreed to his wish that they dwell together at that place, which has ever since been known as Paḻaṉi (abridged from PTP XIII, 23–73; Shulman 1980, 85).

While the *Paḻaṉittalappurāṇam,* followed on the footsteps of the early Dravidian traditions, sees Murukaṉ primarily as the essence of sweetness, another key feature of the god in his residence at Paḻaṉi has to do with poisons. Indeed, Murukaṉ's physical embodiment at Paḻaṉi is said to be made of an alloy of nine poisonous metalloids (*navapaśaṉam*) and various medicinal herbs and roots obtained from that hill. The idol of the god is said to have been fashioned by an ancient alchemist, Siddhar Pōkar, at the beginning of the *Kali yuga,* the age of moral deterioration and precariousness. Pōkar, identified in some sources as a Chinese pilgrim and mathematician, collected the poisons and herbal substances from the

Paḻaṉi Hill, and to make the embodiment of Murukaṉ, combined them in a unique proportion, probably by means of an ancient "catalytic agent" (*muppū*), still current among the practitioners of the indigenous medical system known as Siddha,[10] whose headquarters are in Paḻaṉi (Venugopal 1971, Zvelebil 1979).

The mysterious combination of these poisons is said to be unique and to have extraordinary healing and restorative powers, much greater than the usual drugs *Siddha* doctors prepare with similar poisons (Somalay 1975; Somasundaram Pillai 1970). There is a widespread belief that contact with Murukaṉ's embodiment can heal any disease and remove any misfortune. Thus, the god of Paḻaṉi is also commonly known as the "Doctor of the Dark Age" (*Kaliyuga Vaidyanātaṉ*). There are limits, however, to this boon to humanity. The unique proportion in Murukaṉ's embodiment can be lost as a result of deleterious thermic influences due to the variations which the seasons and astral bodies bring with them, or by changes in the god's mood and disposition while attending the continuous requests of his devotees. Should this happen, this incomparable source of life and well-being would become a source of death, a deadly poison, just like *Siddha* drugs are poisonous when not handled properly (Shanmugavelu 1971). Both the everyday and the festive procedures of worship in the temple of this god appear to focus on protecting the god's healing and restorative power by regulating the proportions of his component substances.

Twice a year, in the cold and hot seasons, the idol of the god is said to contract and swell, due, respectively, to an "excess of cold" (*kuḷir tōṣam*) or an "excess of heat" (*cūṭu tōṣam*), and special procedures are adopted to prevent the god from falling into a state of imbalance (Moreno and Marriott, 1989). Thus, these two seasons are the occasions for the two most important festivals in this temple, which are always accompanied by well-attended pilgrimages. *Tai Pūcam* is the winter festival when pilgrims of a trading caste (Nāṭṭukkottai Ceṭṭiyār) bring the god an offering of unrefined sugar (*carkkarai*), which is thought to be a "heating" substance. This sugar is used in the confection of *pañcāmirtam,* the jellylike foodstuff which figures prominently in Murukaṉ's festive bath. *Paṅkuni Uttiram* is the festival of the hot season, and pilgrims of the farming caste (Koṅku Veḷḷāḷār Kavuṇṭar) bring the god pots of water from the Kaveri River for his festive bath, and this water is said to be as "cooling" as water from the Ganges. In this manner, by "warming up" the god when he is "cold" and "cooling" him when he is "hot," the healing proportions of his embodiment are thought to be maintained viable.

After having considered some of the aspects of Murukaṉ's various biographies, it is important to highlight what seems to be a constant feature of his personality, namely, that he is like *rasam,*[11] a composite resulting from combining various substances (flowers, fruits, herbs, metals) and refining them into sweetness or healing poison. In other words, culinary, alchemic, and aesthetic elements figure prominently in the construction of the Murukaṉ's personality and in his worship.

2. The Winter Pilgrims: Nāṭṭukkottai Ceṭṭiyārs

The Nāṭṭukkottai Ceṭṭiyārs (also known as Nagarathar) are a caste of very entrepreneurial traders and bankers, firmly devoted to the worship of Murukaṉ (Rudner 1987), for they view the god as the chairman of their financial institutions. Members of this caste often address the god as *Ceṭṭi Murukā,* "the Sweet Trader," and keep an empty seat for him when they meet to discuss their finances (Natarejan 1968). The Nāṭṭukkottai have traditionally been associated with the Left-hand division of castes, that form of sociopolitical organization which was characteristic of south India until the past century, but whose makeup is still observable nowadays (Appadurai 1974; Beck 1972; Stein 1980). Composed chiefly of artisans, merchants, and traders, the primary concerns of these nonlanded, nonagricultural Left castes are the development of their technical or commercial capacities and the manipulation of tools, goods, or money. Members of these castes display a tendency to symmetrical nonexchanges, minimizing the output and input of bodily substances (Marriott 1976). This strategy is similarly carried out in their patterns of kinship and marriage (nonterritorial *gotra*-like organization and narrow marital alliances), diet (fundamentally vegetarian, with a preference for cool-type foods), occupation (arts and trade), transactional locus (market), social forms of worship (primordially isolated from other groups or domestically oriented), and temperament (aloof and withdrawn).

Members of this Left division (*iṭaṅkai*) consider themselves to possess in their natures a higher proportion of the *sattvaguṇa,* the "Hindu" strand or quality accountable for subtle knowledge and containment, and less of the *rajaguṇa,* quality making for humoral heat, activity, and bodily mixing with others, which characterizes members of the Right division (*valaṅkai*) (Daniel 1983, 186); therefore, their mode of behavior is usually described by them as "cool" (*paccai*) and "contained" (*sāttvika*), closer to the ascetic nature which Left-hand castes tend to emulate (Obeysekere 1975). This last characteristic makes these left-hand castes optimal candidates to control processes involving "coldness" as well as to assist divine persons when they are affected by "excess of cold" (*kuḷir tōṣam*).

The past history of the Nāṭṭukkottai Ceṭṭiyārs contains many episodes of persecution, forced marriages, displacements, and destruction which appear to have been detrimental to these peoples' image and self-esteem (Thurston and Rangachari 1909, 258–60). In modern times, the Nāṭṭukkottai followed the British domination all over southeast Asia as moneylenders, bankers, traders, and contractors of plantations. The end of World War II brought nationalization of land in many places without adequate compensation, with great financial losses to the Nāṭṭukkottai community. With the exception of those in Malaysia and Singapore, most Nāṭṭukkottais returned to India (Natarejan 1968). The losses these traders experienced were not only financial. When questioned about their way of life in those foreign lands, they sadly say that many of them abandoned traditional customs in order to adjust better to the various ways of life of those distant places. Upon their return to India, intense efforts were carried out by the members of this caste to regenerate and reconstitute themselves as a "cold" and unmixed caste in order to regain the lost quality of *sattvaguṇa*. The strategy which these traders have adopted throughout their recent history to reconstruct themselves is "greatness through goodness" (*sāttvika perumai*): giving away a percentage of their profits and refusing to accept any food from others, except the gods. This strategy seems to be working for, nowadays, Nāṭṭukkottais are acclaimed as the most generous sponsors of temple reconstruction, the active patrons of Vedic and Śāstric schools, the founders of hospitals and modern colleges, and more particularly, the great performers of *an̲natān̲am,* the "gift of food" to others.

This strategy finds its best example in these traders' annual pilgrimage of *Tai Pūcam* (usually in the second half of January), the most important collective endeavor of this caste, which coincides with the closing of their financial year. Virtually all the sixty thousand Nāṭṭukkottai Ceṭṭiyārs of Ceṭṭināṭu[12] come to Paḻan̲i, walking barefoot, covering a distance of some 160 miles across villages and towns, paddy fields and forest areas. All along the way, these pilgrims refuse the kind gifts of food and beverages offered by pious villagers who gather to welcome them. Instead, these Traders organize impressive "meal-giveaways" (*a<u>n</u>natā<u>n</u>am*) in which many thousands of people are fed with funds (*makamai*) collected from their business profits. Among these pilgrims, one selected group of males undertakes the pilgrimage in a spirit of great asceticism, overcome by a profound love (*a<u>n</u>pu*) and devotion (*bhakti*) for Muruka<u>n</u>. They carry on their shoulders a yoke (*kāvaṭi*), on which pots of unrefined sugar (*carkkarai*) are tied up. This sugar will be used in combination with other ingredients to prepare *pañcāmirtam,* the principal substance in the god's festive winter bath.

The yoke or *kāvaṭi,* a decorated arched pole, has been, since antiquity, the traditional way of carrying food offerings to Muruka<u>n</u> at Paḻa<u>n</u>i and has inspired a whole genre of songs (*kāvaṭippāṭṭu*) and dances (*kāvaṭicintu*), all connected with pilgrimages to Muruka<u>n</u>. It is said to have been first used by Agastiyar's disciple, the demon Iṭumpam, who took the scepter of Brahma as the rod and the snakes of the earth as ropes to carry the Paḻa<u>n</u>i Hills from the Himalayas. Depending on the thermic nature of the food offerings, two general types of *kāvaṭi* are available, "cool" (*paccai*) and "hot" (*cūṭu*). Most important foodstuffs of the "cool" variety include milk (*pālkkāvaṭi*), clarified butter (*neykkāvaṭi*), coconut milk (*iḷanīrkkāvaṭi*), and water from the Cauveri river (*tīrttakkāvaṭi*), and are the prevalent offerings during the hot season. Hot *kāvaṭis* are used to carry substances culturally considered to warm the body, such as unrefined sugar (*carkkaraikkāvaṭi*), honey (*tēṉkāvaṭi*), and even meats such as pigeon (*pūrakkāvaṭi*) and chicken (*kokkuṭakkāvaṭi*).[13] These offerings are more prevalent during the cold season, particularly around the astrological juncture of *Tai Pūcam,* when the *Pūcam* asterism intersects with the full moon in the Tamil month of Tai (January/February) (Merrey 1982).

While carrying these "hot" and heavy *kāvaṭis* on their shoulders, physical trials and endurance are much valued by these traders, as "strictness" (*kaṭṭāyam*) is an essential part of their code of behavior during the pilgrimage. To relieve their tiredness, these pilgrims sing high-style *Tēvaram* songs and those composed by saint Arunakiri, particularly the *Paḻa<u>n</u>i Tiruppūkaḻ.* They also sing *bajanai*-style songs and *kāvaṭi*-songs, many of them yearly composed by young Ceṭṭiyār poets and printed in pilgrimage booklets. These songs extol the ascetic as well as the sweet nature of Muruka<u>n</u>, and they keep the pilgrims' spirits high when their legs and shoulders seem to give away with pain.[14] Some Ceṭṭiyārs are said to have comforting visions of Muruka<u>n</u>, who calls them and tells them to hurry. And indeed, the sense of urgency greatly increases as the pilgrims get closer to Paḻaṉi. The last leg of the pilgrimage—the circumambulation of the outer and inner corridors of the Hill Temple of Murukaṉ—is a speedy two-mile race, with by-standing devotees encouraging the runners with traditional slogans. After the race, the yokes are lowered from the sore shoulders, and the pots containing the unrefined sugar are untied. The sugar is then collected by priests and taken to the temple kitchen to prepare *pañcāmirtam* for the god's festive bath the next day.

3. Pañcāmirtam

The term *pañcāmirtam* is the Tamil popular corruption of the Sanskrit *pañcāmṛta,* which is often translated as "five (*pañca*) ambrosial things (*amṛta*)" (Kane 1941, 731). As a nonritual beverage, it is first mentioned in the *Baudhayana Gṛhya Śesa Sūtra* as consisting of the juices of any three of the fruits coconut, mango, jack, and banana mixed with honey and sugar (Prakash 1961, 302), a mixture which strikingly resembles the "sweet pulp" (*tēṟal*) in the conclusion of the *Tirumurukāṟṟuppaṭai.* More importantly, as a ritual substance, *pañcāmṛta* (or its Sanskrit version *amṛta*) is conceived as the "elixir of immortality," the most precious stuff to be obtained from the gods' churning of the primeval ocean and opposed to the poison which first emerged from the churning (*Mahābhārata* I.15.5–13; 16.1–40; 17.1–30). The poison was drunk by Śiva and got stuck in his throat, hence its blue hue. In some regions of India, *amṛta* is clearly the product of Śiva and consists of his semen. In Bengal, where the identity of *amṛta* with Śiva's semen is very explicit, there are two forms of *amṛta* used in ritual: the *ugra pañcāmṛta,* which is poured over the embodiment of the god (*liṅgam*) and cannot be consumed, but is sprinkled over everything in sight throughout the difficult parts of the ritual; and the *pañcāmṛta,* which is mixed up in large quantities inside the temple and dispensed to worshippers to consume as *prasād* (Nicholas 1980). Ferro-Luzzi reports the ritual use of *pañchāmṛta* (another written variant) and says that it ideally consists of five components, but in actual fact often more. The components are milk, curds, ghee, sugar, honey, banana, raisins, candy, jaggery, and cardamom. She also states that in Kerala it is often considered identical with *rasayāṇam,* which consists of plantain, jaggery, coconut scrapings, coriander, grapes, mango, jackfruit, honey, and milk (1978, 104).

In Paḻaṉi, there are two types of *pañcāmirtam:* one which has been used in the god's bath and originates only in the temple, and another which has not been used in the god's bath and which can be purchased in the many worship shops as "Paḻaṉi jam." Both are made with identical ingredients (seven and not five as the name would indicate) and according to the same unique recipe (Somalay 1975, 65), which follows.

Paḻaṉi Pañcāmirtam Recipe (for 25 kgs)

Ingredients	*Proportions*
Viruppacci plantains	100 units
Unrefined sugar (*carkkarai*)	10 kg
Seedless dates (*periccam palam*)	1 kg
Raisins (*kīsmis*)	1/2 kg
Sugarcandy (*kalkantu*)	1/2 kg
Clarified butter (*ney*)	1/4 kg
Cardamom (*ēllakkāi*)	25 gr

Process

1. Plantain is fully crushed with hands.
2. Unrefined sugar is mixed.
3. Seedless dates, sugarcandy, and raisins are added.
4. Cardamom and clarified butter are added.
5. The mixture should be stirred continuously with the right hand only until adequate thickness is reached.
6. Before its use or consumption, it must rest for a few hours so that a slight fermentation takes place.

The result is a thick, jellylike substance, dark red in color, with a sweet and slightly pungent taste, which is considered to be the trademark of Paḻaṉi. *Pañcāmirtam* improves with age, and the local saying is that "the older it is, the better it tastes" (Somalay 1975, 65). It is also supposed to preserve very well; some people say forever. By its very nature, it is an optimal symbol of perennial food.

From a culinary perspective, it is interesting to note that while dates, raisins, cardamom, and particularly clarified butter (or ghee), are considered "cool" items in themselves, when combined, the resulting mixture, *pañcāmirtam,* is always considered "very hot," perhaps due to the fact of a slight fermentation taking place

(Beck 1969, 570). It is then also an optimal foodstuff to be used in Murukaṉ's winter bath to warm him up.

Pañcāmirtam for temple use is always prepared in the temple kitchen from local ingredients by temple cooks, who recite verses from the *Kumāra Tantra* in the process. Outside of the temple, *pañcāmirtam* is also manufactured in local cottage industries and even by groups of male pilgrims themselves in their resting houses. Only those who have undergone a prolonged period of ascetic observances, like the Ceṭṭiyār pilgrims, may participate in its preparation. While preparing it, these pilgrims' mouth and nose must be covered with a white scarf or towel to prevent the mixing of salival particles with that substance. Temple-originated *pañcāmirtam* is sold to devotees as *prasād* by the temple. What they get is actually nonritual *pañcāmirtam* which as been mixed with a tiny portion of the actual washings of the god. The contact is believed to transform the whole amount into divine washings. Pilgrims are very explicit when they distinguish the state of *pañcāmirtam* before and after it has been used in the god's bath. Before the bath it is very hot. After the bath, however, it is extremely cold for it carries within it the excess of cold of the god's *pañcāmirtam* washings, these washings are supposed to be very tasty food, with extraordinary power to restore health and the normal functions of the body. Together with the sandalwood paste used to cover the god's chest overnight (see appendix), *pañcāmirtam* is considered the best "medicine" to remove any physical impediment. Its miraculous powers, however, do not come about in a magical fashion; most devotees think that for these powers to be fully realized one must have trust or confidence (*nampikkai*) in Murukaṉ and believe that *pañcāmirtam* is truly an exudation of god's body.[15]

Murukaṉ is bathed with this substance various times every day (see appendix). In the winter festival of *Tai Pūcam,* when Murukaṉ is said to be affected by "excess cold" (*kuḷir tōṣam*), the bathing is an elaborate affair and *pañcāmirtam* is then the principal substance, just like sacred water from the river Kaveri is in the god's summer bath. One of the seven ingredients required for its preparation is the sugar brought by the Nāṭṭukkottai Ceṭṭiyār pilgrims in their *kāvaṭi* yokes. This sugar comes from Kangeya, an area in central Koṅku well known for the quality of its sugar cane crop.

The pilgrimage itself is an intensely emotional experience of god for all the Ceṭṭiyārs, but particularly for those who carry the *kāvaṭi* yokes. I went along with the Ceṭṭiyārs in this pilgrimage in 1980, and I was deeply moved by their devotion to Murukaṉ and their physical endurance throughout the long and occasionally tortuous trek. To most pilgrims, the greatest moment of the pilgrimage is when the *pañcāmirtam* is poured over Murukaṉ's body during his festive bathing (*abhiṣéka*). The following is a brief excerpt of what when, together with many other pilgrims, we were facing the chamber where the embodiment of Murukaṉ resides: "Having been attracted by the love of god, moving with extreme urgency in the last stages, they (the yoke carriers) had finally reached the magnetic center, the enclosure where the god resides. There they could see their beloved god being awakened and warmed with a substance which they had themselves carried with extreme difficulties, as part of themselves. Their shouts and cries of praise and victory, their gestures pointing out their sores to the god spoke more intensely than any hymns could do of their joy in warming the god and their expectation of receiving the god's excess cold" (Moreno 1982, 205).

The *pañcāmirtam* washings are entrusted to the leaders of the Nāṭṭukkottai Ceṭṭiyārs to be mixed with the *pañcāmirtam* made in the resting houses and later distributed to all Ceṭṭiyār pilgrims as *prasād*. As Tamil Brahmans do with the water they bring from the Ganges, *pañcāmirtam,* Murukaṉ's washings, is taken daily by these Ceṭṭiyārs in the belief that, by consuming Murukaṉ's excess of cold, they can restore in their natures the greatness and goodness (*sāttvika perumai*) qualities they lost in the past.

Conclusion: God as Rasam

As divine washings, *pañcāmirtam* stands as an optimal symbol of the cosmic qualities of food—restorative, perennial, sweet, and given by the grace of god. But not just any omnipotent, autonomous god, but rather a personal god which needs also to be fed, warmed, and cooled down from time to time, particularly with the passing of the seasons. As a god, Murukaṉ has a particular personality, made out of various components. In that, he resembles *rasam*—a mixture, concoction, essence of various products—in his case particularly of sweetness and poison. The term *rasam* (Sanskrit, *rasa*; Tamil, *irasam*) has multiple meanings in Tamil, of which three are most basic. One meaning is related to food, particularly to very sweet fruit juices, as well as to the peppery water which flavors most

Tamil meals. Another is related to alchemy, for mercury is *r̄ajarasam,* the king of drugs in Siddha medicine, a universal remedy for all kinds of diseases either as *pāṭarasam* (quicksilver) or as *vaḷairasam* (sublimated from *liṅkam*) (Shanmugavelu 1971). The third meaning is linked with Indic aesthetics, at least since Abhinavagupta, and it is the expression of a human emotion (*bhāva*) in a particular mood (*rasam*). In Sanskrit poetics, "the standard analogy (for *rasa*) is that of a blend of a basic food, such as yoghurt, with a number of spices; the resulting substance has a unique flavor (*rasa*), which is not identical with any of the single elements comprising it" (Wulff 1986, 674). It is clear that these three meanings apply to the god Murukaṉ. He is "the fruit" par excellence (*paḻm ni*) whose juices are the sweet *pañcāmirtam* washings from his body. Like mercury, he is also poison of extraordinary healing potency. Indeed, he is the *Kaliyuga Vaidyanātaṉ,* "the Doctor of the Dark Age." Aesthetically, he incorporates the essence of the hills; indeed, his name derives from *muruku,* which is in Tamil a poetic term for the qualities of freshness, vigor, youth, beauty, and sweetness.

If these *rasam*-like features define the personality of Murukaṉ, it would seem then appropriate to conceive of his worship also as a *rasam*-like experience. And indeed, it is particularly in pilgrimage, where the worship of Murukaṉ touches many cords in devotee's bodies and souls. There is first the very active and highly kinetic aspects of moving along the pilgrimage trek, a key aspect of pilgrimage, since "pilgrimage" in Tamil is "traveling to a sacred place" (*tiruttalappirayāṇam*). In the case of the pilgrimage of the Ceṭṭiyārs, walking is painful, but is alleviated by Murukaṉ's magnetism, which they say attracts them to his temple. The sweet smells of the Hill of Paḻaṉi also attract them, even at a very long distance, as is expressed in the songs they sing while walking. When they reach Paḻaṉi, and once in front of the god, pilgrims seem to cease being actors and change into receptors of multiple-sensory stimuli, through which they experience the grace of Murukaṉ. They hear the temple singers, the priestly mantras, the bells, and the thousands of *ōms* from as many devotees. They see the god being adorned with the *alaṁkāras* of a king, a hunter, and an ascetic, and the show of circling of lights (*ārati*) with many types of lamps and flames of various sizes, which later they touch with the palms of the hands. The smells of incense, attar of roses, kasturi musk, *sambaraṉi,* and other perfumes being burned totally fill the area of worship. Finally, with all their senses open and as a culmination of their pilgrimage, devotees experience Murukan̲ as food when they eat the sweet and potent exudation of his body, the *pañcāmirtam* washings.

Appendix: God Murukan̲'s Daily Feeding and Bathing Schedule

1. *Paḷḷiyarai* worship at *uccākkālam* period—5:50 A.M.
The god is given a snack of grapes, raisins, plantain, and betelnut. The leavings are consumed by the attending priests.

2. *Viśvarūpa* worship at *pirātakkālam* period—6:30 AM.
Removal of sandalwood paste covering the god's chest with god's loincloth soaked in water. Sandalwood paste is given to devotees as *prasād*.

3. *Vil̲a* worship at *kālamattyacanti* period—7:30 A.M.
Bathing of the god with the following consecutive substances: gingelly oil (*tāyilam*), sacred water (*tīrttam*) from local Varatar river, *pañcāmirtam*, milk (*pāl*), sandalwood paster (*cantan̲am*), sacred ashes (*vipūti*), and rosewater (*pan̲n̲īr*). Washings of sacred water and ashes are given to devotees as *prasād*. *Pañcāmirtam* washings are given to sponsor as *prasād*.
The god is given breakfast, which includes boiled rice (*cātam:* rice without salt with a few drops of ghee) in summer or sweetened boiled rice (*carkkarai poṅkal:* rice, green gram, jaggery, ghee, cashew nuts, coconut scrapings, cardamom) in winter, curry fried in ghee, and dried ginger with sugar (*cukku carkkarai*). The leavings are consumed by the attending priests.

4. *Cirukkālancanti* worship at *vittyakālacanti* period—9:00 A.M.
Bathing of the god as in no. 3.
The god is given a mid-morning meal of wheat/corn/millet bread (*roti*) with butter, and a special boiled rice (*ven̲ poṅkal*: rice, green or red gram, ghee, cashew nuts, pepper, ginger, salt, cumin or turmeric, cloves and nutmeg). The leavings are consumed by the attending priests.

5. *Kālacanti* worship at the *mattyacanti* period—10 A.M.
The same actions as in period no. 4, with feeding of special boiled rice (*ven̲ poṅkal*) only.

6. *Uccikkālam* worship at *matiyān̲am* period—12:00 (Noon)
Bathing of the god as in periods 3, 4, 5 with two new substances added: young coconut water (*iḷanīr*) and curds (*tayīr*). Washing of sacred water and ashes are given to devotees as *prasād*. *Pañcāmirtam* washings are given to sponsors as *prasād*.
The god is given the most substantial meal of the day which includes tamarind rice (*puḷicātam*: boiled rice with salt, tamarind, black gram and

asafoetida) in summer or curd rice (*tayīrcātam*: rice, curds, milk, salt, curry leaves, mustard seeds, oil, green chilles, ginger) in winter, a sweet pudding (*pālpāyacam*: rice milk, jaggery or sugar), peppery water (*rasam*) and betelnut (*verrilai-pākku*) as digestive. The leavings are consumed by the attending priests.

7. *Cayaraccai* worship at *cayaṅkālam* period—5:30 P.M.

Bathing of the god as in period no. 4. The god is fed either tamarind rice (*puḷicātam*) or sweetened boiled rice (*carkkarai poṅkal*). The leavings are consumed by the attending priests.

8. *Irākkālam* worship at the *irākkālam* period—8:00 P.M.

This is the most elaborate daily period of worship. The god's bathing includes the same substances as in period no. 6. The god's chest is then covered with a thick layer of sandalwood paste—which has been mixed with a small quantity of fresh camphor (*paccai karuppuram*)—to be removed the next morning in period no. 2. The god's menu is very elaborate, with a display of local delicacies. It usually includes plain boiled rice (*cātam*), rice cakes (*āppam*: rice flour, red gram, jaggery, coconut scrapings, cardamom fried in ghee), savories (*vaṭai*: black gram flour, rice flour, pepper, salt, cumin, ghee, ginger; *tenkural*: fried spiral of rice flour, green gram, salt, and spices), uncooked sweet porridge (*tinaimāvu*: hill millet, ghee, cardamom, cinnamon, coconut pieces, jaggery, and honey poured on), and betelnut as a digestive. The leavings are consumed by the attending priests, with the exception of the unique sweet porridge, which is the only food to be distributed to devotees as *prasād*.

9. *Paḷḷiyarai* worship at the *arttacānam* period—10:00 P.M.

The god's portable feet are taken to the bedchamber to spend the night. While temple singers sing lullabies to him, the god is fed milk and raisins.

Notes

1. Tamil terms are transliterated according to the system used by the University of Madras' *Tamil Lexicon*; other Indic terms are transliterated according to established conventions in the literature.

2. The notion of "feeding on others, who are feebler, smaller, and lower" (Manu V, 29–30), pinpointing the famous "law of the fishes" (bigger fish eat littler fish), should not be disregarded in this context. For a discussion of this ideology in ancient India, see Smith 1990.

3. It could be argued that washings are more intimate than leavings, particularly since oftentimes washings are considered "exudations" or "secretions" of the body, while leavings are not. Tamil does not make a linguistic distinction between them, and both are labeled *piracātam* (*prasād*).

4. The field research on which this study is based was conducted in Tamilnadu from November 1979 until May 1981, with the support of a doctoral fellowship provided by the Social Science Research Council. An early version of this paper was written and presented at the NEH Summer Seminar for College Teachers on "Anthropological Perspectives on Food and Food Ways," Charlottesville, June–August 1987. I would like to thank the director of the seminar, Professor R. S. Khare of the University of Virginia, for his interest in this project. Special thanks are also due to Dr. P. Subramaniam of Pal̲an̲i Āṇḍavar College of Indian Culture.

5. The use of the term "sacramental" may be questionable in the context of Hindu ritual. My use of the term here is closer to the Roman Catholic theological sense of transformative and efficacious sign than to the Protestant sense of symbol as a spiritual reality.

6. Besides the Sanskrit term *naivédya,* which is commonly used by Tamil Brahmins to designate "food for the gods," the most frequent Tamil words used by devotees include *paṭaiyal* ("offering") and *amutam* ("food," "boiled or unboiled rice").

7. According to Ferro-Luzzi 1977a, the distinction between the gentler nature of Viṣṇu and the more violent character of Śiva is consistently stressed also by the spices used in their respective foods. For instance, in most Vaiṣṇava temples of Tamilnadu chillies are not acceptable to Viṣṇu, while Śiva has a special liking for green chilies. In general, the opposition between Viṣṇu and Śiva is expressed by the relative abundance of foodstuffs for eating in the case of Viṣṇu, and for bathing in the case of Śiva.

8. It should be noted that sandalwood paste and sacred ashes received as *prasād* are both used externally was well as internally by most devotees. Sandalwood paste is particularly applied to the forehead and arms, but is also drunk diluted in water, especially the sandalwood paste which has covered the chest of the god overnight (see appendix). Sacred ashes may be applied to various parts of the body, but it is not infrequent for many worshippers to place a pinch of them in the mouth.

9. The Arul̥migu Śrī Tanṭāyutappan̲iswami Tirukkōyil, the official name of the Hill Temple of Pal̲an̲i, is after Tirupati, the second richest temple in South India, in terms of assets and revenues.

10. Siddha is one of the three major branches of indigenous medical systems practiced in India, the other two being Unani and Ayurveda. Siddha medicine is confined to the South, and it differs from the other systems, particularly Ayurveda, in emphasizing the use of poisonous substances, especially minerals.

11. As it will be argued in the conclusion, I am using the term *rasam* in its various culinary, alchemic, and aesthetic meanings.

12. Ceṭṭināṭu is a region nowadays integrated in the district of Ramanathapuram, Tamilnadu. It traditionally consisted of ninety-six *nakarams,* of which presently only seventy-eight exist. The business center of Ceṭṭināṭu is the city of Karaikuṭi.

13. These non-vegetarian *kāvaṭis* may be a relic of the past and are not accepted as offerings by the temple authorities. Nevertheless, devotees, particularly from Kerala, continue to bring them. The handling of these nonvegetarian offerings appears to be indicative of the general goal to be obtained in the worship of Murukaṉ. A pigeon or a chicken (often also a snake) are cut into pieces and these are deposited in a container which is tied to the *kāvaṭi* yoke. It is said that upon opening the container at the top of the Hill which houses the temple, the pigeon or chicken comes to life by the power of Murukaṉ. To corroborate this belief, devotees often quote a verse from a poem written by the Tamil saint Arunakiri which says that Murukaṉ can extract milk even from a dead branch.

14. I recorded a large number of these songs, which were transcribed by Dr. P. Subramaniam of the Paḻaṉi Āṇḍavar College of Indian Culture. A Tamil-English publication and study of these songs in collaborative with Dr. P. Subramaniam is forthcoming. The sweet nature of Murukaṉ is particularly extolled in these songs, and *pañcāmirtam* is referred to as an "exudation" or "secretion" of Murukaṉ's body.

15. The necessity to believe and trust in Murukaṉ as a condition for his power to be manifested in miracles is an aspect which Ceṭiyār pilgrims particularly emphasized to me. Their songs reflect this point too.

References

Appadurai, Arjun

1974 "Right and Left Hand Castes in South India." *Indian Economic and Social History Review* 11, nos. 2, 3: 216–60.

1981 "Gastro-Politics in Hindu South Asia." *American Ethnologist* 8: 494–511.

Babb, Lawrence A.

1970 "The Food of the Gods in Chhattisghar: Some Structural Features of Hindu Rituals." *Southwestern Journal of Anthropology* 26:287–304.

1975 *Divine Hierarchy: Popular Hinduism in Central India.* New York: Columbia University Press.

1983 "The Physiology of Redemption." *History of Religions* 22:283–312.

Beck, Brenda E. R.

1969 "Colour and Heat in South Indian Ritual." *Man* n.s. 4:553–72.

1972 *Peasant Society in Könku. A Study of Right and Left Subcastes in South India.* Vancouver: University of British Columbia Press.

Breckenridge, C. Appadurai
1986 "Food, Politics and Pilgrimage in South India, 1350–1650 A.D." In R. S. Khare and M. S. A. Rao, eds., *Food, Society and Culture: Aspects in South Asian Food Systems,* 21–53. Durham N.C.: Carolina Academic Press.

Bühler, G., transl.
1886 *The Laws of Manu.* Delhi: Motilal Banarsidass.

Cantlie, Audrey
1981 "The Moral Significance of Food among Assamese Hindus." In Adrian C. Mayer, ed., *Culture and Morality. Essays in Honour of Christoph von Fürer-Haimendorf,* 42–62. Delhi: Oxford University Press.

Clothey, Fred W.
1978 *The Many Faces of Murugan: The History and Meaning of a South Indian God.* The Hague: Mouton.

Daniel, E. Valentine
1983 "Karma Divined in a Ritual Capsule." In Charles F. Keyes and E. Valentine Daniel, eds., *Karma: An Anthropological Inquiry,* 83–117. Berkeley: University of California Press.

David, Kenneth A.
1977 "Hierarchy and Equivalence in Jaffna, north Sri Lanka: Normative Codes as Mediators." In K. A. David, ed. *The New Wind: Changing Identities in South Asia,* 179–226. The Hague: Mouton.

Diehl, Carl G.
1956 *Instrument and Purpose. Studies of Rites and Rituals in South India.* Lund: Hakan Ohlssons Boktryckeri.

Eggeling, Julius, transl.
1966 *Satapatha-Brāhmaṇa according to the text of the Madhyadina School.* Delhi: Motilal Banarsidass.

Ferro-Luzzi, Gabriella E.
1977a "Ritual as Language: The Case of South Indian Food Offerings." *Current Anthropology* 18:507–514.

1977b "The Food Disliked by the Gods in South India." *Estratto da Annali dell-Istituto Orientale di Napoli, Vol.* 37 (N.S. XXVII):357–73.

1977c "The Logic of South Indian Food Offerings." *Anthropos* 72:529–555.

1978 "Food for the Gods in South India." *Zeitschrift für Ethnologie,* vol. 103, no. 1:86–108.

Greenough, Paul R.
1982 *Prosperity and Misery in Modern Bengal. The Famine of 1943–1944.* New York: Oxford University Press.

1983 "Indulgence and Abundance as Asian Peasant Values: A Bengali Case in Point." *Journal of Asian Studies,* XLII (4):831–850.

Griffith, Ralph T. H., transl.
1973 *The Hymns of the Ṛg Veda.* Edition revised by J. L. Shastri. Delhi: Motilal Banarsidass.

Harris, Marvin
1985 *Good to Eat: Riddles of Food and Culture.* New York: Simon and Schuster.

Harriss, Barbara
1986 "The Intrafamily Distribution of Hunger in South Asia." Paper for WIDER Project on Hunger and Poverty, Seminar on Food Strategies, Helsinki.

Hume, Robert E.
1977 *The Thirteen Principal Upanishads.* 2nd edition revised. Oxford: Oxford University Press.

Jolly, Julius
1928 *Hindu Law and Custom.* Calcutta: Greater India Society.

Kane, P. V.
1941 *History of the Dharmaśāstra.* Vol. II, pt. 2. Poona: Bhandarkar Oriental Research Institute.

Kavirayar, Balasubrahmaniya
1903 *Paḻaṉittalappurāṇam.* Ed. with Preface, Paraphrase and Notes by N. Kadiraver Pillai. Madras.

Khare, R. S.
1976a *Culture and Reality: Essays on the Hindu System of Managing Foods.* Simla: Indian Institute of Advanced Study.

1976b *The Hindu Hearth and Home.* New Delhi: Vikas Publishing House.

1982 *Eating and Feeding as Categories of Culture and Nutrition in India.* (Mimeo.)

1986a "The Indian Meal: Aspects of Cultural Economy and Food Use." In R. S. Khare & M. S. A. Rao, editors, *Food, Society, and Culture: Aspects in South Asian Food Systems,* 159–183. Durham, N.C.: Carolina Academic Press.

1986b "Hospitality, Charity, and Rationing: Three Channels of Food Distribution in India." In R. S. Khare & M. S. A. Rao, editors, *Food, Society, and Culture: Aspects in South Asian Food Systems,* 277–96. Durham, N.C.: Carolina Academic Press.

Khare, R. S. & M. S. A. Rao, editors
1986 *Food, Society, and Culture: Aspects in South Asian Food Systems.* Durham, N.C.: Carolina Academic Press.

Lévi-Strauss, C.
1966a "The Scope of Anthropology," *Current Anthropology* 7 (2):112–123.

1966b *The Savage Mind.* London: Weidenfeld & Nicholson.

Madan, T. N.
1975 "The Gift of Food." In B. N. Nair, ed., *Culture and Society: Festschrift for Professor Aiyappan,* 84–96. New Delhi: Thomson Press.

Mahābhārata
1973 Vol. 1, *The Book of Beginnings,* Trans. and ed. J. A. B. Van Buitenen. Chicago: University of Chicago Press.

Malamoud, Charles
1978 "Cuire le Monde." *Puruṣārtha,* 1:91–135.

Marriott, McKim
1968 "Caste Ranking and Food Transactions." In M. Singer and B. S. Cohn, ed. *Structure and Change in Indian Society.* Chicago: Aldine Publishing Company.

1976 "Hindu Transactions: Diversity Without Dualism." In B. Kapferer, ed. *Transaction and Meaning: Directions in the Anthropology of Exchange and Symbolic Behavior.* Philadelphia: Institute for the Study of Human Issues.

1978 "Intimacy and Rank in Food." Paper presented during the International Congress of Anthropological and Ethnological Sciences, 10–16 December; New Delhi.

Mauss, M.
1950 *Sociologie et Anthropologie.* Selected essays ed. by C. Lévi-Strauss. Paris: P.U.F.

1967 *The Gift.* London: Cohen and West.

Merrey, Karen L.
1982 "The Hindu Festival Calendar." In G. R. Welbon and G. E. Yocum, editors. *Religious Festivals in South India and Sri Lanka.* New Delhi: Manohar.

Moreno, Manuel
1982 *Murugan, a God of Healing Poisons: The Physics of Worship in a South Indian Center for Pilgrimage.* Unpublished Ph.D. dissertation. University of Chicago, Department of Anthropology.

1987 "Agriculture as a Sacrament: A New Approach to the Cycle of Rice in South India." *Lambda Alpha Journal of Man,* 18:53–62.

1990 "Esbozo de una teología agraria hindú." *Estudios de Asia y Africa,* vol. XXV, no. 2:185–208.

Moreno, M. & McKim Marriott
1989 "Humoral Transactions in Two Tamil Cults: Murukan̠ and Māriyamman̠." *Contributions to Indian Sociology* (n.s.) vol. 23, no. 1: 149–167.

Nakkīrar
1978 *Tirumurukāṟṟuppaṭai.* Tamil annotated edition by P. V. Somacuntaranar Avarkal. Tirunelveli: Saiva Siddhanta Nurpatippu Karakana.

Natarejan, M.
1968 "The Nāṭṭukkottai Ceṭṭiyārs of Ceṭṭināṭu." In *Proceedings of the Tamil International Conference.* Kaula Lampur.

Navaratnam, Ratna
1978 *Kartikeya, the Divine Child.* Bombay: Bharatiya Vidya Bhavan.

Nicholas, Ralph W.
1980 Personal correspondence, April 2.

Nichter, Mark
1986 "Modes of Food Classification and the Diet-Health Contingency: A South Indian Case Study." In R. S. Khare & M. S. A. Rao, editors, *Food Society and Culture: Aspects in South Asian Food Systems,* 185–221. Durham, N.C.: Carolina Academic Press.

Nikhilananda, Swami, transl.
1963 *The Upanishads.* New York: Harper Torchbooks.

Obeyesekere, Gananath
1975 "The Left-Right Subcastes in South India: A Critique." *Man,* n.s. 10, no. 3:462–468.

O'Flaherty, Wendy D.
1973 *Eroticism and Asceticism in the Mythology of Śiva.* Delhi: Oxford University Press.

Prakash, Om
1961 *Food and Drinks in Ancient India.* Delhi: Munshi Ram Manoharlal.

Ramanujan, A. K.
1969 *The Interior Landscape.* Bloomington: Indiana University Press.

1973 *Speaking of Śiva.* Baltimore: Penguin Books.

1981 *Hymns for the Drowning.* Princeton: Princeton University Press.

Rig Veda
1968 *Die Hymnen des Rigveda.* Wiesbaden: Harrassowitz.

Rudner, David
1987 "Religious gifting and inland commerce in Seventeenth Century South India." *Journal of Asian Studies,* 46:361–379.

Shanmugavelu, M.
1971 "Mercury, the Universal Remedy for Almost All Diseases, According to Siddha's Concept." In *Proceedings of the 2nd International Conference Seminar of Tamil Studies,* Madras.

Shulman, David Dean
1980 *Tamil Temple Myths: Sacrifice and Divine Marriage in the South Indian Śaiva Tradition.* Princeton: Princeton University Press.

Sitapati, Pidala
1969 *Sri Venkateswara, the Lord of the Seven Hills, Tirupati.* Bombay: Bharatiya Vidya Bhavan.

Smith, Brian K.
1990 "Eaters, Food, and Social Hierarchy in Ancient India. A Dietary Guide to a Revolution of Values." *Journal of the American Academy of Religion* 57(2):177–205.

Somasundaram Pillai, J. M.
1970 *Pa<u>l</u>a<u>n</u>i, the Sacred Hill of Muruga<u>n</u>.* Pa<u>l</u>a<u>n</u>i: Sri Dandhayuthapani Swami Devasthanam.

Somalay
1975 *Pa<u>l</u>a<u>n</u>i, The Hill Temple of Muruga.* Pa<u>l</u>a<u>n</u>i: Arulmigu Dandhayuthapani Swami Temple.

Srinivas, M. N.
1952 *Religion and Society among the Coorgs of South India.* Oxford: Claredon Press.

Stein, B.
1980 *Peasant State and Society in Medieval South India.* Delhi: Oxford University Press.

Thite, G. U.
1982 *Medicine: Its Magico-Religious Aspects according to the Vedic and Later Literature.* Poona: Continental Prakashan.

Thurston, Edgar and Rangachary K.
1909 *Castes and Tribes of South India.* Vol. V. Madras: Government Press.

Toomey, P. M.
1986 "From the Mouth of Krishna: Socio-Religious Aspects of Sacred Food in Two Krishnaite Sects." In R. S. Khare & M. S. A. Rao editors, *Food, Society, and Culture: Aspects in South Asian Food Systems,* 55–83. Durham, N.C.: Carolina Press.

Torry, William I.
1986a "Morality and Harm: Hindu Peasant Adjustments to Famines." *Social Science Information* 25 (1):125–160.

1986b "Drought and the Government-Village Emergency Food Distribution System in India." *Human Organization,* 45 (1)11–23.

Vanamanalai, N.
1979 "Skanda-Muruga Synthesis." In R. Nagasamy, editor, *South Indian Studies.* Madras: Society for Archaeological, Historical and Epigraphical Research.

Venugopal, P. M.
1971 "Muppū." In *Proceedings of the 2nd International Conference Seminar of Tamil Studies.* Madras.

Waghorne, J. P. & N. Cutler editors
1985 *Gods of Flesh, Gods of Stone. The Embodiment of Divinity in India.* Chambersburg, Pa: Anima Books.

Wulff, Donna M.
1986 "Religion in a New Mode: The Convergence of the Aesthetic and the Religious in Medieval India." *Journal of the American Academy of Religions* LIV (4):673–688.

Yalman, N.
1969 "The Meaning of Food Offerings in (Buddhist) Ceylon." In R. F. Spencer, editor, *Forms of Symbolic Action. Proceedings of the 1969 Annual Spring Meeting of the American Ethnological Society,* 81–96. Seattle: University of Washington Press.

Zimmermann, Francis
1987 *The Jungle and the Aroma of Meats: An Ecological Theme in Indian Medicine.* Berkeley: University of California Press.

Zvelebil, Kamil V.
1979 "The Ideological Basis of the Siddha Search for Immortality." *South Asian Digest of Regional Writing* 8:1–9.

6

Food Essence and the Essence of Experience

✱

H. L. Seneviratne

This chapter explores classical Indian conceptions concerning the ingestion of food and the process of aesthetic creation as analogous with each other. It suggests a relation between aesthetic and religious experiences as well. All three spheres appear to be concerned with the seeking of essences appropriate to each, the aesthetic sphere occupying an intermediary position between food absorption and the nourishment of the contemplative life. In conclusion, the chapter uses a sample of ethnography from one Indic culture, Sri Lanka, to illustrate how these classical conceptions present themselves in everyday behavior.[1] I wish to suggest that the process of food distillation, on the one hand, and of aesthetic creation, on the other–both of which are interior to the individual—find a parallel in the culinary process, which is exterior to the individual. The latter is, however, internal to a larger corporeality, the house, which shares with the individual the semantic properties of being.[2] The theory we are concerned with is elaborated in ancient medical and aesthetic texts and their descendent literature.[3] It must be stated that the conceptions found in these two areas do not constitute an integrated whole. There is great divergence of opinion in both fields.[4] Nevertheless, we have a meaningful core of ideas which are generally accepted, and it is this body of ideas which we arbitrarily refer to as "classical."

The Ingestion and Transformation of Food

According to the medical texts, the human body consists of the five elements (*bhūtas*): earth, water, fire, air, and ether. These are modified into seven essences (*dhātus*) which maintain the integrity of the organism. These are flavor (*rasa*),[5] blood (*rakta*), flesh (*māṁsa*), fat (*medas*), bone (*asthi*), marrow (*majjā*), and semen (*śukra*). Air (*vāyu*), bile (*pitta*), and phlegm (*kapha*), often called the three humors, are also sometimes considered essences. While these are in a state of constant flux, normally they exist in a state of balance or equilibrium (*dhātu sāmya*). The science of medicine aims at assisting the individual to maintain this equilibrium through diet, medication, and the routinization of behavior.

The function of food is to generate the essences. That is, food is "of the essence" for the continued existence of the body. Food must be selected carefully, cooked, and ingested properly. The digestive fires of the stomach cook the food intracorporeally and transform it into *rasa*, and then into blood, flesh, fat, bone, marrow, and semen. Some of these essences increase and decrease in the body, and so do the allied constituents of the body. Therefore measures must be taken to ensure their equilibrium. That is, a person must take foods of varying forms, tastes, and attributes. This is essentially a theory of a "balanced diet," except for the binary nature of the qualities which inform the dietary ingredients: foods must be a balance of hot and cold, solid and liquid, chewy and tender, dark and light, heavy and light, savory and bland. Such dietary discretion ensures that no single essence gains an undue dominance, which would result in the subservience of others and in the disequilibrium of the organism as a whole. Further, food is also important for its crucial function of kindling the digestive fire, which seems to find an appetite on what it feeds. An inextinguishable digestive fire is indispensable for health, strength, growth, luster, and life. When it rages within, a person is healthy and long-lived. When it is low, he is diseased; when it is gone, he no longer lives. The digestive fire therefore must be constantly fueled.

The two best known classical sources, *Caraka* (first to second centuries A.D.) and *Suśruta Saṁhitas* (ca. fourth century A.D.), emphasize the importance of food and discuss at length its properties, its proper use, and related matters (Ray and Gupta 1965; Ray, Gupta and Roy 1980; Sharma and Dash 1976. See also note 2). Like the body, food items consist of the five elements. Each body element is nourished by the identical element found in food items. However, foods are more than a mere summation of their constituent elements. They possess qualities (*guṇas*), the most important of which is taste, or flavor (*rasa*). Flavor[6] is sixfold: sweet (*madhura*), saline (*lavaṇa*), sour (*amla*), bitter (*kaṭu*), pungent (*tikta*), and astringent (*kaṣāya*). Each of these contains all five elements, but in variant combinations, which accounts for their distinction. Each *rasa* could produce beneficial or detrimental physiological effects. Through the essences, the *rasas* nourish the body.[7]

The *Caraka* (Sharma and Dash 1976) mentions other qualities which are paired: heavy and light, hot and cold, dry and oily (wet), mild and sharp, compact and loose, tender and hard, separative and slimy, rough and smooth, intricate and gross, solid and liquid. Heavy and light receive particular emphasis in this work, as light foods are conducive to the maintenance of digestive fires and can be consumed in abundance, whereas heavy foods burden the fire and should be consumed only in moderation. Digestion starts with the action of life breath (*prāṇa*), which pushes the food down to the stomach. All food in the stomach is liquified before the digestive fire cooks it, producing the nutritive *rasa* and the waste matter (*mala*), which is excreted. A further process of cooking is involved in transforming *rasa* into essence (*dhātu*). This is an intricate process and requires the action of five elemental fires (*bhūtāgnis*), and seven essential fires (*dhatvāgnis*; that is, fires of essences). Each essence has to be cooked by its own particular *dhatvāgni*. For example, flesh-forming fire (*maṁsāgni*) acts on blood to form flesh, the fat-forming fire (*medhāgni*) to form fat from flesh, the marrow-forming fire (*majjāgni*) to form marrow from fat, semen-forming fire (*śukrāgni*) to form semen from marrow, and so on. The essence of semen produces a still finer essence termed *ojas,* which returns to the heart from whence it is distributed throughout the body as the supremely vivacious substance. It will be seen that this is the third digestive process we have encountered, and that each essence yields a finer essence which successively serves as the basis for the next essence.

The successive subjections of food to fire, or "cookings," produce both a fine essence and waste products. The latter are of two kinds: (1) *mala,* the waste product of digested food which pollutes and must be banished from the corporeal realm; (2) *prasāda,* the finer wastes produced by the fires of the various essences. The latter are beneficial and indeed necessary for the maintenance of the body, which entitles them the dubious honorific "waste-essences" (*mala dhātus*). These run appropriate errands; for example, the waste matter of the bones sustains hair and nails. We may note parenthetically that cutting hair and paring nails are, thus, forms of excrement and, while they are essential, they are not honorable tasks. The recurrent role of fire is obvious. It occurs in processes beyond those mentioned here. In addition to the fact that each essence has its own fire which cooks its *rasa* into the appropriate *dhātu,* we might recall the five elemental fires which enable the digestion of the five elements contained in food.

Rasa: The Essence and Relish of the Aesthetic World

Aesthetic ideas, like medical ideas, while not uniform, exhibit a general integration and consensus regarding fundamentals. The literature, as in the medical corpus, is vast, but what is relevant to us is the central area of aesthetic conceptualization, known as the theory of *rasa*. And, as we noted in the foregoing, *rasa* is also the central concept in the medical theory regarding the transformation of food. The *rasa* theory is about aesthetic creativity and how artistic effect takes place. It was developed primarily in relation to drama in Bharata's *Nātyaśāstra* (Rao 1967; see also note 2), but it is generally valid for all artistic genres. It was elaborated, like the medical texts were, by a large number of subsequent schools, and it continues to be elaborated to the present time, although the fundamentals proposed by Bharata (possibly as early as the second century), are not challenged, but only elaborated, commented upon, and modified in matters of detail.

How is aesthetic effect created? Stated simply, this is a process in which the artist experiences a significant emotion and subsequently re-creates it in an external form, so that the audience is enabled to experience the emotion too. There is one difference, however. The emotion experienced by the artist, whether pleasant or unpleasant, becomes refined, elevated, and transformed when re-created in the audience, so that it produces aesthetic enjoyment. That is, even an unpleasant experience, when re-created in artistic form, produces a pleasant state of mind. The process, to use analogies familiar to the Western reader, is one of finding "a local habitation and a name"[8] or an "objective correlative"[9] for one's private experience. In artistic creation, the artist stimulates the general susceptibility which human beings share, by endowing private and individual experiences with qualities and forms which make them universally accessible and appealing. A work of art is therefore a generalization of experience (*sādhāraṇīkaraṇa*).

Bharata, as well as later theorists, explained and elaborated this apparently simple process in great detail, with profound insight into human psychology and behavior and with remarkable analytical skill. To begin with, there are two givens. The first is the experience of the artist. The second is the potential of the audience to receive the aesthetic message, that is, the capacity for appreciation and responsiveness which, though more pronounced in some than others, is assumed to be shared by all. This is called *sthāī bhāva,* the responsive predisposition in men that exists unmanifested. The artist's experience could be described theoretically, but such a description would fail to evoke aesthetic joy, or *rasa,* and would remain no more than *vārtā,* mere reportage, lacking in the liveliness of the experience's essence. To transcend this bland process and to communicate the experience aesthetically, the artist must present, in an objective and external mode, certain stimuli which represent his experience and which are capable of activating the desired sentiment in the audience.

Several terms are used to explain how artistic effect is created. First, *sthāyī bhāva,* as already mentioned, signifies the innate human capability for responding emotionally to stimuli. Second, the term *vibhāva* refers to an external stimulus. The poet wishing to create aesthetic effect must present a stimulus, for example, a heroine, who would be an external semblance of his internal emotion—an emotion which, had it remained merely internal, would have been no more than an "airy nothing," inaccessible to others. In acting her role, the heroine acts as a stimulus to create the poet's emotion or inner experience in the audience. This stimulus can be made more effective in stagecraft by elaborations, called "enhansive stimuli" (*uddīpana vibhāva*), as opposed to the "suspensory stimulus" (*ālambana vibhāva*), which the heroine personifies.

Moreover, the heroine can extend the stimulative process by suggestive behavior such as glances and body movements, which are called *anubhāva.* The exteriority of sentiment or emotion also can be enhanced with extras, or "frills," which are the ancillary or transient emotions (*vyābhicārī bhāva, saṁcāribhāva*); for example, joy in love and anxiety in separation. These further the communicative process by emphasizing and dwelling upon the sentiment of love (which is at that point openly visible in the heroine and her gestures). All the above combine to fashion a dramatic situation, or—with appropriate differences—a poem, a painting, a musical composition, and so on, as the case may be. Such an objective correlative to the artist's inner experience is devoid of the grossness of the experiential world or the nature of worldly things (*loka dharma*) and is distilled and refined into partaking of the nature of dramatic things (*nāṭya dharma*). Its effect on the mind of the receptive audience (*rasika*) is *rasa,* or aesthetic enjoyment (*āsvādana*).

The similarities between this analysis of aesthetic experience and the culinary and ingestive processes of the medical theories are inescapable. First and most obvious, the concept of *rasa* is common and central to the two areas. Just as the *rasa* of food is an essence derived from cooking the gross material of the ingested food by the action of the digestive fires, the *rasa* of aesthetics is a fine emotion born of the transformation of gross and mundane experience by the multistaged extractive and distillative deliberation involving *anubhāva, vibhāva,* and *vyabhicāribhāva.* Many other terms of the vocabulary of food, such as *rasana* (relish), *carvaṇa* (gestation), and *āsvādana* (taste), recur in the vocabulary of aesthetics. Next, we have the striking similarity between the two areas in their attention to the details of the processes. The aesthetic process almost seems to model some of its descriptions on the medical; for example, it describes the involuntary gestures (*sāttvika bhāvas*) of the heroine—blushing, perspiration, horripilation, and so on of the heroine—as "symptoms" of her emotional state.[10]

Moreover, both theories are concerned with integration: the medical, with the balanced integration of the organism; the aesthetic, with the integration of an experience which is beyond the boundaries of the person, but which embraces the artist and his audience in the generalization (*sādhāraṇikaraṇa*) of experience. Related to this, there is the further parallel of the possibility of disrupting the equilibrium, conceptualized in the shared notions *guṇa* and *dośa.* In the physiological example *guṇa* is a beneficial quality whose absence, conceptualized as *dośa,* will disturb the organism's salutary equilibrium. In the aesthetic example, *guṇa* is a quality involving a high aesthetic evaluation which, when absent, is replaced by *dośa,* which is the result of the combination of inappropriate emotions, analogous to the discordant levels of bodily elements of the medical theory. Still another parallel is found in the place the heart occupies in the two schemes. In the medical theory, the final essence derived from food through the digestive process, *ojas,* visits the heart and is circulated throughout the body, vitalizing it and suffusing it with luster and majesty (a physical quality often attributed to the king, a person who is not lacking in the economic means to take care of his nourishment). The aesthetic theory similarly envisages the centrality of the heart in aesthetic enjoyment, as expressed in the concept of *sahṛdya,* a "person of like heart" such as a poet, gifted with supreme artistic receptivity and sensitivity. Artistic enjoyment fills the heart with pleasure (as the daffodils did to Wordsworth) and suffuses the entire body with its thrill.

In concluding this section, we might extend the parallel we have examined toward a third area, that of the spiritual. The ingestion of food is patently an exercise which has as its purpose the mundane end of nourishing the body. The aesthetic sphere occupies an intermediary position between the concerns of the body and the sphere of ritual and transcendental action. Whereas in the gastronomic process, essences of varying degrees of refinement are identified, they still remain substantial and material. This includes *ojas,* the most refined essence, which primarily produces material consequences, such as the radiance of the skin. In the aesthetic sphere, we are confronted with a blend of the material and the qualitative, with emphasis on the latter. For an artist to conceive an artistic creation and to give birth to it, he must possess an artistic gift (*pratibhā*), which is a quality. The aesthetic process, even if it might involve a human agent such as the heroine, is clearly superorganic. Indeed, if it remains mundane, it is gross and unrefined. Thus when human agents are involved, they are simply the insubstantial media of the aesthetic process. They are outside time and space and are mere disguises—hence the appropriateness of masks, makeup, costumes, and so on, in plays. The whole aesthetic process is designed to erase the mundaneness of the experience upon which the artistic work is founded. The expressions (*abhinaya*) of the heroine are worn like a mask and, though based on the body, are essentially noncorporeal. They are not necessarily an indication of the existence of any emotion within her.[11] When, through the mediation of the heroine's dramatic action (or any other objective correlate of the artist's experience), emotion is evoked in the audience (the persons with the same heart as the artist), it is totally devoid of experiential grossness and is suffused with the blissful aesthetic joy of *rasa* alone.

In its earliest usage in the *Artharva Veda, rasa* refers to the juice of plants. In the Upanishads, the term gains a further meaning, bliss, with spiritual connotations. *Rasa* of the Upanishads is the essence of the universe. The objective of the holy seeker is to experience this *rasa*. It stands for the illumination of consciousness (which incidentally recalls the bodily illumination brought about by the material essence of *ojas*). Aesthetic *rasa* enlightens and makes the inner self serenely joyous. Hence it is "the brother of the spiritual experience" (*brahmāsvādasahodara*). In the moment of perfect aesthetic appreciation, self is submerged in the bliss of *rasa* and freed from worldly bondage—a state not too far from the meditative bliss of the ascetic.

Food in Sri Lanka: Variation on a Classical Theme

What follows is a description of some aspects of food among the Sinhalese of Sri Lanka. We may start by mentioning two properties of food which make it physically and culturally meaningful in Sinhalese thought, *rasa* and *guṇa*. *Rasa* refers to the flavor of food and literally means "flavor," while *guṇa* refers to its nutritional value. These two implicitly or explicitly carry their opposites, *nīrasa* and *aguṇa*. A flavorless or bland food, devoid of *rasa*, is therefore *nīrasa*. *Aguṇa*, however, is not just the absence of nutritive quality, but is plainly detrimental to health in a culturally conceived way, primarily in terms of being excessively hot or excessively cold. ("Hot" and "cold" here, do not refer to temperature, but to specific culturally defined properties.) Both excesses are harmful because they disturb the humoral balance of the body. Since food ideally must be healthy, it is necessary to avoid excessively hot or cold foods: or at least, an excess of one must be countered by an excess of the other. This echoes the theory of equilibrium found in the classical texts.

The meaning of *rasa* in relation to the main meals centers on certain valued flavors such as hotness (in the burning, spicy sense), saltiness, sweetness, and so on. Sweetness is separated from all other desirable flavors and, though highly valued, is never mixed with the spicy or salty flavors which dominate the main meal. Thus "sweet and sour," such as we find in Chinese cuisine, would be quite unacceptable to the Sinhalese as part of a main meal. The idea of a sweet drink (for example, fruit juice, carbonated drinks, or sweetened tea), as an accompaniment to the main meal would not be at all in keeping with traditional Sinhalese taste.

The Sinhalese are meat eaters. Fish in particular, either in fresh or dried form, is universally consumed. In the cities and towns where meat is available, it is part of the regular diet of those who can afford it. On the fringes of the wilderness, villagers hunt and eat the meat of deer, sambhur, wild fowl, wild boar, rabbit, and so on. Thus, unlike the common consumption of fish, meat eating is concentrated in the two extremes of the society, the urban areas and the vicinity of the forest.

The carnivorousness of the Sinhalese has baffled many who reason that since Buddhism proposes nonviolence toward all beings, the Sinhalese, who are Buddhists, should not eat meat. This is certainly a logical expectation, but the ordinary Sinhalese people think differently. They hold that what is non-Buddhist is killing, and not eating—a position which is perfectly in keeping with the doctrinal Buddhist idea that *karma* is volition and not action. The large majority of the Buddhist Sinhalese do abhor killing, often hesitating to kill even pests, and certainly avoid killing for purposes of food. Who then does the killing? Muslims and Christians: the former control the meat business, and the later control the fishing, with seaside village churches playing an important organizational role.

A more difficult logical problem faces those Buddhist Sinhalese who actually do kill, such as the seafaring communities of the southern and southwestern seaboard. The dilemma is solved by resort to the well-known distinction, made by peasants in many Buddhist societies, between merit (*pin, puṇya*) and demerit (*pav, pāpa*). These fisherman admit that when killing fish, they actually commit unwholesome karma, which produces demerit. But they believe that merit gained by good works cancels the demerit. How do these fishermen gain merit? By avoiding fishing on the sacred full-moon days and by feeding Buddhist monks with a portion of the catch.

A further area of relevance emerges when the fact that Buddhists eat meat is considered in relation to the paradigm of the Buddhist life exemplified in monkhood. The Buddhist monk is a *bhikkhu,* who begs for his food and is unconcerned with what food he eats. Ideally, his begging is universalist, that is, he goes from door to door without exception, from the house of the high to that of the low. He is expected to mix together whatever food he gets and eat it with no desire for it. Mixing erases the social origin of the portions of foods received, as it does the distinctiveness of the items of food. By doing so, the mendicant transcends the worldliness of eating. He does not taste a variety of delicate flavors. This is analogous to the monk's injunction not to look at parts of a woman's body. For to do so would be to savour them as it would be to savor distinctive flavors. Buddhists in general, like Buddhist monks, mix their food before eating, except that in mixing it, they are enhancing flavor in a culturally conceived way rather than seeking ascetic indifference to it. One treats what is on one's plate as food and not as fish or meat, so that the question of killing simply does not arise.

The specific Buddhist attitude to food deserves special comment. Food occupies a central place in Buddhist philosophy and is understood in a broader sense than the merely material. This is signified in the Buddhist "first question" (*eko dhammo*) and its answer, "all beings subsist on food" ("*sabbe satta aharaṭṭhitika*"). This statement is so important that to fully understand it would release one from *saṁsāra*. In it is condensed a very high valuation of food as subsistence, as well as an equally strong devaluation of food as having any significance beyond the purely subsistive. Subsistence is understood as a necessary condition of proper contemplation and mental discipline which leads to enlightenment.

Food is the basis of all life, biological, psychological and social, and, therefore, of all action. Life is understood both as the present one and as the cycle of existence. Both are sustained by food, of which there are four types. The first is *kabalinkara āhāra,* "that which is consumed in morsels," or material food, which can be gross (*olarika*) or fine (*sukhuma*) and which sustains the body. The second is *phassa ahāra,* "food of contact," which nurtures the senses, giving pleasure, displeasure, or neutral feeling. The third is *manosamcetana āhāra,* volition, the food of the mind which sustains becoming. And the fourth is *viññana ahāra,* consciousness which produces body and mind, name and form (*nāma rūpa*). The source of all four of these sustenances is craving. Their effect is not just the continuity of this life but the process of regeneration. Thus, food has to be approached with the greatest caution. It must not be consumed for pleasure, indulgence, personal charm, or beauty, but solely for subsistence. The practice of the path to liberation is only possible when body and mind are in a healthy and vigorous state. Hence the Buddhist rejection of the two extremes, self-indulgence (*kāmasukhalli kānuyoga*) and self-mortification (*atthakhiḷamathānuyoga*), both of which are described as unworthy and unprofitable. Food is merely a necessity, explicitly compared to a medication which one must consume to sustain the body—a comparison which recalls the recurrent medical imagery of Buddhist literature and the characterization of the Buddha as the physician teacher (*Bhaisajya guru*) who treats the illness of *saṁsārik* existence. Many things we consider luxuries or comforts are seen by the Buddhists as medications for specific pathologies, for example, perfume as a medication to dispel bodily odor. The view of food we see here is also consistent with a basic Buddhist doctrine, that of causality. Food (all four types mentioned above) is the cause of life. These food categories are also causes because when they are taken away, their effect—existence—is taken away too. In the ideal Buddhist life, that of the monk, food is to be ingested merely as necessity. The practice of begging for food eradicates both the social origin and the uniqueness of food items and flavors and thereby expresses indifference to those qualities such as texture and flavor which are so important in the food ingestion of the laity. The inevitable mixing of food which takes place in this method of food gathering, considered to lower flavor, is repeated in the monk's conscious act of mixing immediately before ingestion. In the terminology we have used, the Buddhist monk consumes food solely for *guṇa* and not for *rasa*.

A further ramification of the idea that food is a mere necessity which should not be savored lies in the belief that merit for the lay donor of food is maximized by the proper attitude of the monk toward the gift of food received. To generate maximum merit, the monk should think of the food as neither a source of enjoyment nor of physical prowess, but only as sustenance which enables his pursuit of the pure life. Food must be ingested with the reflection (*pratyāvēkṣa*) that it is done for sustenance alone, which makes possible contemplation and spiritual progress. We are reminded here of the Buddha's realization, which set him on the path to Enlightenment, of the futility of rejecting food, and of the incapacity of the weakened body to engage in healthy, rigorous, and meaningful contemplation. Thus, there is no rejection of food in Buddhism.

The thoroughgoing instrumentality of food envisaged in these ideas also helps to explain a significant contrast between Buddhist and Hindu practices surrounding food offering. It is well known that in Hindu ritual, food is offered to the gods and is later consumed by the devotees as *prasād,* or leftovers of the offering, which contains divine substance. Food offered to the Buddha is never consumed later by the devotees. It is typically thrown away, often to be eaten by birds and animals, the commonest being crows and dogs. Unlike the leftover food of the gods, which is auspicious and affirmative of life, food offered to the Buddha or to the monks is the food of the ascetic, devoid of uniqueness of item, flavor, texture, and social origin—qualities which would have defined it as enjoyable, worldly, and life-affirming. It is food which is fit only for those spiritual seekers who have renounced the world, and unfit for worldly beings. Hence the belief that consumption of such food is not meritorious and will cause rebirth as crows and dogs—the visible consumers of discarded food offerings. The undue use of the property or produce of religious establishments is prohibited in some ancient inscriptions on pain of mystical retribution that such users will be reborn as crows or dogs. Large quantities of food offered twice daily at the Palace of the Tooth Relic in Kandy are given to beggars, a practice which affirms the rule that devotees do not consume the discarded offerings.

In Sinhala, there is no distinction between human and natural causation in the process of food transformation from raw to cooked, since both are said to involve a "ripening." This does not mean that a concept of human agency in cooking is absent. Cooked food in Sinhalese thought is food which has been completely transformed, since there is no trace left of the flavors of the originally raw items. We noted that mixing food in secular eating is a mechanism of enhancing flavor. Here "flavor" does not refer to the original flavors of the raw items which are cooked. Instead, the emphasis is on flavor such as spiciness, hotness, saltiness, and so on, which are generated by the ingredients and by the cooking procedure. If there is any trace of the original flavor left, it is present in a somewhat abstracted way, for example, as aroma, which is a mere reminiscence of the original item and one that is quite different from its aroma in its raw state. Besides, that aroma—being insubstantial—may mingle freely with its counterparts derived from other cooked items. The act of cooking thus unifies the remnants of flavors which were originally separate in their raw state. Yet this unification preserves an element of diversity based on the dimensions of the major flavors such as spiciness, saltiness, and sourness. Thus, when one eats properly transformed food, one is, in fact, eating flavor. This is, of course, in the secular realm, where flavor, or *rasa,* reigns supreme over nutritive value, or *guṇa.* In the sacred realm this relation is reversed. Accordingly, the consumption of flavorful food is sometimes accompanied by an underlying anxiety that, by definition, such food is not nutritious and may even be unhealthy—a phenomenon socially expressed in taboos or restrictions on foods and in beliefs that desirable foods attract the eyes of malevolent spirit beings, and psychologically in food phobias.

In relation to the transformation of food, two areas may be mentioned as suitable for exploration. First, the transformation of food in Sinhalese cuisine (which I believe it shares with the broader south Asian pattern) stands in contrast to that in China and in the modern West, both of which share the notion that cooking should not fully transform the original raw items. The culinary techniques of both China and Western cultures exemplify this. In China, for example, raw food items are brought into sudden and intense contact with heat for a brief period and the food is considered cooked. Procedures productive of comparable effect are followed in the West. The result is a blend of the raw and the cooked, where the outer layer of a piece of food, such as a steak in the West or a slice of carrot in a Chinese meal, is cooked while the interior remains relatively raw. Thus, in a Chinese dish the raw items—pieces of carrot, peppers, cabbage, and other vegetables or chunks of meat—retain a close affinity in both flavor and texture to their uncooked state. There is, of course, an encompassing flavor in the dish, but this is in dialogue with the distinctive flavors of the constitutive items. In contrast, the slow simmering of the south Asian style enables the spices, salt, and other ingredients to penetrate the raw items totally and bring about their transformation, thereby reducing, in the logical extreme of the style, the raw items into mere flavors such as spiciness and saltiness. The south Asian preoccupation with excessive cooking, or total transformation, is exemplified in the practice of second cooking found either in its real form, such as the Bengali mode of frying fish before cooking, or in the more symbolic form, such as the nominal frying of cooked food (tempering) in the Sinhalese cuisine. (We may note that in the two examples cited, the Bengalis fry before cooking, while the Sinhalese cook before frying.) Either way, an obsession with total transformation is manifest.

Since in the social sciences there is a general belief that the world has been going through a process of secularization, we may consider food preparation to have once been associated with religious attitudes. We may look upon the examples of overcooking and second cooking as expressive of such attitudes. All cooked foods, offered twice every day at the highly formal food offering at the Palace of the Tooth Relic in Kandy, Sri Lanka, are tempered after cooking. Practices such as this, where food is ritually offered to sacred beings, may well be related to the pollution concept of South Asia because the preoccupation with cooking—to the point of overcooking—suggests an attempt to rid the original raw items of their natural grossness and impurity. The modern notion of "tempering" is perhaps a vestigial second cooking, now secularized and elevated into the culture of high cuisine. The term is significant, for we need to temper something only if it is gross or wild and intemperate. The emphasis on cooking and recooking is reminiscent of the multiple intracorporeal cookings of the medical texts. Both are ways of transcending grossness and achieving finer essences.

From these general observations, I must now turn to a description of the Sinhalese meal. The universal use of meat in varying forms and quantities was already mentioned. I hasten to add that this does not suggest that meat is primary in the Sinhalese meal, as it is in the modern West. Meat in the Sinhalese meal is but another dish in an intricate constellation of dishes. It indicates the relative affluence of the consumer. Not everybody can afford a proper meat dish as opposed to a nominal one.

The central food of the Sinhalese is rice. Traditionally, the Sinhalese ate three rice meals a day, breakfast, lunch, and dinner. Children could snack on more rice in between meals, especially between lunch and dinner. Even today this pattern is sometimes followed in the countryside, but it is not common and appears to be on the wane. Many areas of culture such as language and religious ritual express the centrality of rice in the Sinhalese meal. When one is ready to eat, one does not say, "let us eat," one says, "let us eat rice." Eating is synonymous with rice eating.

During the rice shortages of World War II and its aftermath, a new element was introduced into the food of the Sinhalese: wheat flour. The cultivation of millet had all but ceased, due largely to its uneconomical nature, and a cheap substitute was available in wheat bread. However, there was a great deal of cultural prejudice against bread, particularly among the rural gentry. The urban dwellers and the poor took to it with little protest, and it has today become accepted even in rural homes as edible for breakfast. The westernized upper classes and the middle classes now eat bread seven days of the week. These same groups also may eat some other nonrice meal such as hoppers (pancakes) and string hoppers (spaghetti), even though these may be fully or partially made out of rice flour. We see in these examples a new perception that rice is monotonous, a change which reflects a newly acquired taste for variety in carbohydrates. The vast majority of the Sinhalese, however, the inhabitants of the countryside, still feel a sense of starvation and deprivation if they do not eat at least two rice meals a day. The ideal of three rice meals still lingers. For example, if one were to offer breakfast to Buddhist monks, rice would certainly be the central dish. Rice, therefore, has been described, without exaggeration, as the staple of the Sinhalese. It has enjoyed this status for as long as we have records—more than two millennia. The traditional epic history of the island, known as the *Mahāvaṁsa* (Geiger, ed. 1960), glorifies the kings who made possible the greater cultivation of rice by the construction of extensive waterworks. No other activity has been historically more important to the Sinhalese than the cultivation of rice. The cycle of rice cultivation is hedged with ritual and ceremonies which express the public significance of rice production. The harvesting of rice, the culmination of this productive process, is especially celebrated in ceremonial, festivity, and taboos.

The centrality of rice is visually expressed in the arrangement of the table. A large dish of rice is placed at the center of the table, with a number of vegetable and nonvegetable dishes of relatively smaller size occupying the periphery. The Sinhalese table is like a solar system in which all dishes are peripheral to the sunlike bowl of rice. All dishes are seen as aids for consuming rice rather than as foods in themselves. In eloquent Sri Lankan English, curries are simply "rice pullers." They are seen as flavorings for rice and, therefore, act as agents to transform rice into greater gastronomic acceptability. The curries, fiery with spice, recall once more the different digestive fires of the texts, which transform the grossness of the staple into fine essence.

With the centrality of rice established, we can further assess the status of meat in Sinhalese food. Like other peripheral dishes, it is clearly a flavoring—although relatively large quantities of meat may be consumed whenever it is available and affordable. As we have already noted, the large majority of the people live neither in the cities nor in the fringes of the jungle, the polar locations of meat, but in the infinitely greater interstitial ecological area which constitutes the countryside. In these villages and hamlets, the majority may never eat meat at all or only on very rare occasions because it is a food beyond their reach in more than one sense. More frequently they have the opportunity to eat fish, especially seasonally. Even fish eating may not be possible more than once a month. However, for practically every meal, all except the poorest will eat some form of meat—dried fish of some kind being the most common. Even here the quantity consumed may be quite modest, being only a few ounces, cooked in a rather thin gravy of the milky juice of grated coconut and spices. Where even this small amount of dried fish is not affordable, a housewife will cook a dish similar to the one just described using about an ounce or two of dehydrated fish known as "Maldive fish."

These examples of the minimal use of meat are instructive and show that the purpose of meat in Sinhalese cuisine is to provide flavor, and not nourishment. Flavor is an agent in consumption, the halfway point between the fully exterior culinary process and fully interior digestive process, both of which use the agency of fires. Flavor is the fire that envelops the real food, which is rice, in the process of ingestion. Being so, meat can be ritually neutral—in contrast to its untouchability or ambiguity in most of the subcontinent.

As we have seen, the classical texts are meticulous in their details about the process of intracorporeal cooking, including its agencies, its digestive fires, and its objective of producing essences out of gross material. What we have in the above examples of culinary practice is highly reminiscent of these processes. The slow and repetitive cookings and the copious use of spices overpower the grossness of the original raw foods and thereby achieve the goal of producing culturally edible food. This culinary process is but the first in a series of cookings, of which the intracoporeal cookings constitute the rest. The essences instrumental in these internal cookings are produced inside the stomach. The essence of exterior cooking—cooked food—is produced in the kitchen, the stomach of the house.

The numerous curry dishes which form the periphery of the rice dish in the Sinhalese meal constitute several sensory opposites: white and dark, hot and cold, wet and dry, spicy and mild, smooth and rough, salty and sour, and so on. All these are considered essential elements of a proper meal. White curry contrasts with red, brown, or black curry. Hot and cold are meaningful both in terms of inner properties of the respective items capable of influencing humoral balance and in terms of physical hotness or coolness (that is, the contrast between a cooked dish and a saladlike dish which, though uncooked, is transformed by the use of salt, lime juice, chopped green hot peppers, and other spices). Wet and dry brings us to dishes such as Maldive fish gravy, on the liquid extreme, and on the dry extreme, a dish known as *mallun,* which is cooked without the use of water or any other liquid, whose water content, through constant stirring, is largely made to evaporate, leaving a dehydrated dish. In the next pair, spicy and mild curries are complimentarily used. Often white curries are milder than dark ones, although none is ever free from the supremacy of hot spices. Rough and smooth refer to texture—although here again excessive cooking has a leveling effect—but the saladlike dishes and their approximations retain a chewiness, as opposed to the easier mutability of others. The last pair on our list, salt and sour, usually refers to no more than one or two dominantly salty and/or sour dishes. Here again, both kinds are liberally spiced. The rice dish, by its particular cultural gravitational pull, keeps these sensory opposites harmoniously mediated and poised, so we could say that the Sinhalese have a cosmically balanced diet. These oppositions recall the foods types of the *Caraka,* but of greater relevance is the balance between them, which reflects the equilibrium of the elements and essences emphasized in the texts. The central rice dish with its peripheral curry dishes visually represents this equipoise. Since the set table represents the moment before ingestion, it also represents a temporal equipoise.

It is unnecessary to labor any further the centrality of rice in Sinhalese food, but we may in passing make brief mention of the ritual expression of this high evaluation. Rice cooked in the milklike juice of grated coconut is the ritually and festively most valued food among the Sinhalese. To give an example from a more strictly ritual sphere, the formal food offerings at the Palace of the Tooth Relic in Kandy dramatize the significance of rice in two rituals: first, in the daily food offering made in the morning, not only are the rice dishes arranged to occupy a spatially central position, but these dishes are made of gold, a material that reaffirms their centrality, in a potent South Asian metallic metaphor. Second, at the annual ceremony of New Rice at the Palace of the Tooth Relic, which celebrates the rice crop and facilitates its prodigious increase, three colossal bowls of rice are offered to the Sacred Tooth Relic, with great ceremony. A more exaggerated metaphoric representation is hardly imaginable.

Since vegetarianism and meat eating are important South Asian thematic opposites, we might briefly explore some of the dynamics and dimensions of these two phenomena in the food and society of the Sinhalese. We have noticed that although meat is universally eaten, it is a peripheral dish. But the kinds of meat are diverse, and they form a hierarchy in which beef occupies the lowest position. Could this be considered an echo of the Hindu taboo on beef eating? This could well be the case—especially if the same evaluation prevailed in ancient times. However, some other factors have been at work, particularly during the past five centuries or so. We may here consider the implications of the fact that Muslims control the meat business. And meat is not the only business of the Muslims. They also control other businesses, such as retail trade, in which they and their Buddhist compatriots are in competition with each other. In the nineteenth century an enterprising Buddhist mercantile and professional class grew out of the caste of fishermen concentrated in the southern and southwestern seaboard of the island. We have considerable evidence which suggests that antibeef sentiments were fanned and financed by this aggressive group. Considering who controls the beef business, this can hardly be considered the result of pure religious fervor. These antibeef movements and sentiments are religiocultural expressions of entrepreneurial antagonisms.

With the swelling of the nationalist movement in the nineteenth and early twentieth century, we have another sociological source with which to evaluate the practices of beef eating. This lies in the fact that the British were conspicuously beef eaters. The Sinhalese business leaders of the aforementioned antibeef group were parties to conflict in this instance too. Their target this time was not the Muslims but the Western-oriented Sinhalese elites who had actually become "brown-skinned Englishmen," speaking the language of the colonial masters, doing their jobs, and eating their food. By these adaptations, this group acquired privileges which the aggressive Buddhist entrepreneurs found both intolerable and unprofitable. Propaganda controlled by the latter group ridiculed the British and their darker counterparts of native origin as beef eaters. We must understand these antibeef sentiments, and even periodic calls for vegetarianism, as protests against obstacles to profit making which colonial domination and the westernization of local elites engendered for the contending group. Thus, while the antibeef sentiments of the subcontinent may have some influence on Sinhalese Buddhists, we have even more forceful explanations closer home.

Acknowledgments

I wish to thank Professors Ashok R. Kelkar and David Shulman for their comments on this chapter.

Notes

1. The ethnographic material used in this paper is based on my fieldwork in Sri Lanka in 1975–76 which was supported by the Social Science Research Council.

2. See Daniel 1984, chap. 3, for a perceptive discussion on the South Indian conception of a house.

3. According to tradition, Indra taught medicine to Atreya and surgery to Dhanvantari, each of whom had six pupils. The works of two of these, Agnivesa and Bhela, are extant and are known as the *Caraka Saṁhitā* and the *Bhela Saṁhitā,* respectively. Suśruta the surgeon wrote the *Suśruta Saṁhitā.* Of the three, the *Bhela* has survived only in a corrupt form. Thus the *Caraka* and the *Suśruta* form the basis of classical Indian medicine as it is known today. These authorships and genealogies are far from clearly established. The *Caraka* as it exists today is considered the work of not one

but three authors—Agniveṣa, a disciple of Atreya, and Caraka and Drdhabala, both Kashmiri physicians. The best known commentator is Cakrapāṇi ca. 1066, who elucidated both the *Caraka* (Sharma and Dash 1976) and the *Suśruta* (Ray, Gupta, and Roy 1980) in his works *Caraka Tātparya Tīkā* or *Ayurveda Dīpikā* and *Bhānumatī,* respectively. Of the latter, only the section on *Sūtra Sthāna* has survived. The best known extant commentary on the *Suśruta* is Dallana's *Nibandha Saṁgraha,* ca. twelfth century. Arunadatta ca. 1220, wrote *Sarvāṇga Sundarī,* a commentary on the work of Vāgbhata II. Modern works are numerous. One of the most authoritative is Surendranath Das Gupta 1932. See also J. Filliozat 1964, *The Classical Doctrine of Indian Medicine: The Origins and Its Greek Parallels.* Translated by D. R. Channa, Munshiram Manoharlal, New Delhi 1964; P. Kutumbiah (1962) The *Caraka Saṁhitā* is available in manuscript form in a dozen major libraries in India, England, and Germany. Printed editions go back to the nineteenth century. Complete English editions are Sharma and Dash 1949 and the six-volume edition by the Shree Gulabkunverba Ayurvedic Society, Jamnagar 1949. Other languages in which the *Caraka* is available are Hindi, Urdu, Gujerati, Bengali, Marati, Telegu, Tibetan, Persian, Arabic, and Sinhala.

Some material to which I refer is based on my memory of the Sinhala *Caraka,* a copy of which is not available to me. Hence my inability to provide more exact references.

The classical works on aesthetics are more numerous. The source of all of them is the *Natyaśāstra* of Bharata. Bharata's work is placed between the second and seventh centuries, and we have an unbroken tradition of literary thought until about the thirteenth century. Bhamaha, Dandin, Vamana, Udbhata, Lollata, Anandavardhana, Kuntaka, Abhinavagupta, Ksemendra, and Mammata are only a few among the galaxy of these thinkers. Numerous modern works exist in English, which include A. B. Keith 1954; P. V. Kane 1961; G. H. Tarlekar 1975; S. K. De 1960, and Edwin Gerow, *Indian Poetics* 1977. For an authoritative yet concise account see S. K. De, *Sanskrit Poetics as a Study of Aesthetic,* 1963.

4. Controversies about details are numerous and lively. A particularly symbolic expression for the medical field is the meeting of the great sages celebrated in the *Caraka Saṁhitā*. Having assembled at the Caitrāratha forest to discuss questions relating to foods and flavors, no two sages agreed about as elementary a question as how many flavors there are. Bhadrakapya maintained that there was only one flavor while Kankayana argued for an infinity of flavors. The other participants each held an opinion, proposing various numbers. (See Das Gupta 1932:357–358; William Alwis, editor 1967:90–91). For aesthetics, the different schools such as Rasa, Dhvani, and Alaṁkāra provide ample examples of hairsplitting. A significant example, as Shulman (1988) points out, is the contrary views expressed by Bharata and Abhinavagupta. For Bharata, *rasa* is an

effect, as discussed above, but for Abhinavagupta, it is a preexisting reality which only needs to be unveiled by removing the impediments of normal consciousness.

5. The texts distinguish between two *rasa-s:* 1) the essence of digested food (*āhāra-rasa*), and 2) *rasa-dhātu* or *rasa*-essence produced from the *āhāra-rasa,* which is a constituent of the body (Kutumbiah 1962, 40).

6. We know that this is controversial. See note 3 above.

7. Rasa here, though qualitative, has a substantial aspect while in modern popular usage, it is merely a quality, namely, flavor.

8. Shakespeare, *A Midsummer Night's Dream,* act V, sc. I. lines 12–17 (Wells and Taylor 1986, 371):

The poet's eye, in a fine frenzy rolling,
Doth glance from heaven to earth, from earth to heaven
And, as imagination bodies forth
The forms of things unknown, the poet's pen
Turns them to shapes, and gives to airy nothing
A local habitation and a name.

9. "Hamlet and his problems," in T. S. Eliot 1950.

10. This is the only instance in the *rasa* theory which concedes that the heroine or actor feels the emotion being enacted. Even here it is not clear whether this is actually so, the emphasis being on the externalization of the emotion. But for this exception, which is doubtful, the Indian theory is diametrically opposed to the Stanislavskian.

11. With the possible exception of *sāttvika bhāvas,* alluded to in note 10, above.

References

Alwis, William (editor)
1967 *Dravya Guṇa Viññanaya* (in Sinhala). Navinna, Sri Lanka: Ayurveda Research Institute.

Bhatt, G. K.
1986 *Bhārata nāṭya manjarī.* A selection from Bharata's *Nāṭyasāstra.* Poona: Bhandarkar Oriental Research Institute.

Daniel, Valentine
1984 *Fluid Signs.* Berkeley: University of California Press.

Das Gupta, Surendranath
1932 *A History of Indian Philosophy,* vol. II. Cambridge: Cambridge University Press.

De, S. K.
1960 *History of Sanskrit Poetics,* 2 vols. (Second and Revised edition). Calcutta.

1963 *Sanskrit Poetics as a Study of Aesthetic*. Berkeley: University of California Press.

Eliot, T. S.
1950 *Selected Essays*. New York: Harcourt Brace.

Filliozat, J.
1964 *The Classical Doctrine of Indian Medicine: The Origins and Its Greek Parallels*. Translated by D. R. Channa. New Delhi: Munshiram Manoharlal.

Geiger, Wilhelm (editor)
1960 *The Mahāvaṁśa or the Great Chronicle of Ceylon*. Colombo: Ceylon Government.

Gerow, Edwin
1977 *Indian Poetics*. Weisbaden: Otto Harrasowitz.

Kane, P. V.
1961 *History of Sanskrit Poetics*. New Delhi: Motilal Banarsidass.

Keith, A. B.
1954 *The Sanskrit Drama*. Oxford: Oxford University Press.

Kutumbiah, P.
1962 *Ancient Indian Medicine*. New Delhi: Orient Longmans.

Rangacharya, Adya
1986 *Nātyaśāstra*. English translation with critical notes. Bangalore: I. B. H. Prakashana.

Rao, P. S. R. A.
1967 *A Monograph on Bhārata's Nāṭyaśāstra*. Hyderabad: Natyamala Publication.

Ray, P. and H. N. Gupta
1965 *Caraka Saṁhitā*. New Delhi: National Institute of Sciences.

Ray, P., H. N. Gupta and Mira Roy
1980 *Suśruta Saṃhitā*. New Delhi: Indian National Science Academy.

Sharma, Ram Karan and Bhagwan Dash
1976 *Agnivesa's Carakasaṁhitā: text with English translation and critical exposition based on Cakrapāṇi Datta's Ayurveda Dīpikā*. Varanasi: Chaukhamba Sanskrit Series office.

Shulman, David
1988 Personal communication.

Tarlekar, G. H.
1975 *Studies in the Nāṭyaśāstra*. New Delhi: Motilal Banarsidass.

Wells, Stanley, and Gary Taylor (editors)
1986 *William Shakespeare: The Complete Works*. Oxford: Clarendon Press.

7

Annambrahman:
Cultural Models, Meanings, and Aesthetics of Hindu Food

*

R. S. Khare

Background

What follows requires a brief prologue. A specific activity conducted during the Mysore conference—Professor Marriott's "SAṀSĀRA" game—started me thinking about different interrelationships among cultural models and meanings of food and their relationships to *saṁsāra* (Marriott 1987). When asked to play the game, I had declined. Instead, I simply observed, reserving an opportunity to reflect on the game in relation to Hindu conceptions of food. This chapter, in a way, provides me with such an occasion. Essentially, there are two issues which concern me here: first, the Hindu's conception of gross (*sṭhūla*) and subtle (*sūkṣma*), with a distinct approach to the "world" (and the worldly), or saṁsāra.[1] Second, what is the relationship between food, self, and the otherworldly? Though Professor Marriott's "saṁsāra game" may have become an instigating occasion for what follows, there is no attempt made here to interpret or evaluate his approach to the Hindu world.

During the saṁsāra game, a focus on the anthropology of Hindu transactions was obvious.[2] Transactions—verbal (and nonverbal), social, material, and evaluative—"flowed" via the players (moral agents), back and forth, involving ("marking") the Hindu within his everyday rural life. Scoring sheets of the inventor of the game recorded the markings gathered and erased as the players went through their rounds of "saṁsāra." We are told of what underlies all of this:

> Players aim to maintain or alter their markings, their wealth, or their people during one or more births in SAṀSĀRA, or to get out of SAṀSĀRA, or any combination of these aims.
>
> In pursuing these aims, players' problems are (a) to understand SAṀSĀRA, and themselves; and (b) to learn to act appropriately. To solve these problems they need (c) to record and score their actions" (Marriott 1987).

Marriott's definition of saṁsāra, provided below, frames these aims:

> "Saṁsāra" is the natural and human world or universe, understood as a "flowing together" (of everything), hence as a "cosmic flux." The "saṁsāra" of living things is their "life passage," or "cycle of birth and death." It is also a word for "family," or "family life."

Roughly, the goal of each player during the game was to conduct one's life—birth, harvesting, marriage, accumulating wealth, increasing crops, feuding, and dying—with minimum "markings" (a technical term for "action" or karma which the game's background document explains, to let the positive and negative actions cancel themselves out). A winner was a player "with no markings." The game started with a "source person," ranked higher, who began with no markings, and he or she tried to stay that way to retain his or her position within the game, with a "recycling bin" (and transactional capabilities) in hand. Since the source could not cook, others must feed him; he inspected, intervened, and negotiated during the game, but he had to do all of this without gaining any "personal markings." In short, the simulation game tried to replicate Marriott's transactional approach to the Hindu world and in the process illustrated an interplay among what the Hindu calls strands or qualities, (*guṇas*), elements (*mahābhūtas*), humors (*dośas*), and aims (*puruṣārthas*).[3] Producing, procuring, and eating food remained integral to Marriott's simulation of "saṁsāra," for in foods also fully participated the above four essential constituents of the Hindu cosmology. However, the game concerned itself with wide-ranging social exchanges and they implicitly commented, as the game proceeded, on the nature of Hindu "saṁsāra."

We will consider in this chapter a few ways in which the Hindu posits close interdependence between self-dharma-saṁsāra in terms of certain distinct learned as well as popular cultural models of food. My general argument is that (a) Hindu food, by definition, conjoins this worldly goals and consequences with those otherworldly; (b) the Hindu world, accordingly, carries an appropriate chain of formulations, models, and discourses; and (c) there is a cultural logic—such models ("webs of significance") help us reach not only a more accurate conception of Hindu food but also reveal those languages of discourse which such food generates.

Gross and Subtle

While observing the saṁsāra game, I was reminded of a cultural assertion of some of my Hindu informants (interviewed and consulted on the subject in Lucknow, during 1980) that food for them was *annadevtā* ("food god"), though it appeared in the material form in everyday life. Food for them concerned matters of the otherworld (i.e., *sūkṣma* states and *paramārthika* goals), especially for expressing a host of interrelationships between one's body and self, self and saṁsāra. Food also related to conditions of bondage and freedom (for a general discussion of long-held philosophical positions, see Potter 1965). Thus, if food thoroughly represents everyday moral order and individual action—*dharma* and karma—it also becomes, at the cosmological level, a self-evident essence of the Absolute (*Annambrahaman*), and at the level of yoga, a medium for acquiring self-control.

As we will illustrate in the following discussion, food is integral to all major models and meanings of the Hindu world, though these are philosophically diverse. Concerns of the worldly and the otherworldly (characterized as *asāra* and *sāra,* in popular terms) closely define the "essence" (*sattva, mūla tattva*) and experience of food for the Hindu. Simultaneously, food is continually taken into account for personal health, self-identity, and group status. It is a medium open to forces of personal and social history, with attention to material and practical conditions. To make sense of such diverse concerns, Hindu yogis, sadhus, and renouncers often become crucial "synthesizers" of worldly goals with the otherworldly. In the process, they address internal conflicts and expand on the scope and influence of Hindu gastrosemantics.

Food at the gross level presents a picture of hunger and survival, of sensual indulgence and satisfaction, and of worldly desires and bondage. As a part of saṁsāra, gross (*sthūla*) food refers to worldly give-and-take (*ādāna pradāna*) and "worldly life" (*saṁsārika jīvan*), and therefore causes succession of births. On the other hand, food in its subtle form, as a classical expression puts it, stands for "breath" or "breath of life" (i.e., *prāṇa*). It contrasts with the outermost "sheath" (*annamaya kośa* or the nutriment-based vesture or "visible body in the world of sense" [see Apte 1965, 89]). However, a living being (*jīva*) to the Hindu is comprised of vital breath, five (gross to subtle) vestures, and the indestructible soul (i.e., *prāṇa, pañcakośa,* and *ātman;* for a schematic discussion, see Nikhilananda 1963, 55–56, 364, 371–372, 375).

The Hindu never considers food bereft of its subtle (i.e., its hidden essential) properties. There is *no* simply "material" or "substantive" view of food without such subtle dimensions. As my informants put it, some properties of food are directly perceived upon ingestion (including those of *tāsīr*—hot and cold, light and heavy, etc., which concern an Ayurvedic doctor), some from social exchanges, and others from one's personal intentions and actions, on the one hand, and by supernatural forces, on the other. Though only those spiritually prepared and sensitive grasp messages of the last kind, food is widely seen as a combination of hidden "elements, humors, strands, and other flaws" affecting one's mental states. As says a hymn from the *Chāndogya Upanishad:*

> When the food is pure, the mind becomes pure. When the mind is pure, the memory becomes firm. When the memory is firm all [worldly] ties are loosened (in Nikhilananda 1963, 347; also Kane 1974, 757; my interpolation).

We understand such "conjoining" of gross and subtle properties of food better if we start with the Hindu's assertion that food for him is not only integral to the general moral condition and cosmology but that its materiality and transactions are always manifestations of one's dominant karmic imprints and otherworldly efforts. Even the slightest bad (or good) intentions, emotions, and karma readily stain foods in a subtle way, though only a yogi (with pure heart—*pavitra antaḥkaraṇa*) is able to detect them and become affected by them. Severely "blemished food" could even cause the death of a Brahman, according to Manu (V, 4). Since the unknown sins of a food-giver can freely attach themselves to foods, the receiver must be constantly on guard. Even eaters sitting in the same row pass the sin unseen to one another.

Models and Meanings

In contemporary India, orthodox householders, accomplished saints and ascetics, genuine aspirants (*sādhaka*), and devout women constantly worry about the "flaws" (*dośa*) and bondages (*bandhana*) foods bring to them from diverse sources. Though the renouncer must, in principle, freely beg food to feed himself, he actually avoids defiled (*dūṣita*) foods, including those that come from a sinner. Such heterogeneous cultural notions make us wonder if the Hindu food rests on any distinct cultural model or models. If so, what is their general cultural emphasis and rationale? In answer to both questions, we will discuss below three cultural models which, together, try to account for various "seen" and "unseen," and gross and subtle properties and consequences of Hindu food. Since the overarching goal of this food is to represent/evoke comprehensive interrelationships between the worldly and the otherworldly (with ultimate emphasis on the latter), our three models will help show how such goals are pursued in each other's terms within the Hindu world, *without* posing a dichotomy between idea and practice. Each model not only generates a distinct system of contextual meanings but also a distinct discourse on life goals, contextual situations, and cosmology. These models and discourses, together, illustrate distinct styles of "Hindu cultural reasoning" (see introduction, this book), allowing us to see how the Hindu goes about conjoining material with nonmaterial, and transactional with nontransactional (or supratransactional), properties of Hindu food.

Our models try to highlight certain dominant themes and concerns of Hindu life (whether of the learned or the commoner). However, they obviously are not exhaustive, nor can they claim to explain all anomalies and exceptions.

Model I: Axiomatic and Ontological

The first axiomatic model of food rests on what constitutes *prāṇa* ("breath of life") for the Hindu.[4] As will be presently explained, let us call it the "thread-soul" model of food. It is, in one classical scheme (the scheme also recalled in part by one of my informants), depicted as a wheel with fourteen spokes radiating from the center (see *Chāndogya Upanishad;* Nikhilananda 1963, 337–347). The fourteen spokes of *prāṇa* are: name, speech, mind, will, consideration, meditation, understanding, strength, food, water, fire, space, memory, and hope. However, in another formulation of the same model, each succeeding item on the list is found to be the ground for the previous one, and the whole hierarchical chain culminates in *prāṇa,* or "the self of all," the vital force which pervades all the living creatures. Thus, if *prāṇa* is synonymous with life, then food enables one "to see, hear, reflect, become convinced, act, and enjoy the result" (*Chāndogya Upanishad*; Nikhilananda 1963, 341). In popular Hindu ideology, therefore, as one of my informants remarked, both food and *prāṇa* remain grounded in that "thread-soul" (*sutrātamana,* Brahman, Hiraṇyagarbha, or simply the *sūtra*—the first manifestation of Brahman in the relative cosmos) which attracts all the relative (the cognitive, affective, and material) diversity of the saṁsāra around itself as "the hub" attracts spokes.

These two formulations of the thread-soul model provide us with an essential cultural foundation (and rationale) for food to be transactional, substantive, and indispensable to the Hindu at all different levels of creation. Food becomes synonymous with the creator's presence; it is one of his primordial acts. Within such an ideology, food (in its availability and consequence) reflects of one's (a moral agent's) total karma-dharma condition. Food closely reflects one's being and becoming (ontology), until liberated from the cycle of birth and death. The classical tradition insists that we do not treat the two formulations of Model I separately. For an anthropological analysis, it means that we treat subtle ideals and gross transactions in each other's terms. If the scale of the fourteen criteria conveys to us the primacy of one's *prāṇa* (microcosm) in everyday life, then the fourteen-spoke wheel provides us with a process view of interrelationships between food, self, and creation (macrocosm).

Model II: Transactional and Therapeutic

The "thread-soul" is fundamental to all the subsequent Hindu cultural models and schemes of food. Its axiomatic position and explanatory force variously pervade most of the Hindu world, setting the basic parameters of the cultural logic of food within this-worldly and otherworldly contexts. The second major model of food, transactional and therapeutic, exemplified best by the *Dharmaśāstra* literature and the Ayurveda, treats food as a domain of appropriate ritual and moral regulations, on the one hand, and "ecological" es-

Model I: First formulation—*Prāṇa* as a (hierarchical) scale of fourteen properties.

PRĀṆA > 1 hope > 2 memory > 3 space > 4 fire > 5 water > 6 food > 7 strength > 8 understanding > 9 meditation > 10 consideration > 11 will > 12 mind > 13 speech > 14 name.

Model I: Second formulation—*Prāṇa* as the (processual) wheel of fourteen spokes.

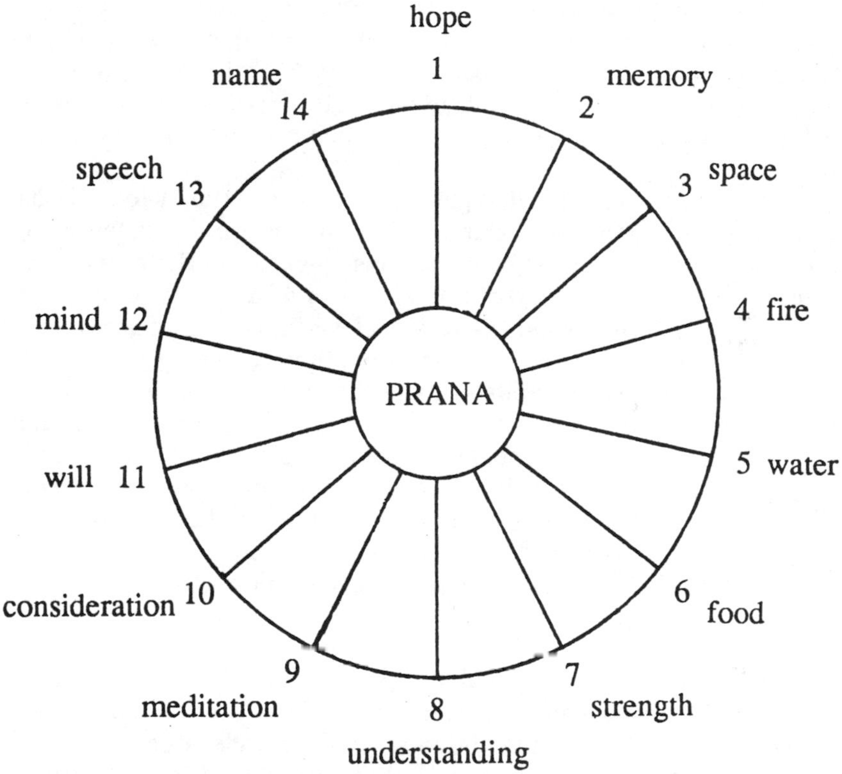

(Note: Numbers in this figure refer to the same categories as in the first formulation.)

sences and humoral conditions, on the other (e.g., see Kane 1974, chaps. 20–22; Zimmermann 1987). The goal of the second model is to distinguish physically injurious and morally improper foods (by identifying agents, actions, and consequences) from those that are proper, preferable, and healthy. Only morally just food (a subtle property) can be the truly healthy food for the Hindu.

Recent anthropological studies of food provide us with a representative picture of how everyday Hindu food rests on a variety of "transactions" (i.e., a gloss for the crucial and comprehensive Hindu notion of *saṁcālana* or transmission)—reciprocal and nonreciprocal, and minimal and maximal among different castes, humans and gods, and across various other "constituents" of the Hindu cosmos (Marriott 1968, 1976, 1984). In model II, the essence of food lies in the conjoining processes of such gross and subtle transactions (i.e., from *ādāna pradāna* to *saṁcālana*). The essence of *anna* (food), as the Hindu popularly says, rests in the *annadāna* (giving of food). The giver earns religious merit while the receiver accumulates a form of debt (*ṛṇa*), to be repaid sooner or later, in this life or the next.

The essence of food also gets expressed in other ways. Foods, once ingested produce their subtle "inner" and otherworldly (*ātamika, pāralaukika*) effects and consequences on the eater. Most importantly, the gross and subtle effects of food closely follow each other in Ayurvedic terms, the humoral configuration of wind, bile, and phlegm within the eater's body, and, in yogic terms, the expression of three *guṇas* (strands)—goodness (*sattva*), passion (*rajasa*), and darkness (*tamasa*) within his or her self. Both humors and strands are dependent on some form of transaction (i.e., *saṁcālana,* meaning motion, oscillation, transmission, passage) to express themselves. Both, only together, complete the Hindu notion of body (*déha* or *śarīra*), acquired by a soul (*jīva* or *ātman*). Within Hindu thought, soul acquires body, formed of five elements (*bhūtas*—ether, air, fire, water, and earth), and tries to maintain it disease free, among other things, by performing morally appropriate actions (*sukarma*) and eating physically agreeable foods (*samucita āhāra*).

The food essence and experience in model II are therefore based on *circulation* of elements, humors, and strands among natural agencies and among beings with bodies. Food absorbs "nature" (Zimmermann 1987, 21) and is absorbed by both souls and their bodies according to their karma and dharma. Food mutually nourishes and cures the body *and* soul of a Hindu. Strictly speaking, there is no notion of only a physical cure in the Ayurveda (see Kakar 1982, on healing). Comprehensive healing (i.e., of both body and soul) is more important than physical cure, and food (as *pathya*), faith, and medicine, together, meet this expectation of the patient. Such therapeutic conceptions of diet and the resulting logic of Ayurvedic dietary regulations are widely shared, most often across regional differences (e.g., Zimmermann 1987, chap. 5; Nichter 1986; Rizvi 1986).

As Zimmermann notes (1987, 131), "The paramount point [in the Ayurveda] is that the arrangement of the whole of 'immobile and mobile' living creatures within the category of food signifies, as a matter of principle, the exclusion of even the possibility of a botanical or zoological classification: the beings themselves are no longer of any interest, only their dietetic and therapeutic qualities." India's notions of appropriate diet and therapy depend on "a combinative system" of essences and properties of foods matched to those of people and their environment. The multiple essences and properties of various foods and medicine contribute to the content of Ayurvedic learning and medicine. An Ayurvedic physician refines his therapy as he learns to "read" better the interdependencies between the patient's disease, body, and diet.

Returning to food as essence and experience in general, we see how our model II gives us an entry into an entire domain of ritual rules and therapeutic classifications, on the one hand, and into a "grammar" of logic, tradition, and poetic expressions, as Zimmermann shows (1987, 133–158), on the other. The ritual (*dharmaśāstra*) literature, therefore, readily incorporates the "intrinsic" properties of foods as a primary classifier (e.g., three *guṇas,* three *dośas,* four modes of ingestion, six flavors, and twenty qualities; for a quotation on these qualities from an Ayurvedic text, see Zimmermann 1987, 130; for ritual criteria, see Kane 1974, chap. 20–22). If the therapeutic part emphasizes various combinations of humor-balancing properties of foods, then the transactional part deals with food's moral essence, social nature, possession, contact, exchange, ingestion, and consequence. (Marriott's [1987] "Saṁsāra game" explicates many of these transactional properties as it conjures up Hindu rural life).

The Hindu view of food essence and experience also changes with one's life phase (*varṇāśrama*) and rites of refinement (*saṁskāras*). The regulation and control of daily diet increase with age, usually with an eye toward health and otherworldly welfare. One excludes foods which one cannot digest any more. The "unlimited hunger of childhood" and "foods of youth" are left behind with a nostalgic feeling. With age, the essence of food does not lie in desire and sensoria, but increasingly in morally appropriate and physically agreeable nourishment.

Model III: World Critical and World Redefining

As many of my informants have over the years insisted, model II, by itself, remains incomplete. To get more out of this model, we must see it firmly grounded within the first (i.e., the Upanishadic) model, and pursued along a third one, where different "paths" (i.e., of action, knowledge, devotion, or heterodoxy—*karma, jñāna, bhakti,* or *tantra,* or a suitable combination of these) criticize and redefine the worldly (vis-a-vis the otherworldly). The role of Bhakti movement has been particularly crucial to such a critique and redefinition. The third model thus underscores the fact that Hindu food faithfully reflects the internal critiques of Hinduism's classical (i.e., Vedic, Vedantic, and *dharmaśāstric*) worldviews and that a revaluation of the worldly and the otherworldly (*laukika* and *alaukika*) is integral to Hindu gastronomy. Given the constraints of space, we will only briefly consider some aspects of popular Bhakti and Tantra to illustrate the place of food within them.

The Bhakti and Tantra movements have produced new emphases for Hindu gastronomy by (a) locating the otherworldly (the divine) within this world, (b) opening fate and past karmas to personal deities (for seeking their divine intervention), and (c) displacing ritual authority by ascetic spiritual power. In such a situation, food starts by faithfully reflecting the Hindu's changing philosophic values toward the worldly existence. Under rigorous renunciation and asceticism, therefore, we find that sensual, aesthetic, and culinary distinctions of Hindu food become simpler, even atrophy. Though food still symbolizes a ritual-cosmic essence, its physical, material, and substantive social transactional domains lose dominance. Even the therapeutic is subordinated to ascetic powers (*tapas*) since these are dispensed as a blessing to one's disciples. Gifting and exchange of food become *tapas*-coded with ascetic-like householders.

On the other hand, the same ascetic-like householder is still the hub of food exchanges—unequal, equal, or intimate, with all creatures, immobile and mobile. He is also often a devotee who ultimately seeks divine grace for social prosperity as well as personal liberation. For him, if saṁsāra still is like "caterpillar's saliva" which binds the "spinner" until the caterpillar dies, the supreme deity (*parmātamā*) is the compassionate "deliverer." As my knowledgeable informants in Lucknow repeatedly emphasized, the householder surrenders his fate to the deity, as he is exhorted to get out of this saṁsāra by dissolving "I" and "mine," and "thou" and "thine" (*maiñ aru mōr tōr tain térā*—part of a couplet quoted from Tulsidasa's *Rāmacharitamānas*).[5] Total resignation before the divine (*prapatti*) is considered the easiest way for the householder. By implication, asserted my world-redefining informants, the orthodox textual rules of purity, prescribed elaborate rituals, and severe penances are accorded the second place. Increasingly more people are ignorant about them in urban surroundings. All of this is justified because devotion is considered necessary and sufficient to replace intricate rituals in this Kali age. Even the supreme goals of one's life is modified: It is not the "release" (*mukti* or *mokṣa*) any longer. Instead, it is the unconditional devotion to the divine, which alone can assure proximity with the divine (usually of four kinds—*sālokya, sārupya, sāmipya,* or *sāyujya,* meaning nearness to the divine by residence, form, bodily contact, or complete absorption).

Such a goal recasts orthodox ritual rules of the Brahmanic system, on the one hand, and establishes supremacy of divine grace (Hari's *kr̥pa*), on the other. One only needs to cultivate genuine personal faith and disposition (*śraddhā* and *bhāva*) of devotion by appropriate reflection and practice (*manana aur abhyāsa*). God's name (*bhagvān nāma*), devotional texts like the *Gītā, Rāmāyaṇa* and *Bhāgavata,* and the company of the devout (*satsaṅga*) are considered to be of greatest help in such a path. God's devotion, thus pursued, transforms the ephemeral saṁsāra into the divine residing "universe" (*jagata;* see Barz 1976 and Kapoor 1977, for the Bhakti schools' formulations). The illusory world (*māyāmaya saṁsāra*) of the non-dualist is displaced by the divine-immanent real world (*bhagvadamaya jagat*). Similarly one's body becomes divine's temple. There is really nothing to give or to receive here since everything is already of (and for) the divine. Even one's own senses, perceptions (including pleasure and pain), and actions, once surrendered to the divine, are divinized. Such an existence transcends all transactions.

Ideals of ascetics and renouncers also do not remain unaffected by such developments. The devotional saints and sadhus, in particular, as we discuss them below as "synthesizers," award full recognition and authority to such a change brought on by the devotional movement. The Bengali saint Ramakrishna, as my informants recalled, combined devotion with Vedantic nondualism, proving the validity of both paths.

With devotional movement, food particularly became an eloquent medium with saints and saint-poets for conveying the profoundness of change which the Bhakti movement envisaged. Food as a divine offering (*naivéyda*) breached the regular rule of the giver being always higher than the receiver. Intoxicated with devotional love, the devotee and divine even reverse the order of eating of "leftovers" (*prasāda* or *bhoga;* see chapter 3 in this book, where the divine eats the devotee's leftovers). In such a mood there is no room for distinguishing ranks between giving and receiving, since the devotee says "I offer your things to you . . . " (*tvadīyama vastu goviṁdama tubhya méva samarpayēta* . . .) for your pleasure. Such an offering in the devotee's eyes is either nontransactional or supratransactional (*sāmanya ādāna-pradāna sé paré*), but no ordinary transaction.

Similarly, since taste, smell, appearance, culinary variety, order (or its lack), and the quantity of food come to represent the divine wish (*bhagvat ichā* or *Hari ichā*), these are no more mundane, worldly (*saṁsārika*) accountable properties. They are not subject to the nondualist's notion of *māyā* (illusion), but an authentic ground for divine play (*bhagvat līlā*). With total faith and self-surrender (*prapatti*), the devout lives in a God-intoxicated world (*bhagvadmaya jagat;* see Kapoor 1977, 203ff.), where food as a divine substance communicates divine presence, intimacy, disposition, and bliss (*prasāda*). Hunger, fasting, feasting, and even culinary excellence and gluttony become highly meaningful, divine-charged contexts. As regal majesty of the divine is contemplated, the devout's sensoria get attracted to the luxurious. But in such a pursuit, the devout transforms the seemingly worldly indulgence into a divine "service" (*bhagvadsévā*). Without qualms, therefore, Krishna's devotees in Mathura and Vrindaban, as Toomey reports (chapter 4 in this book), become sated, carefree gluttons (*chaké mastarāma*).

Food does not speak to the devotee in worldly terms; it is always about the divine service, "taste," wish, and their associated aesthetics (e.g., Krishna likes butter and certain milk sweets; Rama requires sedate regal offerings; Hanuman favors specific gram-flour sweets). The devotee feeds the divine in a mood of love and intimacy, as a part of his worship. His worship is his highest otherworldly goal (*paramārtha*), treating the "ocean of saṁsāra" as a divine sporting ground (*līlā sthala*). Similarly, locating the divine within his "heart," the devout does *not* neglect his body; he cares for it—and feeds it well—because in it resides the divine, and it allows him to love and worship the divine within this world.

Food most often is the favorite medium for expressing personal love between devotee and the divine. Culinary art, aesthetics, and communication directly expand and elaborate as the devotee houses and cares for the divine in temples and domestic shrines. Even a renunciant (*vairāgī*) saint is not free from such caring, and is therefore found lamenting that he is a "prisoner of Krishna." He spends life looking after Krishna's comforts in a well-endowed temple!

Within a generalized view of devotion, at least in popular conception, also appears the Tāntrika approach to food and its communicative powers. Briefly, the *Shākta* model is most often about the pursuit of Goddess as the divine mother, who feeds and protects her children from all kinds of obstructions, calamities, grief, and evil forces. The goddess, riding the world of opposite forces and feelings (e.g., birth and death, beauty and ugliness, and fear and devotion), variously represents difficult-to-control divine power, energy, and force. With one mood, she feeds on cosmic vices and demons; with another, she becomes the provider (*annapūrṇā*), the nurturer, of the universe, even during famines and droughts.

In contrast to Rama and Krishna, her food is full of abominations (blood sacrifice, wine, and *tāmasika*—"darkness"-producing foods). Her devotee, a Tāntrika yogi, reflects a corresponding preference toward the abnormal as he takes to five M's (i.e., *madya* or wine, *māṁsa* or meat, *matsya* or fish, *mudrā* or parched cereal, and *maithuna* or sexual union; see Avalon 1978, 590–648). Though on a different path, both Goddess and Tāntrika also unveil the same ultimate truth as those worshipping Vishnu. Tāntrika, also a yogi, is after self-control, but by pursuing the path of sensual indulgence (Tucci 1969; Bharati 1965). He turns "drinking, eating, and procreation" into tests of his self-control, by tapping into the power of Goddess. This path's principle is, "The man must be taught to rise by the means of those very things which are the cause of his fall. 'As one falls to the ground, one must lift oneself by the aid of the ground' " (*Kaulārṇava Tantra* quoted by Avalon 1978, 633).

Synthesizers

For our exercise, the three cultural models just discussed exemplify a general profile of how Hindus interpret their "food and food essence." Still, the picture must remain particularly complicated because (a) all three models are found, in thought and practice, overlapping and simultaneously valid in life (yielding multiple realities of food); (b) the dominant message of one model is variously interrelated with the other two to yield the composite gastronomic ethos of the contemporary Hindu (e.g., *anna* or food is also body, medicine, divine offering, and food god—*annamayakośa, auṣadhi, prasāda,* and *annadévatā*); (c) consequently, appropriate multichannel expressions and action-paths are encountered which are at once receptive to sensual and suprasensual properties and to a redefinition of this-worldly and otherworldly goals. But the Hindu habitually uses such a diversity for expanded cultural communication and expression via food. Food (*annama*) for him covers a wide connotative ground (Apte 1965, 89)—from boiled rice to water, earth, the sun, Vishnu, Śiva (*annada*), Durgā (*annadā, annapūrṇā*), Agni (*annapatiḥa*), and the Brahman (as in *annambrahman,* the grossest of five vestments). He is used to handling the foods of gods and goddesses which are at once auspicious but impure, or pure but inedible (e.g., the neutralized or nonneutralized poisonous offerings to Śiva; sacrificial blood before Kali; see Edholm 1984; Kinsley 1986).

More important, all this is made intelligible by those who deal with the holy. Devotional saints, austere and detached in life, paradoxically become major "synthesizers" of the essence and experience of food within the Hindu world. They do so with considerable ease once they see the divine within food, and they celebrate this relationship with aesthetic sensitivities, poetic afflatus, and tropic creativity (chapter 8 in this book). The deeper the internal unresolved ambiguities and contradictions between the worldly (*saṁsāra*) and the otherworldly (*paramārtha*), the greater is the reliance on creative expressions to make sense of the unusual and the suprasensual.

As exemplars of the otherworldly sensibilities, power, and authority, Hindu sages, saints (or sants), and renouncers are crucial because they provide the ordinary person with new messages and meanings on traditional gastronomy. The saints relive ideals, overthrow dead traditions, initiate social reform, and reinterpret unchanging values. Within such a domain of cultural innovation, a yogi's fasting is as meaningful as a devout saint's sensorial aesthetics and indulgence (to please the divine). Without caring for contradictions between austerity and indulgence, a saint may freely dwell on food to convey a spiritual message, to denounce a social rigidity, and to deepen and extend the spiritual essence of food over social and ritual rules. His influence rests in the superiority of spiritual power over worldly experiences and ritual authority. He knows the reality better than the worldly householder; he clearly sees the play of *māyā* in everyday activity.

In popular terms, the "fire" of a saint's *tapas* (austerities) helps him rise above ordinary ritual rules and distinctions. Thus while the traditional (i.e., the *dharmaśāstra*) formulations elaborate on ritually pure and proper food and eating, the devout saint is ultimately guided by the supreme goal of divine devotion (*bhagvad-bhakti*). Actually, there is an ambiguity. Without denying the efficacy of austerities and self-control, the śāstric texts warn that a renouncer, a learned Brahman or a saint or a yogi must never underestimate the bondage foods produce within saṁsāra (see Kane 1974, 767–786, for the purifiers and the defilers of the row of diners). Popular Hindu culture also remains ambiguous on the issue. It sways with the dominance of a prevailing authority figure. For example, while an ordinary householder, a Brahman pundit, and even a sadhu may continue to observe intricate ritual rules about excluding forbidden and defiled foods, a renowned saint, like Ramakrishna, declares a "higher truth" (but with a necessary caution for the novitiate; see Diwakar 1956):

> He who eats the food of the gods, namely, simple non-stimulating vegetable food, but does not desire to attain God, for him that simple food is as bad as beef. But he who eats beef and desires God, for him beef is as good as the food of the Gods (Abhedananda 1946, 150).

To illustrate a similar cultural ambiguity, I quote the remark an informant made to me in Lucknow in 1979, where "cooking" becomes a metaphor for ritual observances as well as spiritual progress with the help of one's guru:

> Both saṁsāra and rites of passage (*saṁskāras*) help "cook" or "ripen" a soul (*jīva*). They prepare him to learn the significance of a guru and the true knowledge (*satjñāna*) he imparts. A disciple is like an unripe fruit, and one's guru is a great cook who knows how long to cook each fruit to get the maximum flavor out of it. Once appropriately cooked, the disciple is ready to progress on a path that would take him beyond the cycle of births and deaths.

Such a comment could also be seen as representing multiple semantic discourses in terms of guru as a cook and samsara a form of cooking, with roles for traditional rituals, *māyā*, and the divine. India's food culture is full of such discourses, alerting us to the centrality of *tropic food*. Cooking and eating acquire special significance. (For a comparative semantic analysis of terms of cooking in the context of Lévi-Strauss's culinary triangle, see Lehrer 1969, 39–55). Cooking and ripeness become a metaphor for capturing a person's progress in distinguishing between reality and illusion and in recognizing the significance of nonreciprocal and disinterested giving and receiving (see Parry 1986, 453–473, for raising the issue of disinterested gifting).

Overview

Our discussion draws attention to the following: (a) The essence, meaning, and aesthetics of Hindu food vary with changing values given to the world (*bhavasāgar*), the "experience" of pleasure and pain (*bhoga*), and divine devotion (*bhakti*). (b) The values of food (*anna*) and food essence as represented by "food god" (*annadevatā*) become markedly complex with synthesis-inclined (heterodox) philosophical and religious movements in India, fostering conflicting "logics" of exclusion and simplification (via austerity and detachedness), complicated reversals (via Tantrism), and emotive inclusion (via the sensorial, social, and aesthetic world-reforming formulations of the Bhakti movement). (c) The food in Hindu conception and practice must always remain a conduit for helping realize the Brahman. In such a pursuit, food variously becomes a communicator of hidden knowledge about one's own body and self, suprasensual experiences, and subtle divine intimations.

The three models of food illustrate how the Hindu interrelates his worldly concerns with those otherworldly. He does so in idea and practice, personally and in groups. It is so natural for him that, as reflected by the models, it has become a part of his everyday "cultural reasoning" and learned discourses. If food for the Hindu is at once action, meaning, and "text," then each model displays a correspondingly distinct discourse and its relational property. The "thread-soul" model, for instance, underscores *interconnectedness* between parts (i.e., the fourteen properties represented by spokes) and the whole (the *prāṇa,* the "hub"). But it is done to show interrelation between the here-and-now of food to that which is ideal and the ultimate. The therapeutic or "karma-dharma" model is based on the *appropriate matching* of distinctions and transactions, often determined by the contexts and purposes set in motion by the four goals of Hindu life (dharma, *artha, kāma,* and *mokṣa*). Here the social, the personal, and the instrumental acquire the center stage. An Ayurvedic search for personal health and longevity via special diets and controlled eating are parts of this scheme. Still, the overarching otherworldly values are never far away or in doubt. For some sort of liberation remains the ultimate purpose of all Hindu distinctions. The third Bhakti-Shakti model expands on this purpose by resorting to divine *pervasiveness,* where the divine, male or female, inundates, controls, and runs both this-worldly and otherworldly domains. Here is recognized the supremacy of divine wish and grace (*bhagvat ichā* and *kṛpa*). Major philosophical shifts, ritual syntheses, and social reforms are a part of the third model, with food as integral to the sublime communication of divine name, form, play, and abode (*nāma, rūpa, līlā, aur dhāma*). It is also with such an inspiration that the Hindu food becomes subtlest, eternal, and nontransactional or supratransactional. It becomes (rather than only represents) the *prasāda* (divine grace rather than only divine leftovers).

All the three models thus widely comment on the spheres of the seen and the unseen, gross and subtle, and the essential and the experiential for which Hindu food is responsible. But such food's goal does not end in body, health, longevity, or even appropriate karma and dharma. Instead, being self-evident, its ultimate goal is the ultimate Reality, when understood in the Upanishadic sense. Translated in human terms, food becomes one with the language and discourse of different "paths" for pursuing the ultimate goal, whether it is the orthodox goal of liberation or the devout person's nearness to the divine.

Notes

1. *Saṁsāra,* a concept central to the Indic—the Hindu, Buddhist, and Jain—cultures in one form or another, most often means succession of births to the Hindu and, by extension, the round of "worldly life" (*saṁsārika jīvan*), as against, say, the otherworldly or heavenly life. In an overall sense, *saṁsāra* becomes one's temporary passage through mundane existence; it is a soul's intermediate step toward deliverance. Rites of refinement (*saṁskāras*) mark one's life-passage through the *saṁsāra,* which is for some (i.e., the nondualist or *advaitvādin*) illusory, for others (dualists) a reality. Essentially one's karmic attachments produce *saṁsāra* (which makes one take birth again and again; see O'Flaherty 1980), and the divine illusion (*māyā,* as in the Bhakti tradition) causes the *saṁsāra* to appear like a "magic show" (e.g., see Potter 1965, 166–167; for a detailed analysis of these categories, see Satprakashananda 1965). Some of these conceptions will be considered later in the context of food.

For simplicity, I shall refer to *saṁsāra* as saṁsāra (or "saṁsāra," to refer to Marriott's pedagogic template in the beginning pages).

2. The reference is to Professor McKim Marriott's way of approaching and analyzing the Hindu (and more generally the South Asian) sociocultural universe. From his standpoint, then, Hindu saṁsāra is a multidimensional "flow" of "transactions." It is nothing less, and it need be nothing more. Marriott's "saṁsāra game," proceeding on such a premise, variously attempts to imitate clusters of activities of Hindu life, "verifying" the transactional causation and explanation of saṁsāra.

3. But an uninitiated reader should not look for these criteria explicitly stated in the game. As in his previous work, Marriott (1989) develops a distinct analytic language necessary for his explanatory schemes by supporting his perspective on a range of ethnographic "reports" collected and published by others. As he does so, Marriott still leaves the reader largely to his own devices to decipher how exactly Marriott employs different Western (and American) sociological approaches to "explain" India.

4. Alongside karma, dharma, and saṁsāra, *prāṇa* is a crucial cultural principle. It is a multidirectional metaphor for life and self (hence it also denotes the vigor, strength, and power of the soul). The term *prāṇa* means, among other things, the air inhaled, digestion, and anything or a person which is held dear or vital (see Apte 1965, 679). *Prāṇa* is basal, and it is sensorially self-evident as "breath" in creatures. A hidden manifestation of the cosmic energy, it is ultimately an epithet of Brahman (the Supreme Spirit). Within individual body, food, once digested, supports breathing. Food sustains *prāṇa,* the breath which moves as wind (*vāyu*) in different directions within one's body. Thus, while the *apāna* wind moves downward to eject waste (urine and feces), *vijāna* pervades the entire body, *samāna* carries nutrients to the whole body, and *udāna* moves upward (including at the time of death for ejecting the soul). The *prāṇa,* comprising these five "winds," constitutes an essential worldly template of the Hindu's self. Ayurveda, Yoga, Tantra, and Bhakti—all employ it as a bridge between evanescent body and immortal soul (*ātman*).

5. This provides us with a popular definition of saṁsāra. "I-ness" and the distinction between "mine" and "yours" constitute the crux of the matter, according to many of my informants. Such feelings fetter a person to one's near and dear ones, to one's property, and to one's desires. An ordinary person's "round of life" (as in Marriott's "saṁsāra" game) goes on in terms of securing these worldly goals and desires. They cause the worldly transactions to appear, but only as "a feast of illusion" (a phrase used by one of my informants).

References

Abhedananda, Swami
1946 *The Sayings of Rāmakrishna.* Calcutta: Ramakrishna Vedanta Math.

Apte, Vaman Sivaram
1965 *The Practical Sanskrit-English Dictionary* (Revised and Enlarged Ed.; originally published in 1912). Delhi: Motilal Banarsidass.

Avalon, Arthur
1978 *Shakti and Shākta.* New York: Dover Publications.

Barz, Richard
1976 *The Bhakti Sect of Vallabhācārya.* Faridabad: Thomson Press (India).

Bharati, Agehananda
1965 *The Tantric Tradition.* London: Rider & Co.

Diwakar, R. R.
1956 *Paramhaṁsa Srī Rāmakrishna.* Bombay: Bhartiya Vidya Bhavan.

Douglas, Mary
1975 *Implicit Meanings: Essays in Anthropology.* London: Routledge and Kegan Paul.

Edholm, Erik
1984 "Caṇda and the Sacrificial Remnants: A Contribution to Indian Gastrotheology." *Estratto da Indologica Taurinensia.* 12:75–91.

Kakar, Sudhir
1982 *Shamans, Mystics and Doctors: A Psychological Inquiry into India and Its Healing Traditions.* Delhi: Oxford University Press.

Kane, Pandurang Vaman
1974 *History of Dharmaśāstra* (vol. II, pt. II; vol. IV). Poona: The Bhandarakar Oriental Research Institute.

Kapoor, O. B. L.
1977 *The Philosophy and Religion of Srī Caitanya.* Delhi: Munshiram Manoharlal.

Khare, R. S.
1976a *Hindu Hearth and Home.* Delhi: Vikas Publishing House.

1976b *Culture and Reality: Essays on the Hindu System of Managing Foods.* Shimla: Indian Institute of Advanced Study.

Kinsley, David
1986 *Hindu Goddesses: Visions of the Divine Feminine in the Hindu Religious Tradition.* Berkeley: University of California Press.

Lehrer, Adrienne
1969 "Semantic Cuisine." *Journal of Linguistics,* 5:39–55.

Marriott, McKim
1968 "Caste Ranking and Food Transactions: A Matrix Analysis." In *Structure and Change in Indian Society.* Milton Singer and Bernard S. Cohn (eds.). Chicago: Aldine.

1976 "Hindu Transactions: Diversity without Dualism." In *Transaction and Meaning: Directions in the Anthropology of Exchange and Symbolic Behavior.* Bruce Kapferer (ed.). Philadelphia: Institute for the Study of Human Issues.

1984 "A Description of *Saṁsāra:* A Simulation of Rural Hindu Life," mimeographed (Draft of December 19, 1984).

1987 "A Description of *Saṁsāra:* A Realization of Rural Hindu Life." Chicago: Civilization Course Materials Project, University of Chicago.

1989 "Constructing an Indian Ethnosociology." *Contributions to Indian Sociology.* vol. 23, no. 1: 1–39.

Nichter, Mark
1986 "Modes of Food Classification and the Diet-Health Contingency: A South Indian Case Study." In *Food, Society and Culture.* R. S. Khare and M. S. A. Rao (eds.). Durham: Carolina Academic Press.

Nikhilananda, Swami
1963 *The Upanishads.* New York: Harper Torchbooks.

O'Flaherty, Wendy D.
1980 *Karma and Rebirth in Classical Indian Traditions.* Berkeley: University of California Press.

Parry, Jonathan
1986 "The Gift, the Indian gift and the 'Indian gift.' " *Man,* vol. 21, no. 3: 453–473.

Potter, Karl H.
1965 *Presuppositions of India's Philosophies.* New Delhi: Prentice-Hall (India).

Rizvi, Najma
1986 "Food Categories in Bangladesh, and its Relationship to Food Beliefs and Practices of Vulnerable Groups." In *Food, Society and Culture,* R. S. Khare and M. S. A. Rao (eds.). Durham: Carolina Academic Press.

Satprakashananda, Swami
1965 *Methods of Knowledge.* London: George Allen and Unwin, Ltd.

Tucci, Guiseppe
1969 *The Theory and Practice of the Maṇḍala* (Translated from the Italian by Alan Houghton Brodrick). London: Rider and Company.

Zimmermann, Francis
1987 *The Jungle and the Aroma of Meats: An Ecological Theme in Hindu Medicine.* Berkeley: University of California Press.

8

Food for Thought: Toward an Anthology of Hindu Food-Images

*

A. K. Ramanujan

One of the aims of this chapter is to capture the common sense about food of someone like myself who grew up in a bilingual South Indian Brahmin household in Mysore—the commonplaces acquired from proverbs, tales, attendance at life-cycle ceremonies (weddings, births, death ceremonies) or from being subjected to old women's or Ayurvedic pundits' medical remedies. Though I cite sources, I have used them chiefly as an aid to memory—to help me sift through what I knew as a boy without quite knowing what I knew. The ethnographic writings of Khare especially, and those of Beck, Ferro-Luzzi, and Marriott have been most useful, and I am indebted to them. Most of my folklore examples are from Kannada, unless otherwise indicated.

This essay/anthology/collage/primer falls into two parts: both cite poems and passages from Indian literature to exemplify certain principles regarding food. Each passage displays a different paradigm in which food participates. Each paradigm presents food in a different aspect, gives it a new "interpretant," a new "translation." The first section will draw from these well-known passages a system of signification (in Eco's sense of the term).

Communicative acts presuppose signification systems, as *parole* presupposes *langue,* as pragmatics presupposes syntactics—or even better, I would say, as poetry presupposes language. Cultural systems in use are more like poetry, or at least more like the poetic use of language than like ordinary language. So terms of rhetoric and poetics are more useful in describing a system like food or clothing than terms developed for a linguistics that can describe sentences but nothing larger (like discourse), which cannot adequately and elegantly describe a metaphor.

The second part of this chapter cites passages which illustrate the actual uses of food and its meanings that breed further meanings by metaphor and metonymy, making figures out of basic language. I believe with Peirce that "symbols grow" and semiosis is "unlimited."

My concern here is synchronic; I wish someone would explore the social history of these images and ideas.

Food Cycles

The basic "language," or the set of structures, underlying Hindu commonplaces about food, seems to consist of a cycle, a triangle, and four sets of distinctive features, all of them well known to specialists as well as to natives, though the latter may not state them explicitly.

In early childhood we heard about the world being food (*annamayam jagat*). When we heard a Sanskrit passage like the following in a *harikathā* recital, it rang more than a bell:

Food Chain

From food, from food
creatures, all creatures
come to be.

Gorging, disgorging,
beings come
to be.

By food they live,
in food they move,
into food they pass:

food, the chief
of things, of all things
that come to be,

elixir,
herb of herbs
for mortals.

Food, food, Brahman is food:
only they eat

who know
they eat their god.

For food is the chief
of things, of all things
that come to be:

elixir,
herb to herbs
for mortals.

From food all beings
come to be,
by food

they grow,
into food
they pass.

And what eats is eaten:
and what's eaten, eats
in turn.

(After the Sanskrit, *Taittirīya Upanishad,* translated by the author)

Food is Brahman because food is what circulates in the universe through bodies which in turn are food made flesh and bone. According to this view, in the organic world there is no other stuff: food is the primal substance; all animate beings are its forms. One may go further and see this cycle as including inorganic matter as well. All forms arise out of food and return to it—which is, after all, one of the descriptions of Brahman, the ground of being. In the transformations of food, inorganic becomes organic, one form is metamorphosed into another; the eater is eaten, big fish eat little fish, and if you wait long enough, little fish eat big fish.

This cycle is part of a large cycle that includes the gods, as in the following passage. Though there are ambiguities here, one may summarize the cycle thus: *humans- sacrifice- gods (Brahman)- work- rain- food- contingent beings (which includes humans):*

The Bhagavadgītā, III, 11–16:

(11) With this shall ye sustain the gods so that the gods may sustain you [in return]. Sustaining one another [thus] ye shall achieve the highest good.

> (12) For, [so] sustained by sacrifice, the gods will give you the food of your desire. Who so enjoys their gifts yet gives them nothing [in return] is a thief, no more nor less.
>
> (13) Good men who eat the leavings of the sacrifice are freed from every taint, but evil are they and evil do they eat who cook [only] for their own sakes.
>
> (14) From food do [all] contingent beings derive and food derives from rain; rain derives from sacrifice and sacrifice from works.
>
> (15) From Brahman work arises, know this, and Brahman is born from the Imperishable; therefore is Brahman, penetrating everywhere, forever based on sacrifice.
>
> (16) So was the wheel in motion set: and whoso here fails to match his turning [with the turning of the wheel], living an evil life, the senses his pleasureground, lives out his life in vain (trans. Zaehner 1969).

And food, in a more direct, obvious, and mundane way, is part of a life-death cycle:

When Death Is On Holiday

The son of the Sun God,
Time, King of all things right and true,
the God of Death,
is on holiday.

No death in the human world.
The world is full
of old people.

They cannot die
for Death is away
and cannot be reached.

Grandfather's father
is still here
and so is his grandfather's
grandfather.

The five-hundred-year-old
are mere babies here,
for they have their grandfathers
alive with them.

No gruel, not by any chance,
in any house,
for eight or ten vats
are not enough
for a round.

Just millions of people
milling in a house,
people without teeth,
moving like painted dolls.

Some cannot see.
Some cannot hear.
Some bald heads
shine like silver plates.

Starve them for ten days,
they do not die.

But there is no decrease
of births. Babies are born,
here, there, now, then,
everywhere.

I should stop.
I cannot describe it.

(Kunjan Nambiyar, Malayalam, eighteenth century; translated by K. M. George and the author)

Entropy and its Products

Now, the larger cycle is replicated in, or replicates, the social realm. In Marriott's (1968) apt image: "The circulation of food is the lifeblood of caste rank." But this circulation depends on a three-way distinction, the Indian food triangle: food/leftovers/feces (Khare 1976), a sort of entropy. For entropy, a linear progression, or decay within each unit of the cycle, is part of cyclical systems: the days of a week or the seasons in a year or *yugas* in cosmic time are linear; but weeks, seasons, *yugas* are cyclical. Our first poem expresses this twofold order very effectively: it moves toward a climax in the middle of the poem and then repeats itself, miming a cycle, and then ends with a second climax. Now for the triangle again.

Food (*anna*) is what you offer the gods; the other two cannot be offered—in the epics, when demons wish to disrupt a sacrifice, they pour garbage and feces into the sacrificial fire. The former is *medhya,* the latter are *amedhya* ("unfit for sacrifice," a common Brahmin euphemism for shit). Leftovers (*eñjalu,* in Kannada) and feces have to do with the two ends of the alimentary canal; both pollute. *Eñjalu* also means "saliva"; leftovers could also mean "uneaten food." As Marriott and others have shown, the giving and taking of these three things places people on the rungs of a hierarchy. I shall say no more about these transactions, as they are well explored (Marriott 1968).

In common parlance, dogs and pigs are low animals, and freely used in proverbs and as abuse terms (as in *eñjalu tinnō nāyi,* "he is a dog that eats leftovers"), because they eat leftovers and feces. The natural cycle of food and feces concerns Ayurvedic physicians, who classify the latter as ripe and unripe. Their first questions to a patient are concerned with *kālapravṛtti,* or the movements of time, which is (at least, was) their technical term for bowel movements. And to all the negative connotations of the left hand is added its association with feces: one eats with the right and washes oneself with the left. In Tamil, the left hand is regularly called *piiccaṅkay,* "the fecal hand"; you neither serve nor take food with it. The right hand is called *sōttukkay,* "the food hand." See Khare for further subtleties of the main cycles and the triangle (Khare 1976:109, 136).

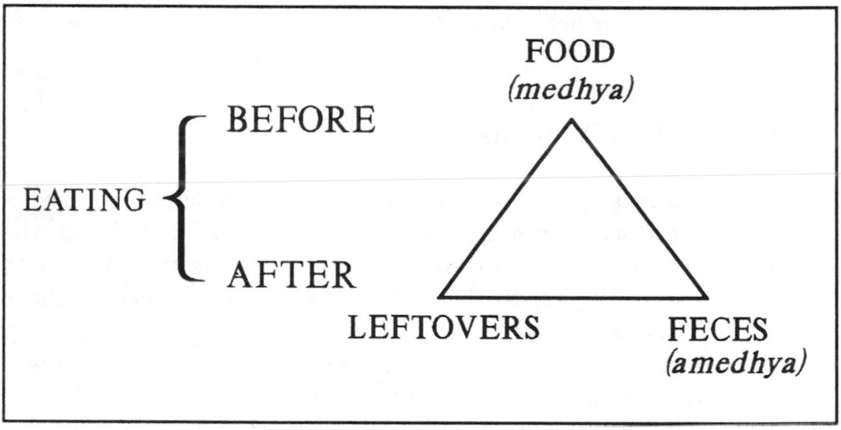

Figure 8.1. The Hindu Food Triangle

These relations and transactions and cycles may be replicated even spatially, as Selwyn (1980) shows in a diagram of the different stages of a village feast (see Fig. 8.2).

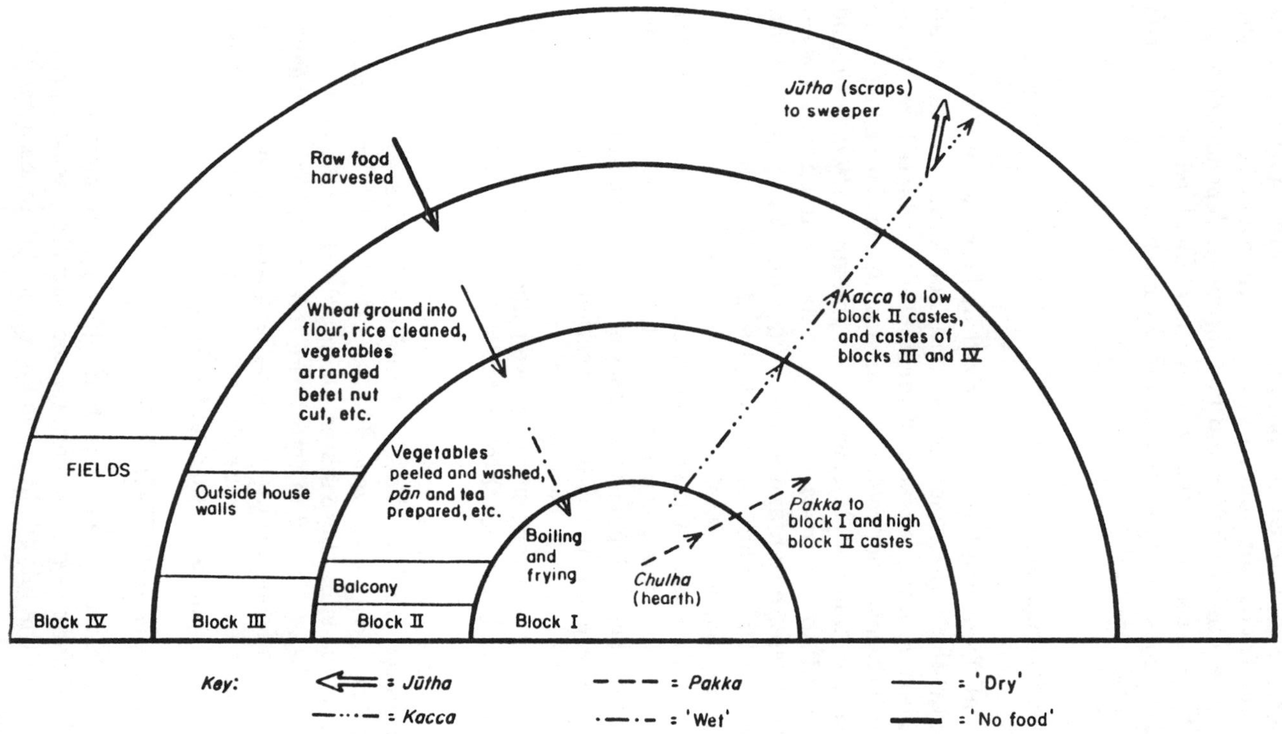

Figure 8.2. The Commensal Structure of a Feast. The figure represents the career of food as it is prepared, cooked, served and eaten at an intercaste feast (*bhoj*). It shows how food is progressively transformed by members of castes from progressively higher blocks before being finally served by Brahman cooks. Reprinted with permission from *The International Journal of the Sociology of Law,* 1980, vol. 8: 297–317.

The diagram points to another expressive pattern: social distance is expressed through distance from the kitchen. The nearest relatives and friends are admitted to the kitchen and fed close to the cooking stove, others farther and farther away, depending on how distant they are socially, ritually, or by caste. The kitchen is so central that the gods too are either part of the kitchen or given a niche or room very close to it.

Distinctive Features

Now, all foods can be characterized by four sets of distinctive features: (a) the three *guṇas,* or "strands" or "constituents," of all things: *Satva, rajassu, tamassu* (Kannada terms adapted from Sanskrit); (b) "heating" and "cooling," *uṣṇa* and *śīta* in Kannada; (c) the three *doṣas,* or "humors": bile, wind, and phlegm—*pittha, vāyu,* and *kapha;* and (d) the six *rasas,* or tastes: sweet, sour, pungent (or savory), astringent, bitter, and salty—*sihi, huḷi, khāra, ogaru, kahi,* and *uppu* (all Dravidian words, except *khāra,* though all six have corresponding Sanskrit terms).

Of these, the last set is sensory, the second and third sets are physiological (and causes of certain effects), and the first is characterological (and causal and explanatory of certain properties). All of them, like the elements of Indian aesthetics, are consumer oriented: they are causes known by their effects.

Such words and concepts were well known to us through the oral tradition at home, not through texts. ("You may not know Sanskrit, you certainly know the taste of pepper," says a proverb.) Anytime we caught a cold, or had a pimple, or felt dizzy, or discussed why certain communities that drink buffaloes' milk are dull-witted, we heard of *śīta* ('cold'), *uṣṇa* ('hot'), *pittha* ('bile'), or *tāmasika* ('gross') foods causing these states. Or in proverbs and abuse: "Your bile (*pittha*) has mounted to your head," meaning, "You're crazy."

The *guṇas* relate food to temperament; you are what you eat, and your taste expresses your character. The *Bhagavadgītā* has a classic and influential passage on the subject:

> The *Bhagavadgītā,* XVII, 7–10:
>
> (7) Threefold again is food—[food] that agrees with each [different type of] man: [so too] sacrifice, ascetic practice, and the gift of alms. Listen to the difference between them.

> (8) Foods that promote a fuller life, vitality, strength, health, pleasure, and good-feeling, [foods that are] savory, rich in oil and firm, heart-gladdening,—[these] are agreeable to the man of goodness.
>
> (9) Foods that are pungent, sour, salty, stinging hot, sharp, rough, and burning,—[these] are what the man of Passion loves. They bring pain, misery, and sickness.
>
> (10) What is stale and tasteless, rotten and decayed,—leavings, what is unfit for sacrifice, is food agreeable to the man of Darkness. (trans. Zaehner 1969)

It is clear that tastes (*rasas*) are related to the *guṇas.* The six tastes are also related to the six seasons, which affect the balance of humors in the body, among other things. All these are held together by a medical view of food: food and medicine are classified together in these four ways. As we saw in the very first passage, food is described as elixir, herb of herbs. The medical texts (as well as mothers and hypochondriacs) take the characterizations of food seriously and literally. All foods have medical properties, not only the proverbial apple a day. Foods are part of the Ayurvedic regimen (*pathya*), even its pharmacopia.

I must add that these four sets of characteristics do not seem to be correlated with each other in any precise fashion, though some correlations are clearly made, as in the passage from the *Gītā* quoted above. There is much disagreement from community to community regarding which items cause "heating," and which "cooling." In South India, but not in the North, papayas are considered extremely "heating"; they induce abortions, and so should not be eaten by pregnant women. For details on Tamilnadu, see Beck (1969) and Ferro-Luzzi (1973); for Karnataka, see Regelson (1972).

I provide a simplified diagram (Fig. 8.3) about one common set of correlations, based ultimately on Caraka. (I am indebted to Vishwajit Pandya 1980 for it. Marriott has a subtler, more complex diagram, but this was closer to what we knew roughly in childhood, or how my mother's cuisine and advice operated).

Meal sequences are orchestrated around these *rasas;* textures, temperatures, smells, and colors also play a part. I do not see a deliberate distribution of "heating" and "cooling" foods in the daily cycle—though they play a big part in the regimen of the sick, lactating mothers, etc., and in food offerings to certain gods (no chilies for Viṣṇu). To the six classical *rasas,* we should add a seventh,

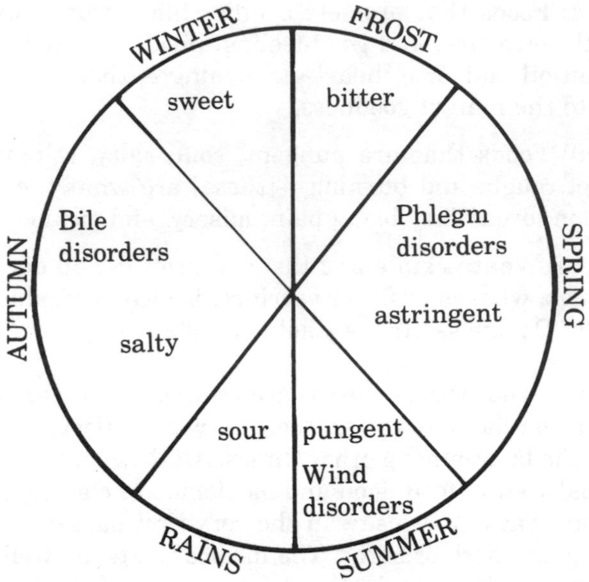

Figure 8.3. Seasons, Humours, and *Rasas*

"bland, insipid" (*cappunu* in Tamil, *sappe* in Kannada), as Regelson rightly suggests. Fig. 8.4 provides a (good) South Indian vegetarian meal sequence from a Tamil-speaking Brahmin family.

In the above meal sequence, course 2 repeats 1, intensified; in a festive meal, 3 is a climax, sweet being the highest of the tastes. Course 4, like the last part of a Sanskrit play, pacifies (*śānta rasa*) the palate with foods white, bland, and sour, with pickle to offset the rest. Even Brahman-style restaurants (in Karnataka and Tamilnadu) follow this order, when they serve a meal course by course. The meal could be topped with betel nut and betel leaf, which supply astringent and spicy tastes that are supposed to help digestion.

A poorer meal would still keep the order, though it may omit, say, course 2 or 1; if it is a single course, 4 is preferred. Course 3, as suggested, is part of a festive, not a daily, menu. We must also note that, within each course, the order of service is as shown, but the eater would mix the elements in each course (except 3) together, and eat them "simultaneously," not in sequence.

Such a meal illustrates a straightforward use of the *rasa* system. If the *rasas,* or tastes, are like motifs, the meal is like a discourse with a climax and a resolution.

	TASTE	ITEMS	TEMPERATURE	STATE	COLOR, TEXTURE
Course 1	savory	vegetable	hot	solid	green, etc.
	bland	rice+ghee	hot	solid	white, soft
	sour	*rasam**	hot	liquid	yellow-brown,thin
Course 2	bland	rice+ghee	hot	solid	white, soft
	extra-savory	*sambar*	hot	liquid	deeper yellow, etc.
	savory	vegetable	hot	solid	green, etc.
Course 3	savory	*vadai*	hot	solid	deep-fried, dark brown
	sweet	*payasam*	hot	semi-liquid	milk brown
Course 4	bland	rice	hot	solid	white
	sour	yoghurt	cold	semi-liguid or liquid	white
	sour, spiced	pickle	cold, pre-prepared	solid	red

Now these features of the food system, the cycle, the triangle, and the distinctive features can be used in a straightforward way or figuratively, obliquely, yielding new meanings by association, reversal, allusion, etc. Various kinds of markings by food, in social and other kinds of contexts, are usually by association or metonymy. Class and caste, male and female, child and adult, ordinary and special occasions, auspicious and inauspicious events, sickness and wellness are all marked by the foods that are associated with them. Certain foods are required, or preferred; others are taboo, in each context by rules of usage. The gods partake of these markings too: for example, they are vegetarian/nonvegetarian, ordinary/special, Śaiva/Vaiṣṇava. One or another of the four distinctive features may be used to justify this association: chaste-minded widows should not eat certain *rājasika* or hot or sweet foods because they are aphrodisiac. Proverbs express and play with these markings, which may also use the order of foods served (in death ceremonies, rice is served first; in weddings, never first), or what it is served in (insiders are served in metal plates, outsiders on leaves), etc. We may classify these contexts and their markers by a diagram (Fig. 8.5).

Kannada proverbs allude to all these markers. Here are some examples, with their obvious social meanings.

> The man drinks gruel, but he needs a man to hold up his moustache. ("Gruel" marks poverty.)
>
> It's better to eat *obbaṭṭu* at a wedding than *vaḍe* on a death anniversary. (*Obbaṭṭu,* a sweet crêpe, served in weddings, is auspicious; *vaḍe* marks inauspicious death ceremonies.)
>
> Work and eat if you're pregnant; sit and eat if you're a *bāṇanti.* (A *bāṇanti* is a woman who has just had a baby. Pregnancy vs. lactation.)
>
> The one who eats once a day is a yogi; the one who eats twice is a *bhōgī* ["enjoyer"]; the one who eats thrice is a *rōgī* ["sick man"]; and the one who eats four times a day—take him away to the burial ground. (Food regimen for health and sickness.)
>
> No feast without a *hōḷige,* no temple-celebration without a chariot. (*Hōḷige,* a sweet crêpe, marks festivity.)

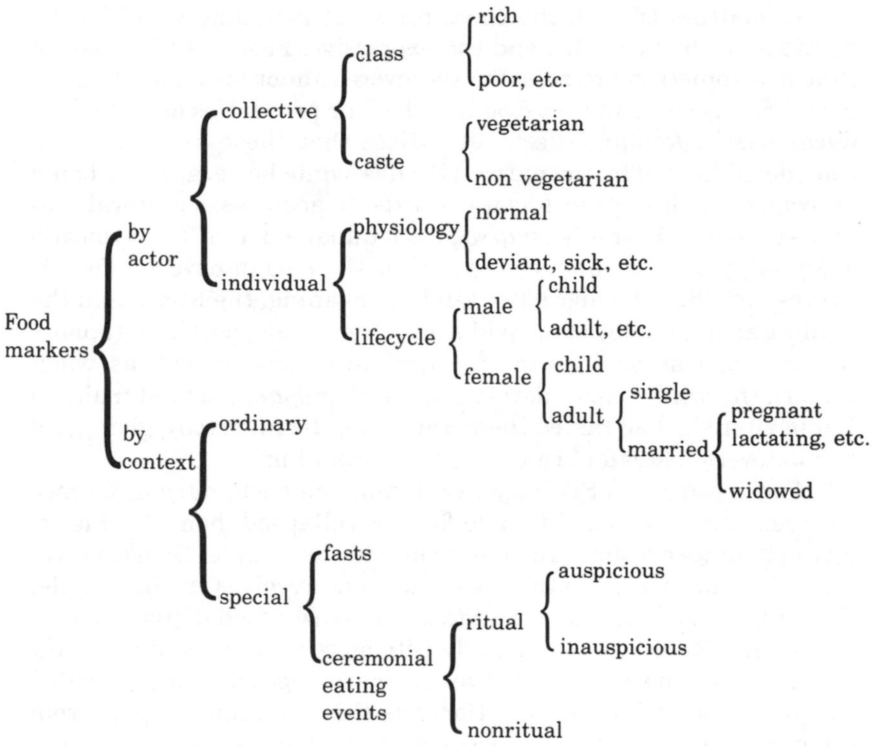

Figure 8.5. Food Contexts (as seen in proverbs, etc.)

Figures of Food

The three central terms of Indian semiotics/poetics, *abhidhā, lakṣaṇa,* and *vyañjana* (*vakrokti, dhvani,* etc.), roughly translated as *denotation, connotation,* and *suggestion* may be useful in our discussion here. In the well-known Sanskrit example, "the village on the Ganges," the phrase denotes a village located *on* the Ganges; as that is not literally possible, one accepts the connotative meaning that the village is really *on the banks* of the Ganges; and because it is on the river bank, the village must have cool breezes blowing over it, etc., which becomes the suggestion.

In matters of food, the three orders of meaning would be the utilitarian, the symbolic, and the expressive. Food is utilitarian in that it is something to be eaten (leftovers cannot be served to a superior or a god), or in that food has the four properties of taste, produces heating/cooling effects, etc. (Note that these properties are considered factual by the native.) Food is symbolic because, by being associated with certain social contexts, it acquires nonliteral values—butter if Kṛṣṇaite, *puḷiyōgare* ("tamarind rice") is typically a Śrī Vaiṣṇava dish; *ambali* ("gruel") is the food of poverty. Food is expressive when the above two kinds of meaning, the literal and the nonliteral, are deployed to yield ironies, reversals, poetic metaphors (in language as well as in the medium of food itself), as when Śabarī, the wild-woman devotee in the *Rāmāyaṇa,* served fruits to Rāma after she had tasted them, reversing the hierarchy, giving god her leftovers instead of receiving them from him.

For instance, in Śrī Vaiṣṇava Tamil, the customary difference between home foods and temple foods is collapsed: home food is referred to in terms that are appropriate to the temple. Drinking water is *tīrtham,* which is the holy water one receives in the temple; the daily cooked rice is *(pra)sādam,* the Lord's food distributed after the service in the temple; other items receive the suffix *amudu* (*amṛta,* divine nectar), so that an ordinary vegetable dish is called *kar(ya)mudu,* etc. This conflation sets this community apart from other groups, and also expresses a conviction that their home is no different from a temple (for details, see Ramanujan 1973). Thus food is used as a metaphor to say that home and temple are alike, even one.

As figures of speech get their effects by both exploiting and violating common language codes, "figures of food" use the system to communicate irony, defiance, appreciation, intimacy, by collapsing commonly held distinctions or reversing them. Take the food/leftover/feces distinctions. In straight usage, these are clearly hierarchic: servants, animals, beggars may eat leftovers; traditionally, an orthodox wife ate off the unwashed plate of the husband to show her love and submission to him. In Hindu *bhakti* practice, all food is first offered to the household god, and his leftovers received back as his *prasāda.* In stories like the following Hindi one, told all over the country, even a god's feces may confer favor on the devout.

Filthy Lucre

Two sisters-in-law lived in a village. The younger sister-in-law was very poor and worked for the older one, who was rich. The day of Sakaṭ came. The younger sister-in-law said to the elder, "Give me something from which I can make my offerings to Sakaṭ: things like *laḍḍū, peḍā,* sesame *bukrā.*" The older woman grudgingly gave her a handful of broken rice. The poor one took it home, pounded it, and did her best to make the proper kind of food for the god. Then she did *pūjā.*

That night the god came and said, "I'm hungry, mother, give me something."

"I've nothing much to give. Only some *laḍḍū* made out of a handful of broken rice." So he ate it.

Soon he said, "Now I've indigestion. I've to shit."

"Go to the toilet," she said.

"Where should I go? I can't wait," he said.

She said, "If you don't want to go outside, go into a corner of my hut." So he did, in the four corners.

Then he said, "I must wash. Where can I wash myself?"

She said, "We don't have any water. Clean yourself with my hair." So he wiped himself on her head.

When she woke up at dawn, she found she had gold ornaments on her hair, and gold in the four corners of her hut. She didn't go to work that day.

Her older sister-in-law came up and said, "You didn't come to work today."

The younger one said, "Why should I? You do my work for me today. God Sakaṭ has given me everything."

The older one looked around and said, "He gave you everything? How did he give you all this?" The younger one told her how the god came at night and ate up all the *laḍḍūs* she had made with the handful of broken rice the older woman had given her. "Then he gave me everything," she said.

A whole year passed. Then the older one did the very same things the younger one had done with broken rice. That night, Śakaṭdevatā came. He said he was hungry. She said, "Eat what I've kept there. Just as you did at my sister-in-law's." Then he wanted to shit. She said, "Go inside the house, don't go out."

"Where shall I wash?" he asked next.

"Here, here, on my head," she said. And in the morning, she found shit everywhere, bad smell and shit in all four directions, and on her head as well. (Hindi folktale, after Susan Wadley's translation.)

In common belief, god's *prasāda* never becomes feces; it feeds only the spirit. For ritual purification, one eats *pañcagavya,* or the five products of the sacred cow, mixing milk, ghee and curds (the best foods) with cow's urine and cow dung. On New Year's Day, one is served bitter neem-sprouts mixed with jaggery, a mixture of sweet and bitter, to symbolize the bittersweet nature of the year's blessings. In all such cases, opposites meet in a kind of oxymoron.

In the god/man relation, the food triangle is reversed, expresses a paradox. And so it is in the case of *saṇyāsins* (renouncers, the most respected stage): they must eat leftovers (at least symbolic ones). And certain *yogis* are said to recycle it all and eat their own excrement. None of these instances would have their expressive charge if the original triangle (figure 8.1) and hierarchy of food/leftovers/feces were not commonly accepted. The taboo of saliva and leftovers is also lifted for children:

Children

Even when a man has earned much
of whatever can be earned,
shared it with many,
even when he is master of great estates,
if he does not have
children

who patter on their little feet,
stretch tiny hands,
scatter, touch,
grub with mouths

and grab with fingers,
smear rice and ghee

all over their bodies,
and overcome reason with love,

all his days
have come to nothing.

(Pāṇṭiyaṉ Aṟivuṭai Nampi *Puṟanāṉāṟu* 188 [Ramanujan 1985, 160])

And between lovers—the male eats from the woman's mouth and gets a charge out of it. As I said earlier, Śabari, the old woman in the *Rāmāyaṇa,* waited for years for Rāma and, when he arrived, lovingly fed him fruit that she had bitten into first—to make sure it was sweet enough for Him. Bhakti poems go one step further and ridicule the food/leftovers distinction itself:

Milk is left over
from the calves.
Water is left over
from the fishes,
flowers from the bees.

How can I worship you,
O Śiva, with such offal?
But it's not for me
to despise leftovers,
so take what comes,
lord of the meeting rivers.

(*Basavaṇṇa* from Kannada; Ramanujan 1973)

Or, once a social and symbolic distinction between rich and poor foods is recognized, food snobbery becomes a possibility. Proverbs make fun of it: "The man eats only gruel, but he needs a man to hold up his mustache." In a Telugu story, a poor man who did not want anyone to know about the poor food he ate always had a small pot of rice and curds made and smeared it on his mustache before he came out of the house wiping it off ostentatiously—till one day his little daughter gave it all away by saying loudly, "Daddy, the cat ate up all your mustache rice today!" (I owe this story to V. Narayana Rao.)

Food Metaphors

As food is such a basic preoccupation of the culture, food metaphors and parables occur even in political situations. People think with them, as in the following two examples. In the first, a bowl of *khicaḍī* serves as a metaphor for military strategy (reminiscent indeed of King Alfred). In the second, sugar in milk suggests the way immigrants may mingle and become one with the existing population.

> Ahmad Shah of Gujarat was defeated and exiled. He could not enter his own city. As he wandered about in exile, he met a *sanyāsī* who gave him a bowl of hot *khicaḍī* [a low food, given at funerals]. Ahmad Shah was very hungry. Impatiently, he plunged his fingers right into the *khicaḍī* and scalded them. The *sanyāsī* said, "When things are that hot, begin at the edge of the pot." Ahmad Shah saw in that sentence a metaphor for his own military strategy. He befriended neighboring chieftains on the periphery of his kingdom, and was soon able to regain his city (Vishwajit Pandya, personal communication, 1984).
>
> When the Parsis first came to Gujarat, the king didn't want them to settle there. He had already too many people in the kingdom. So he sent the Parsi community a diplomatic, symbolic message: a full glass of milk, to indicate the glass could contain no more. The Parsis poured a spoonful of sugar into it and stirred it, and sent back the glass of milk: indicating that, like sugar, they would mix with the population, take no extra space, and sweeten it all. The king was pleased and persuaded. The Parsis came to stay (Veena Oldenberg, personal communication, 1984).

Food is a frequent metaphor for sex (not unknown elsewhere; for instance, terms of endearment in English like honey, sweetie pie). In various parts of India, pimps, I have heard, ask likely customers, "Has the gentleman eaten?" In Telugu, you cannot ask a woman for food, if she is alone, lest the request be misunderstood. The following examples are variations on the theme of food and sex.

The first speaks of the way food is transformed into sexual fluids; the second appeases the cannibalistic hunger of goddesses with fellatio; the third suggests that a person who has no sexual pleasure will compensate for it by eating, till sexual potency is restored. The fourth and fifth, from Telugu, use food and eating as metaphors for seduction. The fourth (like the lusty chicken-eating scene in the movie *Tom Jones*) describes how an artful man may suggest the sexual by the way he nibbles on a piece of meat. The fifth makes one see the dishes at a feast as the seductive parts of a lovely woman.

(1) *Bastu* or *bīrya* [seed] is generated inside the body of a man and *rati* [the seed of a woman] is generated in the body of a woman after the intake of food. Food is converted into blood, and from the blood itself are generated *bīrya* and *rati*.

(2) The demon Ruru with his army attacked the gods, who sought refuge with Devī. She laughed, and an army of goddesses emerged from her mouth. They killed Ruru and his army, but then they were hungry and asked for food. Devī summoned Rudra Paśupati and said, "You have the form of a goat and you smell like a goat. These ladies will eat your flesh or else they will eat everything, even me." Śiva said, "When I pierced the fleeing sacrifice of Dakṣa, which had taken the form of a goat, I obtained the smell of a goat. But let the goddesses eat that which pregnant women have defiled with their touch, and newborn children, and women who cry all the time." Devī refused this disgusting food, and finally Śiva said, "I will give you something never tasted by anyone else: the two balls resembling fruits below my navel. Eat the testicles that hang there and be satisfied." Delighted by this gift, the goddesses praised Śiva.

(3) [A man saw a beautiful maiden] and he wanted to devour her, for he had no penis and he could only find pleasure in swallowing. [Mahādeo came there] and between her legs with his nails he made an oval opening. [He made a penis and testicles for the man out of his own thumb and the two swellings on his ears.] The world was saved. (quoted in O'Flaherty 1983, 280–81)

(4) When a woman comes close to serve him food, this artful man takes a piece of red doe-meat to his tender lower lip and gently nibbles at it with his front teeth, and the woman smiles shyly turning her face a little away from him.

(5) The cool milk is her smile, the sweet *laḍḍus* of her breasts, the jackfruit segments of her lips, and the *pūris* her sari: the feast seduced the wedding party like a beautiful woman. (from Śrīnātha, ca. 1360–1450, *Śrīṅgāranaishadhamu*, chap. 6: 133, 134; trans. from Telugu by V. Narayana Rao])

Food is seen not only as preparation and foreplay, but the sexual act itself is seen as a man feeding a woman and vice versa. In the following passage from a modern novel [Ananthamurthy's *Saṁskāra*], the Ācārya, a long-celibate innocent, is initiated into the four things all animate beings share: food, sex, fear, and sleep (*āhāra, nidrā, bhaya, maithuna*). This set of four offers another paradigm of which food is a member.

> Touching full breasts he had never touched, Praneshacarya felt faint. As in a dream, he pressed them. The strength in his legs ebbing, Chandri sat the Acharya down, holding him close. The Acharya's hunger, so far unconscious, suddenly raged, and he cried out like a child in distress, "O Amma!" Chandri leaned him against her breasts, took the plantains out of her lap, peeled them and fed them to him. Then she took off her sari, spread it on the ground, and lay on it hugging Praneshacarya close to her, weeping, flowing in helpless tears (Ramanujan 1973, pp. 63–64).

In the Kannada folktale of Hanci, a Cinderella story, the young woman is identified with and by a special kind of rice she makes, not by a slipper. In a wife, food and sex, mother and partner meet; a woman has two breasts, so goes a saying, so that she can give one to the husband and the other to her child. (Note how, in the *Saṁskāra* passage, the man first calls his lover "Amma," or mother.)

One may add that the Sanskrit root *bhuj* means both "to eat" and "to enjoy sex." In the following story, it means many more things:

The Karma Eater

> A demon carried off a Brahman's wife and abandoned her in the forest. The Brahman approached the king and said that someone had carried off his wife while he slept. The king asked him to describe her, and the Brahman replied. "Well, she has piercing eyes and is very tall, with short arms and a thin face. She has a sagging belly and short buttocks and small breasts; she is really very ugly—I'm not blaming her. And she is very harsh in speech, and not gentle in nature; this is how I would describe my wife. She is awful to look at, with a big mouth; and she has passed her prime. This is my wife's appearance, honestly." The king replied, "Enough of her; I will give you another

wife." But the Brahman insisted that he needed to protect his own wife, "For if she is not protected, confusion of castes will arise, and that will cause my ancestors to fall from heaven." So the king set out to find her.

The king came upon her in the forest and asked her how she got there; she told him her story, concluding, "I don't know why he did it, as he neither enjoys me carnally nor eats me." The king found the demon and questioned him about his behavior: Why did you bring the Brahman's wife here, night wanderer? For she is certainly no beauty; you could find many better wives, if you brought her here to be your wife; and if you took her to eat her, then why haven't you eaten her?"

The demon replied, "We do not eat men; those are other demons. But we eat the fruit of a good deed. (And I can tell you about the fruit of a bad deed, for I have been born as a cruel demon.) Being dishonored, we consume the very nature of men and women; we do not eat meat or devour living creatures. When we eat the patience of men, they become furious; and when we have eaten their evil nature, they become virtuous. We have female demons who are as fascinating and beautiful as the nymphs in heaven; so why would we seek sexual pleasure among human women?" The king said, "If she is to serve neither your bed nor your table, then why did you enter the Brahman's house and take her away?" The demon said, "He is a very good Brahman and knows the spells. He used to expel me from sacrifice after sacrifice by reciting a spell that destroys demons. Because of this, we became hungry, and so we inflicted this defect upon him, for without a wife a man is not qualified to perform the ritual of sacrifice."

The king said, "Since you happened to mention that you eat the very nature of a person, let me ask you to do something. Eat the evil disposition of this Brahman's wife right away, and when you have eaten her evil disposition, she may become well behaved. Then take her to the house of her husband. By doing this you will have done everything for me who have come to your house." Then the demon entered inside her by his own *māyā* and ate her evil disposition by his own power, at the king's command. When the Brahman's wife was entirely free of that fiercely evil disposition, she said to the king, "Because of the ripening of the fruits of my own karma, I was separated from my noble husband. This night wanderer was (merely the proximate) cause. The fault is not his, nor is it the fault of my noble husband; the fault was mine alone, and no one else's. The demon has done a good deed, for in another birth I caused someone to become separated from another, and this (separation from my husband) has not fallen upon me. What fault is there is the noble one?" And the demon took the Brahman's wife, whose evil disposition had been purified, and led her to the house of her husband, and then he went away (*Mārkanḍeya Purāṇa,* trans. and quoted in O'Flaherty 1981, 30–31).

It is not surprising, given this wide range of straight and oblique uses, that taste and discrimination regarding food is seen as the beginning and, when well developed, the mark of the sensitive, discriminating man:

Taste Makes a Difference

A young adolescent came to a sage to get educated. The sage accepted him into his household, asked him to work for him and learn from him. He told his wife, "Do not serve any ghee on his rice when you feed him. Serve him castor oil instead. Let me know when he complains."

The young man was avid for learning and worked hard for some years. But not once did he complain of the stinking castor oil that was poured on his rice at every meal. He never seemed to notice. After some years, one day he said hesitantly to his guru's wife, "Amma, the food tastes strange today; something bitter about it."

The guru's wife removed the food from his leaf at once and served him fresh rice with ghee and other things. She also promptly reported this change in the young disciple to her husband, who summoned him and said, "I hear that you found the rice bitter today, after all these years. Your education is over. You're ready to go out into the world."

This story is read in two ways. When a man can discriminate between the different tastes, he has learned the basic skills for discrimination in other things as well. Or, all these years the disciple was absorbed in his learning, and did not care about taste; now that he has begun to look for taste in food, he will also be interested in other sensual experiences; so he is ready to go out into the world. How far the sensitivity to taste and flavor can go is suggested by a much older story in the Indian traditions.

The Fastidious Brahmans

> When dinnertime came, the king seated the brahmans at the place of honor and ordered a regal dish to be served of sweet rice flavored with all six flavors. When all were eating heartily, one of the youths, the one who was so particular about his food, refused to eat and pinched his nose disgustedly.
>
> "Why don't you eat, brahman?" asked the king softly. "The dish is quite tasty and well flavored."
>
> The brahman whispered back, "Your Majesty, there is a definite smell of burnt corpses about the cooked rice, and tasty though the dish may be, I can't possibly eat it."
>
> The king ordered everyone to smell the food, but they all said that the rice, which was of a special kind, was perfect and smelled delicious. Nevertheless, the fastidious youth kept his nose covered and refused to eat. Having thought about it, the king made investigations, and he discovered from the cooks that the dish had been prepared with rice that had been grown on an acre near the burning ground of a village.
>
> Most surprised and pleased, the king said to the youth: "You are indeed, sensitive about your food! You must eat something else."
>
> After dinner, when the three brahmans had gone off to their rooms inside the palace, the king had a most beautiful concubine from his own seraglio brought in to him and sent the perfectly shaped and gorgeously adorned woman at nightfall to the second brahman who was so fastidious about his women. Accompanied by the king's flunkies she came to his bedchamber, and, with her face as radiant as moonbeams, she seemed to be the very torchbearer of the God of Love. But when she entered the room, which she

brightened with her splendor, the fastidious youth, pressing his left hand to his nose and nearly fainting, groaned.

"Drag her out. I shall die if she stays! She smells like a goat."

The flunkies took the exasperated courtesan along to the king and told him what had happened. The king summoned the fastidious brahman and said: "This courtesan moves in clouds of the pleasantest perfumes, and she has scented herself with the best musk and camphor and aloe, and yet you declare that she smells like a goat!" But in spite of the king's assurances, the fastidious youth did not give in, and the king began to have his doubts. He inquired and coaxed the courtesan herself into revealing that, when she was a child, she had neither mother nor wet nurse and had been brought up on goat's milk. The king was amazed and praised the fastidiousness of the fastidious brahman (Van Buitenen 1959, 21–22).

Rasa, or taste (as in English), is also the basic metaphor for aesthetic experience: *ruci,* or taste, *asvāda,* or eating, and *rasika,* meaning both gourmet and sensitive man, are part of the technical vocabulary of poetics. As with food, Indian aesthetics would insist that the experience is in the experiencer: "Just as a taste (like sweetness) is created by the combination of different ingredients, a *rasa* (aesthetic 'flavor') is created by the combination of different *bhāvas* or 'affects.' "

I would like to close this little anthology with a widely told childhood story which places the giving of food in the context of other gifts, those of daughters (in marriage), of wealth, and of knowledge: all these gifts (*dānas*) facilitate the cycles of life. Of all these, the gift of food is the best. The folktale also connects this cycle with the other great Hindu cycle, the cycle of Karma, of action and consequence.

The Gift of Food

A widowed mother and her little son lived together. The mother used to work for neighboring women, sweep their floors, and scrub their pots. She earned very little but gave away part of what little she earned and lived on the rest. If too many beggars came to her door, she would save only her son's portion and give away her own food. Her gifts of food were beginning to be famous. The boy grew up and became a young man in such a household. He wondered about his mother struggling to make a living and struggling even more to give away most of her food. If only she didn't just give away so much food every day, she could be comfortable. She might even have been rich.

One day he asked her, "Avva, why do you do this? You give away everything you bring home. What's the point of giving away food left and right like that?"

She answered, "Of all gifts, the gift of food is the best. Riches and poverty are like night and day. They come and go. But if one gives to the poor whatever one can, the merit of such a deed will follow one wherever one goes. Your merit is greater than the rupees you earn."

"What do you mean by 'merit'? What's the measure of this merit you're earning by giving food away?" he asked in turn.

"A mortal woman like me can't explain merit, especially the merit of giving food away. Only god knows about such things. Go ask him," she said.

The young man said, "Well then, I will," and with his mother's blessings he went to talk to god.

He walked far and went through a dense jungle, through trees and underbrush, clambered up several hills and down into valleys. By then it was evening. He didn't know what to do next. Just then a hunter came that way and took pity on the young fellow, who would soon be at the mercy of lions and tigers.

He said, "Young man, it's getting dark. Don't walk about in this jungle. It's full of snakes, tigers, and lions. You'll soon hear the tigers roar. Come stay tonight in our hut and go in the morning."

The young man was waiting for just such an invitation. He went with the hunter. When they reached the hut, the hunter said to his wife, "This boy had lost his way in the jungle. I brought him home. He'll stay the night and leave in the morning. He's hungry. Give him some milk and fruit."

She replied, "I can't do anything of the kind. Give him your portion if you want to."

He gave the young fellow some of his own fruit and milk and asked him to go to bed. "You must be sore and tired," he said, and he massaged the young man's legs. Then he made a bed for his guest with old rags.

As there wasn't room in the hut, the man slept outside with his head on the threshold. That night a tiger came to his door, and ate up the hunter who was sleeping with half his body outside the hut. The taste of blood whetted his appetite. So he entered the hut and devoured the hunter's wife as well. His stomach was too full to take in any more. So he didn't touch the sleeping young man.

When the young man woke up next morning, he saw the shambles all around him—pools of blood and his hosts' bones. "How terrible! How unfair! Alive yesterday, and dead this morning!" he cried, and did his best to bury their remains in that deserted place and moved on.

On the way, he met a king who sat with his head in his hands. The king asked the traveler, "Brother, where are you going?"

"I'm going to talk to god and ask him a question."

"If you're doing that, will you ask him a question for me too?"

"What question?"

"Look, I spent a crore of rupees to build a tank for this town. There's not a drop of water in it. Will you find out why? God will surely know, if anybody does."

The young man agreed, and moved on. Very soon he met a cripple. He too had a question. "Will you ask god why I'm lame?"

In the next lap of his journey, he saw a snake hole with a snake stuck halfway in it, unable to move forward or backward. When the snake heard of the young man's errand, it too asked him for a favor. "Will you ask god the reason for my plight?"

"Yes, I will," replied the young man.

He walked and walked and went all the way to Kailāśa mountain, the abode of Śiva. Śiva and his consort Pārvati sat there, chewing betel nut.

He fell at their feet and asked, "Lord Śiva, you must explain to me the merit one earns by giving away food."

Śiva said, "I'll send you to someone who'll explain it to you. King Śitala's wife is pregnant. When you take my *prasāda* to her, she'll give birth to a baby. Ask that baby. He'll tell you what one gets out of giving away food."

"Before I go away, I have to ask you one or two things."

"Go ahead and ask."

So the young man asked Śiva why the king's tank did not have even one drop of water in it.

The Lord of All Things answered. "The king has a grown-up daughter he hasn't given away. He must find her a suitable bridegroom and give her away in marriage. Then water will flow into his tank."

"Why has the cripple lost his legs?"

"He has all kinds of knowledge in his possession. If he gives it away to someone, he'll regain his legs."

"I saw a snake who can't go in or come out of his hole. Why can't he?"

"If he gives away the jewel in his head to someone, he'll be able to move freely."

After getting all his answers (except the one he came for), he fell at the feet of Śiva and Pārvati, took their *prasāda,* and started his return journey.

He met the snake first. "Did you ask god my question?" it asked.

"Yes, I did. It seems that you have in your head some kind of jewel. If you give it away to someone, you'll move about freely."

"Then you'd better take it yourself," said the snake, and gave him the jewel in his hood. At once, the snake was filled with energy and began to move. In its delight, it spread its hood and danced a dance peculiar to snakes.

Then the young traveler met the cripple. "Did you ask Śiva my question?"

"Yes, I did. If you are willing to give the knowledge you have to someone who deserves it, your legs will be all right."

"Who deserves it more than you?" said the cripple at once. And he transferred all his learning, his sixty-four kinds of knowledge, to the young man in a ritual of transfer, pouring holy water on his hands. His legs grew strong again, and he danced a dance of joy.

The king, who still had his head buried in his hands, got up as soon as he saw the young man on the road. "Did you ask my question?" he asked.

"Yes, of course. You've a grown-up menstruating daughter, don't you? You must give her away in marriage to a suitable bridegroom, and your tank will overflow with water."

"Who's more suitable than you? Come, marry my daughter," said the king, and he married his daughter to the young man. Even before the wedding music had faded, they could hear the springs in the tank bubble up and come alive. By morning, the tank was gleaming, overflowing with water.

The young man moved on, with his new wife, his sixty-four kinds of learning, and his serpent jewel, and came to the country of Śitala, still seeking an answer to his first question. The king's pregnant wife was in great agony, unable to give birth. When he went to the palace and gave Śiva's *prasāda* to the queen, her labor eased at once and she quickly gave birth to a boy. Then the young man asked the delighted king for a favor.

"I need to ask the newborn baby a question. Could you please ask someone to bring the baby here?"

Maids brought the baby on a golden platter.

"The Lord of All Things has sent me to you. What's the merit one earns by giving away food?"

The baby on the platter laughed. The laughter was like nothing on earth.

"You went all the way to see Śiva and still you don't understand. Remember? On our way to see Śiva, you lost your way in a forest. Then a hunter took you home and gave you some fruit and milk. Remember that?"

"Oh yes, I remember. Very well. But they were killed!"

"Yes, I was that hunter. That night, a tiger devoured me. But because I gave you some food, I've been reborn now as a king's son. My wife refused to part with her food, and do you know where she is? She has been reborn in this very town as a pig. Go and check for yourself, if you wish," said the newborn baby.

Then the young man returned home, and he too began to give away food to the poor every day.

(Kannada folktale, Type 460–461B: from author's fieldnotes, 1968]

References

Ananthamurthy, U. R.

1976 *Saṁskāra*. Trans. A. K. Ramanujan. New Delhi: Oxford University Press.

Beck, Brenda

1972 *Peasant Society in Konku: A Study of Right and Left Subcastes in South India*. Vancouver: University of British Columbia Press.

Eco, Umberto

1976 *A Theory of Semiotics*. Bloomington: Indiana University Press.

Ferro-Luzzi, G. Eichenger

1973 "Food Avoidance of Pregnant Women in Tamilnad." *Ecology of Food and Nutrition*. Vol. 2:259–266.

Khare, R. S.

1976 *Culture and Reality: Essays on the Hindu System of Managing Foods*. Simla: Indian Institute of Advanced Study.

Marriott, McKim

1968 "Caste Ranking and Food Transactions: A Matrix Analysis." In *Structure and Change in Indian Society*, ed. Milton B. Singer and Bernard Cohn. Chicago: Aldine Publishing.

O'Flaherty, Wendy Doniger
1983 *Śiva: The Erotic Ascetic*. Oxford: Oxford University Press.

——— (Editor)

1981 *Karma and Rebirth in Classical Indian Traditions*. Berkeley: University of California Press.

Pandya, Vishwajit
1980 *Lakpaktti: A Study in Hindu Culinary and Necronomicon*. M. Phil thesis, Jawaharlal Nehru University, New Delhi.

Peirce, Charles S.
1931 *Collected Papers*, vol. 2. Cambridge: Harvard University Press.

Ramanujan, A. K.
1973 *Speaking of Śiva*. Baltimore: Penguin Books.

1985 *Poems of Love and War*. New York: Columbia University Press.

Regelson, Stanley
1972 *Some Aspects of Food Behavior in a South Indian Village*. Ph.D. Dissertation, Columbia University.

Selwyn, T.
1980 "The Order of Men and the Order of Things: An Examination of Food Transactions in an Indian Village." *International Journal of the Sociology of Law*, 8:297–317.

Van Buitenen, J. A. B.
1959 *Tales of Ancient India*. Chicago: University of Chicago Press.

Zaehner, R. C. (transl. and commentator)
1969 *The Bhagavad-Gītā*. Oxford: Clarendon Press.

Glossary

The following list is provided to help the reader mainly in two respects, first with general meanings of often used words in the text, and second, to draw attention, wherever feasible, to their use within varied gastronomic contexts. (However, it is not a comprehensive glossary of Indian gastronomic terms.) Though often a range of associated or contrasting categories and meanings are also indicated, only a contributor's contextual use and interpretation can provide us with complete guidance. Accordingly, this glossary supplements rather than either summarizes or supersedes the uses within the book.

abhiṣéka
anointing, consecrating or bathing a deity or a holy person.

āhāra, bhojana
meal, "taking food" in general, "diet" in the sense of that which is naturally appropriate to different creatures.

alaukika, adhyātmika
pertaining to the otherworldly affairs, with a focus on cultivating one's self (with yoga, worship and detachedness) for proceeding on a path toward liberation or some similar ultimate goal.

amṛta, nāmāmṛta
"elixir," literally and metaphorically, often exemplified by divine leftovers (*prasāda*) on the one hand, and guru's speech (*gurū vāṇī*), sacred recitals (*pāṭha*) and God's Name (*nāmāmṛta*), on the other.

anna
food in general, staple food, grain, or also the coarsest and the last vesture in which the Supreme Soul (Brahman) manifests.

annadātā
provider of food; also the one who feeds dependents—family, servants, and subjects.

annadevtā

the deity presiding over food; in popular conception, food itself is considered a god.

annamabrahman

the Supreme Soul (Brahman) extant in food.

annāpiṣékam

"bathing" a deity with food or other edible substances as a part of worship.

antardṛṣṭi

"inner-sight," usually reflecting one's spiritual accomplishments and surpassing the domains of normal reasoning and normal sense perceptions; foods can either enhance or reduce such ability.

āpaddharma

one's (usually modified) duties and obligations during distress or adversity; such a situational ethic usually relaxes food taboos.

āśrama

a stage or phase of life, usually referring to one of the four stages—student, householder, forest-dweller, or renouncer; also hermitage.

bandhana

"bondage," as produced by one's past and present karma manifest within this world (*karma bhūmi*); also ritually sullied, morally unjust, and spiritually improper foods that produce bad karmas and hence bondage.

bhakti—dāsya, vātsalya, sakhya, mādhurya

devotion in its four main emotive forms and attitudes where one approaches the divine as a servant, a mother, a friend, and a beloved; each form highlights food presentation to the divine and it's sharing among the devotees.

bhajan

devotional songs sung alone or in groups; also connotes "worship" as done by counting God's name.

bhanḍārā

a ritual feast arranged for feeding a large group, especially at a pilgrimage center on some specific religious occasion.

bhāva

emotion, mood or sentiment (where feeling and experiencing merge) directed toward either this-worldly and otherworldly affairs; as expressed and elaborated by *anubhāva* and *rasas* of aesthetics, and by the devotional and Tantra movements for worshipping a deity, forging rich connections between food and emotion.

bhūtas, mahābhūtas

five primordial elements, variously combined and recombined to produce food and body or *deha*; see *sthūla* and *sūkṣma* for further details.

brhamarṣi, devarṣi

a Brahman sage as Vasiṣṭha; a divine sage as Nārada, Atri, Bhṛgu.

cāṇḍāla

literally, the one cruel or wicked in deed; a person of lowest caste, an outcaste (born of a union between Śūdra father and Brahman mother).

darśana

intent "seeing" or "viewing" of the divine image or any revered being, usually as a part of one's devotion; "seeing oneself" or "seeing" divine within oneself; also a way of viewing the reality, a philosophy.

dharmasaṁkata

an ethical-moral dilemma, especially when no clear choice is available.

dhātus

a primary or elementary substance; also essential bodily substances; in Āyurveda, these overlap and work with *doṣas*; different foods help produce different substances within the body.

doṣas

humors, especially three of the Ayurvedic system of medicine—*pitta* or bile, *vāyu (vāta)* or wind, and *kapha (sleṣma)* or phlegm or mucus; one's diet directly affects the balance of three humors and hence dietary modification is basic to Ayurvedic treatment.

gomāṁsa

beef; a centuries-old abomination for the Hindu; popularly, the word is employed only to designate a taboo of the highest order.

guṇas

the primary constitutive "strands" or qualities of this worldly existence; essentially of three types according to Saṁkhya philosophy—*sattva* (lucidity, goodness, represented by savory, smooth, firm, and rich foods), *rajas* (passion, reflected by bitter, sour, salty, hot, pungent, harsh, and burning foods), and *tamas* (darkness or inertia as carried within stale, unsavory, putrid, and spoiled foods).

hiraṇyagarbha

the primordial "golden embryo" that marks the start of creation; a primordial form of the Supreme Soul, within Hindu cosmology.

jīva, jīvātman, ātman, Ātman or Brahman

a string of formulations used in learned and popular discussions referring to one's own or another's self (or person) with successively greater freedom from the worldly involvement, until the noncontingent absolute, Brahman, is realized; thus, if a *jīva* is a being caught in the illusory world, Brahman is the ultimate Reality that one aims to realize; all major ideas and uses of food variously verify the superiority of these formulations over the bodily and the worldly.

jñāna

knowledge; the path of knowledge, which is generally characterized with a detached stance toward the everyday world.

kaccā or sakharī

foods boiled or cooked in water, especially without the "base" of cooking fat (usually the clarified butter); such foods require special ritual care from the orthodox in sharing and exchanging them outside one's hearth and immediate relatives.

kharif

crop grown during the rainy season; also called "the rainy season crop."

khicṛī

a rice-lentil preparation, found suitable for recovery from illness, since it is considered "light" or easily digestible; also regarded as a *sāttvika* ("good and smooth") food, especially for holy persons.

koṣa

a sheath, vesture; food as one of the five vestures (*panckoṣa*) which constitutes the body (*annamayakoṣa*) enveloping the soul; the other four—successively subtler—sheaths are: vital breath, mind, intellect, and bliss.

kṣīrānna, khīra

sweet "rice-milk" dish, widely considered auspicious and favorite of many gods and deities, including Rama and Krishna, the incarnations of Vishnu; also the favorite medium of blessings and curses.

laukika

pertaining to this-wordly affairs, including everyday food handling within the social life of the ordinary.

līlā

divine sports or "play" within this world and its events; also as reflected by food at the center of many divine events and actions.

manas, buddhi

the "mind-heart," perception, understanding, and intellect; the devout generally emphasize faith and feeling over intellect as they offer food to divine.

mārga

"path" one chooses or belongs to for one's religious or spiritual pursuit; three main paths being action (*karma*), knowledge (*jñāna*), and devotion (*bhakti*); personal food selection and daily diet with the chosen path and its yogic practices.

māyā

a trick, an artifice, "illusion" or unreality; also a name for nature (*prakṛti*).

mokṣa

liberation or freedom in general, especially from rebirth and all the cares and sorrows of the world.

muruku

the quality which incorporates the properties of youth, vigor, freshness, tenderness, and sweetness; Lord Murukan̠ represents such a quality for the Tamil devotee.

naivédya, bhoga, prasāda, piracātam

a comprehensive and crucial cluster of concepts for understanding food offerings to the divine (or to any spiritual superior) in contemporary South Asia; in one popular interpretation, food brought before the deity (*naivédya*) becomes a delectable repast (*bhoga*) during the deity's eating, and it becomes the blessed "leftover" (*prasāda*) afterward for the devout.

pakkā or unsakharī

foods cooked in clarified butter; these foods are widely transactable within the society and are generally considered "pollution resistant."

pañcāmṛta and pañcāmirtam

an auspicious edible substance which appears within the book in two versions, one from the north (Toomey) and the other from south (Moreno); though both versions consist of milk, curds, honey, clarified butter, and sugar, their actual use regionally differs according to local sects and rites.

pañcgavya

five products of cow—milk, clarified butter, curd, cowdung, and urine—mixed together to produce a highly potent medium of purification within the Hindu world; food and its opposite—inedible refuse—in such an instance are brought together to stress the cosmic, exhaustive purity of the "cow mother."

pandās

Brahman priests at a pilgrimage center, who specialize in accosting pilgrims by keeping records of their ancestors' previous visits and who are known for their carefree, hard-edged life style and gluttony.

pāpa, puṇya

notions of religious demerit or merit, widely applicable to self, including while handling food from its production in the field to consumption on one's plate.

prāṇa, prān

vital breath, usually differentiated into ten—five inner, five outer—vital airs within a live being; popularly, this *prān* or life rests on food.

prasādam, or persād

the first is the popular Tamil word for *prasāda*; the second connotes similar meanings in Hindustani (see *naivédya* for full meanings).

puruṣārthas

four comprehensive goals of human life as represented by pursuing moral obligations, worldly business, desires, and liberation—dharma, *artha, kāma,* and *mokṣa*: obtaining minimal food and clothing by appropriate means remains an integral part of the *puruṣārtha* scheme.

rabi

winter crop.

rājarṣi

a royal sage, or a Kṣatriya who, by his pious life and austerities, becomes a sage.

rākṣasa

a demon, an evil spirit, usually considered in contrast to gods.

rasas or rasam or in Tamil *irasam*

the term refers to several sets of meanings: six tastes or flavors—bitter, sweet, salty, astringent, pungent, and acid; nine types of pathos, emotion and feeling—love, mirth, anger, sorrow, energy, terror, disgust, astonishment, and tranquility; and also more generally to pith or essence, or subtle substances in philosophy. All these meanings apply to food one way or another, though the first cluster is most obvious.

sādhū, sant, sannyāsin, paramhaṁsa, avadhūta, siddha, śramaṇa

"holy persons" of Hindu and Buddhist traditions on the subcontinent, reflecting differences of "form" (*rūpa*), sectarian path, and personal accomplishments; most major "branches" of holy persons identify a distinct dietary style, usually by excluding or regulating many foods of the householder or the ordinary person (historically, holy figures have significantly extended gastrosemantics).

saguṇa, nirguṇa

two forms of God, with and without attributes (*guṇas*), requiring different approaches and attitudes from the worshipper; food prominently appears within the first—*saguṇa*—form, where God accepts the food offered and returns it suffused with his grace and blessings; see *naivédya*.

śakti

energy, strength, power, capacity, and prowess, whether natural, human or divine; especially the goddess in any of her various forms (well-regulated food remains the source of one's energy and strength).

saṁsāra

popularly the world and the "worldly existence" and its uncertainties, desires, and sorrows; also referring particularly to one's past karmas and the consequent transmigration of soul from one birth to the next (for a morally proper existence within the world, one exerts self-control while eating and generosity while sharing and exchanging food).

saṁskāra

cultural impression and form one has; also refining, purifying rites and ceremonies; life's rites of passage.

śaraṇa, prapatti

surrender to the divine, without self-doubts and without conditions (food's divine transubstantiation rests on such an intense faith, especially in the path of devotion).

sraddhā

faith, trust, or intense belief, in the divine; only such a faith and attitude converts food into *prasāda* or blessed food.

sṛṣṭi

creation; food is seen as coterminous with creation, and prior to the birth of different creatures, with the important implication that Creator ultimately controls food availability with his unfailing sense of moral justice.

sthūla

the "gross," or "seen" or manifest state of substance, recalling the notion of *dravya,* of which the perceived world is made; food, as seen by the naked eye, exists in a gross form.

sūkṣma

the subtle or the unseen, drawing attention to the five quintessential *tanmātras* of sound, touch, form, taste, and smell; the subtle also stands for domains beyond sense perception and this world.

svadharma

dharma appropriate to one's own given status and location, reflecting one's caste and religious obligations, including rules of food exchange and gifting.

śvapaca

a dog-feeder; a person with abominable food habits.

svarūpa

one's own natural form, nature, character or true constitution (a cultural rule of thumb is that one's food habits generally tend to conform to one's natural form, innate character).

svalpāhāra, mitāhāra

small meal or snack; an abstemious meal.

Tantra

literally a thread, but the reference is to a distinct religious system and its lefthanded rituals for worshipping deities by magical and mystical formulas for acquiring superhuman powers, including eating meat and drinking spirits according to the Tantrik's view of his body, deity and the cosmos.

tapas

austerities of various kinds for self-control, whether by renunciation or indulgence (as in Tantra); a primary route to acquiring "vital force" (*ojas*) and spiritual lustre, heat and glow (*tejas*); dietary control, fasting and abstinence play a crucial part in any austerity and its continued success.

tyāga

relinquishment of various kinds, especially the "fruits" of one's action and moving beyond the conditions of affection and aversion (*rāga aur dveṣa*), including regulated eating and fasting as a common step.

ucchiṣṭa

leftovers or remainders, particularly those provided by sacrificial and devotional rituals, also symbolize continuity of exchanges.

vānaprasthin

the state of forest-dweller (see also *āśrama*).

varṇa, jāti

Hindu's "caste complex," where *varṇa* refers to four principal "kinds" of people (Brahman, Kṣatriya, Vaiśya, and Śūdra) and *jāti* refers more specifically to the group in which one is born; both classifiers remain vital to gastronomic traditions because this is where distinct Hindu "culinary culture" (besides dialect, dress and rituals) develops and is passed on around the domestic hearth, from one generation to the next.

varṇasaṁkara

hybrid, one born of unlawfully "mixed" jātis or varṇas, usually with a corresponding impact on one's culinary culture.

varṇāśramadharma

Hindu's "status-[life]phase" scheme of moral duties and ritual obligations toward one another and toward the cosmos and its creatures; see also *āśrama* and *varṇa* and *jāti*.

yogī, yatī

besides longstanding general terms for holy persons, it is also a popular Hindi phrase applied to yogis specifically known for controlling food, body, mind, and self.

yuga

an "age" of mankind, usually one out of the four—*kṛta, tretā, dvāpara,* and *kali*; where each succeeding age is found shorter in duration, and declining in the observance of proper dharma obligations.

Contributors

Vidyut Aklujkar is assistant professor in Asian Studies at University of British Columbia. She has published poems, short stories and essays in Marathi periodicals and collected in a volume entitled *Mérā Jūtā Hai Jāpānī (My Shoe Is Made In Japan* 1989), scholarly articles in international journals, and *Primacy of Linguistic Units* (1990).

R. S. Khare is professor of anthropology at the University of Virginia. His interests include studies of food and foodways, especially since 1977 when, with Mary Douglas, he launched and chaired the International Commission on Anthropology of Food and Food Problems on behalf of the International Union of Anthropological and Ethnological Sciences. His relevant publications include *The Hindu Hearth and Home; Culture and Reality;* and *Food, Society and Culture* (edited with M. S. A. Rao.)

Manuel Moreno is associate professor of anthropology at Northeastern Illinois University. He specializes in the anthropology of religion. He has written on a variety of cultural aspects of Tamilnadu, including spirit possession, festivals and pilgrimage, agriculture, and marriage.

A. K. Ramanujan is William H. Colvin Professor in the Department of South Asian Languages and Civilizations, and the Department of Linguistics, and is a member of the Committee on Social Thought at the University of Chicago. He is a linguist, poet, and scholar of Dravidian folklore, a translator of Kannada and Tamil poetry, and has written numerous articles and books.

H. L. Seneviratne is associate professor of anthropology and Fellow of Monroe Hill College at the University of Virginia. He is author of *Rituals of the Kandyan State* (1978) and editor of *Identity, Consciousness and the Past* (1989).

Paul Toomey has taught at Cornell and Tufts Universities and is presently an analyst for the U.S. government. He is the author of *Food from the Mouth of Heaven,* forthcoming from Hindustan Press, and several articles on food, pilgrimage, women's rituals, and aesthetics in India.

David White is a lecturer in Religious Studies at the University of Virginia. He specializes in comparative mythology and Hinduism, and is the author of *Myths of the Dog-Man* (1991).

Index